A Unity of Purpose

100 Years of the SBC Cooperative Program

A Unity of Purpose

Tony Wolfe & W. Madison Grace II

EDITORS

B&H PUBLISHING
BRENTWOOD, TENNESSEE

Copyright © 2025 by B&H Publishing Group
All rights reserved.
Printed in the United States of America

978-1-4300-9706-8

Published by B&H Publishing Group
Brentwood, Tennessee

Dewey Decimal Classification: 254.8
Subject Heading: COOPERATIVE PROGRAM / CHURCH FINANCE / CHURCH ADMINISTRATION

Unless otherwise stated, all Scripture is taken from The Christian Standard Bible. Copyright © 2017 by Holman Bible Publishers. Used by permission. Christian Standard Bible® and CSB® are federally registered trademarks of Holman Bible Publishers, all rights reserved.

Scripture references marked KJV are taken from the King James Version, public domain.

Cover design by Darren Welch Design.
Image by detchana wangkheeree/Shutterstock.

2 3 4 5 6 7 • 29 28 27 26 25

Acknowledgments

In 2022, SBC Executive Committee leadership called together a small group of men and women from around the United States to begin thinking through how to celebrate the centennial anniversary of the Cooperative Program (CP) in 2025. The team persisted in its work to plan for a strategic, forward-focused celebration in 2025. I (Tony) was regularly encouraged by the creativity and passion of these Southern Baptist leaders and volunteers. God has been gracious and kind to our Baptist people in gifting this Convention with some of the sharpest minds and most skilled professionals in the country who joyfully focus their energies together in promoting our Great Commission cooperation with excellence.

We would like to express our gratitude to the staff of the SBC Executive Committee, along with the above-mentioned select group of volunteer leaders from across the Southern Baptist Convention, for commissioning this important work at this critical moment in our history. Our deepest gratitude also extends to the Tennessee Baptist Mission Board, the Georgia Baptist Mission Board, and the Alabama Baptist State Board of Missions for underwriting the initial costs of production.

The authors contributing to this volume have undertaken their work as a labor of love. Each of them has been personally blessed by the CP, as you will read in their personal CP testimonies throughout the book. Their contributions are the product of tedious research, careful analysis, compositional excellence, and joyful Southern Baptist cooperation. To them is owed great commendation, for all posterity, for the value added to our Baptist family in this work both now and for generations to come.

Above all, we extend our highest gratitude to the cooperating churches of the Southern Baptist Convention who have sacrificed much to pool their financial resources through the CP these last one hundred years for the advancement of the gospel of Jesus Christ. Many of these churches have given faithfully and sacrificially through the CP instead of hiring an additional staff member, raising ministers' salaries, remodeling buildings, or purchasing new technology. Every generous contribution has cost them something. Some have given 10, 15, or 20 percent of their undesignated receipts whether in seasons of plenty or in seasons of want. Surely, "their abundant joy and their extreme poverty [have] overflowed in a wealth of generosity" (2 Cor. 8:2). Christ has demonstrated his provision to these churches time and time again, always having everything they need though emptying themselves of everything they have. As editors of this centennial work, our hearts are swollen with extraordinary love and admiration for them.

"Now to him who is able to do above and beyond all that we ask or think according to the power that works in us" (Eph. 3:20–21), to him belongs all the glory and the highest praise for the work he has accomplished through the CP giving of our Baptist people these one hundred years. The far-reaching gospel work financed through our cherished unified budgeting strategy will thrive today and tomorrow to the extent that the churches continue to faithfully and sacrificially give through the CP. So, in the words of Earnest Easley in his 1925 Future Commission report at the inauguration of the CP, "May God help our people to see it."

ACKNOWLEDGMENTS

I give thanks to my God for every remembrance of you, always praying with joy for all of you in my every prayer, because of your partnership in the gospel from the first day until now. (Phil. 1:3–5)

Grace and Peace,
Tony Wolfe and W. Madison Grace II

Contents

Foreword xiii
    Jeff Iorg

Introduction 1
    Tony Wolfe and W. Madison Grace II

Part 1

CHAPTER 1: Cooperation—A Biblical Model 15
    W. Madison Grace II

CHAPTER 2: Cooperation in Baptist Beginnings, 1609–1845 32
    Jason G. Duesing

CHAPTER 3: Society and Entity-Based Missions Funding in the SBC, 1845–1925 52
    Adam Harwood

CHAPTER 4: War and Roar: 1910s and 1920s American Context Influencing the Development of the Southern Baptist Convention Cooperative Program 72
    Taffey Hall

CHAPTER 5: Setting the Stage: The $75 Million Campaign as Precursor to the Cooperative Program 92
    Tony Wolfe

Part 2

CHAPTER 6: What Is the Cooperative Program? 115
  Tony Wolfe

CHAPTER 7: What Has God Done in the States? 132
  Leo Endel and Pete Ramirez

CHAPTER 8: What Has God Done in the Seminaries of the Southern Baptist Convention? 150
  Jamie K. Dew Jr. and Chris Shaffer

CHAPTER 9: What Has God Done in the Public Square? 160
  Richard Land and Brent Leatherwood

CHAPTER 10: What Has God Done in North America? .. 182
  Kevin Ezell and Mike Ebert

CHAPTER 11: What Has God Done around the World? ... 197
  Paul Chitwood, Melanie Clinton, and Julie Nall McGowan

Part 3

CHAPTER 12: Current Challenges and Opportunities in the Southern Baptist Convention. 219
  Bart Barber

CHAPTER 13: The Ethics of Kingdom Cooperation. 235
  RaShan Frost

CHAPTER 14: Today's and Tomorrow's Mission Field. 252
  Scott McConnell

CHAPTER 15: A Charge for Our Future 275
 Daniel Dickard

Afterword 295
 Tony Wolfe and W. Madison Grace II

Contributors 299

Notes 303

Foreword

For me it's personal. Just before my thirteenth birthday, a Baptist church shared the gospel with me at a regional fair. There, in an exhibit building just off the midway, my life was changed when I received Jesus as my Lord and Savior. Some years later, I learned that church had joined Southern Baptists only a short time before my conversion. The church cooperated with Southern Baptists (and taught me to be one) because it appreciated their unified mechanism of funding missions through the Cooperative Program (CP).

A few years later, I graduated from a Baptist college funded by the CP. Then it was on to seminary, with reduced tuition made possible by the CP, for both master and doctoral degrees. After pastoring a CP-supporting church for several years, my next major ministry step was moving near Portland, Oregon, to plant a new church. Funding for the church plant came through the CP, jointly supplied by the Northwest Baptist Convention and the Southern Baptist Home Mission Board (now NAMB).

Within a few years, the Northwest Baptist Convention called me as their executive director. My salary was provided through the CP, a major part of my job description was promoting the CP, and my responsibilities included accounting for and distributing CP gifts from churches. After about a decade in that role, my next assignment was president of Gateway Seminary where about one-third of the budget was provided by the CP.

That's why it's personal for me. The CP was the reason the church of my youth became Southern Baptist (and taught me to be one as well). The CP helped provide my education, supported my church plant, funded denominational strategies under my direction in the Northwest, and sustained my presidency of a seminary in a Western location with few Southern Baptists. My life demonstrates that the CP is not a corporate funding mechanism designed to bilk churches and pad bureaucracies. It's a lifeblood for spiritual life and ministry vitality.

The CP is also personal because of the people who make it possible—everyday Baptists who give their tithes and offerings through their local church, like my mother-in-law. She is in her nineties, lives mainly on Social Security, and never misses a month in giving to her church. As a lifelong Southern Baptist, she understands and believes in the CP. She frequently asks, "How is my seminary doing?" because she knows she is one of its main donors!

That's who funds the CP: gray-haired seniors, working-class men and women, and young families trying to make ends meet. Rich fat cats are not the secret benefactors of the CP. Instead, rank-and-file Baptists make it happen a few dollars at a time, resulting in a steady stream of millions of dollars flowing to national and global causes. And, miraculously, they do this voluntarily as their churches adopt annual budgets which specify a percentage or amount of their choosing for the CP. There are no dues, no invoices, and no required allotments or apportionments. The CP is grounded in voluntary cooperation, not contractual coercion.

It's also personal because of the impact the CP has made on the lives of people close to me. For twenty years, thousands of students enrolled while I served as president of Gateway Seminary. Every student benefited from the CP. Southern Baptist students received a tuition discount made possible by the CP. But non-SBC students also benefited since CP resources were used to fund our total budget, not just allocated to SBC students. These were not nameless faces but passionate students we shared life with while they trained.

While serving in the Northwest, we channeled CP resources to support dozens of church planters, collegiate ministers, and regional missionaries. Our CP gifts supported international missionaries, including many who came from churches in our region. Again, these were not anonymous strangers but friends and colleagues we interacted with daily. The CP funds real people, not a faraway religious fiefdom.

Every author who contributed to this volume could have written a similar forward. We have all been personally blessed by the CP. We have given through it, promoted it, expanded it, managed the resources it generates, and been funded by it. For all of us, it's personal. That's why this book is a labor of love, an opportunity to tell an important story and challenge a rising generation to embrace the CP. We hope a similar book can be written in another hundred years, further celebrating this remarkable approach to supporting God's global mission.

For that to happen, a new generation of CP advocates must take up the mantle. That begins not with financial commitments but with a convictional decision to cooperate. This is hard for some Christians for a variety of reasons. Some believe cooperation requires compromise, and they are right. It requires compromising on lesser issues but not on the gospel and the importance of communicating it to every person in the world. Some believe they can do more by themselves than by working with others. That's arrogance, not wisdom, underlying a selfish and faulty conclusion. Some resist cooperation because they get less credit for the results. Again, that's pride talking when a leader cares more about being noticed than getting results. Finally, some Christians resist cooperation because they must surrender management of missional and educational efforts to denominational entities. While that might seem risky, the combined and specialized economy of scale makes it worthwhile.

Leaders who cooperate experience compounding organizational impact. Like compounding interest in a retirement fund, cooperating with other Christians exponentially increases our overall impact. We really are better together!

Cooperation allows us to maximize our strengths while allowing the strengths of others to overcome our weaknesses. When we cooperate, ministry efforts are sustained since they rest on combined efforts instead of depending on a few people. For example, when a hurricane ravages the Gulf Coast and churches in that region give less, CP-funded ministries do not fear loss of revenue. We know the financial base is broad enough to withstand a regional shortfall caused by natural disaster, business downturns, or civil unrest. CP revenue emerges from tens of thousands of churches across the United States which creates remarkable financial resiliency.

Since the CP is supported by so many churches, it eliminates dependency (and the associated risk) from depending on a few donors. A president of an independent seminary lamented his concern about the possibility of losing one of his handful of major donors. If even one died, lost passion for their school, became frustrated with his leadership, or had an economic setback which limited their giving—their school would be in trouble. He concluded by saying, "I wish we had something like the Cooperative Program to depend on." Southern Baptists are glad we do!

Perhaps the most amazing part of the CP is its voluntary and self-determined participation. The only reason Southern Baptists give to the CP is they want to. There is no denominational requirement to give any percentage or amount. Yet churches voluntarily give—some in double digits—a percentage of their unrestricted offerings through the CP. Not only is participation voluntary, but the percentages or amounts of the gifts are all self-determined. Each church decides how much to give and can rescind or revise that amount at any time.

The CP has been an effective tool for so long, it's easy to forget it was once an unproven method dreamed up by frustrated Baptist leaders who were tired of two major problems: perpetual fundraising for every imaginable cause and erratic support from a hodgepodge of fundraising schemes. There had to be a better way. Southern Baptists took a huge risk by creating a financial strategy to fund the totality of their work, built on voluntary cooperation. Their conventions and entities took a similar risk in foregoing direct fundraising and depending on the churches. Billions of dollars channeled to God's mission and millions of lives impacted are our proof of concept. The Cooperative Program works.

As a settled denominational method, it's also easy to overlook the visionary faith of the people who created the CP. These were statesmen who put their reputations on the line to do something never before attempted by any convention, association, or denomination of churches. Their vision was amazing, but it's doubtful they imagined the global impact the CP has made for the past century. Their example, however, motivates us to dream big dreams and trust God to do amazing things!

The scope of what has been accomplished through the CP is outlined in the following chapters. But even these skilled writers can only provide a sketch or summary of all God has done. The original visionaries were concerned about aligning state and national conventions by creating a shared financial channel to resource common missionary and educational enterprises at home and abroad. Those concerns have been satisfied, but the genius of the CP has enabled it to expand to support other aspects of our common efforts as Southern Baptists.

While this book will be a history for some and a textbook for others, my hope is it will do more than catalog facts. As you read it, my hope is the CP will become personal for you as well. When that happens,

- you will become an advocate for cooperation,
- you will insist on giving more generously through the CP,
- you will invest prayerful support in people funded through this channel, and
- you will thank God for revealing such a unifying, resilient funding model.

May God give us similar visionary wisdom, insight, and courage—as demonstrated by our forebearers in creating the Cooperative Program—to reinvigorate our commitment to enhancing it for future generations of Southern Baptists!

Jeff Iorg
President and CEO of the SBC Executive Committee

Introduction

Tony Wolfe and W. Madison Grace II

> May they all be one, as you, Father, are in me and I am in you. May they also be in us, so that the world may believe you sent me. I have given them the glory you have given me, so that they may be one as we are one. I am in them and you are in me, so that they may be made completely one, that the world may know you have sent me and have loved them as you have loved me.
>
> John 17:21–23

Come close, and let's celebrate the story of our Southern Baptist people who rose in their time with courage, solidarity, and faith to diminish what International Mission Board president Paul Chitwood consistently reminds us is "the world's greatest problem: lostness." However, in our celebration, let it not be lost on us that this is our time. As our Baptist parents and grandparents rose to their times, we must rise to ours. Our commission is great. Our message is urgent. Our time is short. These factors call for us to examine Southern Baptist's Cooperative Program (CP) and realize that it is more than a funding mechanism. The CP is a unifying force for Great Commission advance—a conduit for voluntary, cooperative, and sacrificial investment from the churches to the nations. For one hundred years, God has counted this program worthy of his blessing and has shown us favor in our unified efforts. But the success of our Baptist people in these next one hundred years may depend on *our* "unity of purpose and consecration,"[1] as it has depended on the unity of those who have come before us.

The CP is the envy of other evangelical denominations. It is a past treasure, a present strength, and a future promise. But let's not get ahead of ourselves. Allow us first to take you back to where it all began: a Baptist people who owned a unified purpose, a courageous innovation, and an iron resolve to work together for local and global gospel advance in their time.

The dawn woke the morning in the city as the sun broke through the eastern hills, the warmth of its beams quickly stirring activity around the Mississippi River on the city's West bank. There, 4,001 Baptists from across the states began to enter the newly constructed Ellis Auditorium on the corner of Poplar Avenue and Front Street in downtown Memphis, Tennessee. There they were, in "the Crossroads of the South," Wednesday, May 13, 1925—a fitting location for this pivotal gathering in Baptist history. The $75 Million Campaign had promised more than it could deliver, but it left Southern Baptists with a sense of solidarity and an increased denominational consciousness. Eighty years of Great Commission cooperation were behind them, thanks to generations before. But this was their day. This was their time. The need was great, the time was right, and expectation filled the air.

At 9:30 a.m., Southwestern Baptist Theological Seminary's music director and professor of church music Isham Emmanuel Reynolds directed the hearts of the messengers heavenward as they lifted their voices to sing:

> *How firm a foundation*
> *Ye saints of the Lord*

Is laid for your faith
In his excellent word.

Then another:

Let every kindred, every tribe
On this terrestrial ball
To Him all majesty ascribe
And crown Him Lord of all!

T. W. O'Kelly of North Carolina rose to read from the Scriptures.

> Have not I commanded thee? Be strong and of a good courage; be not afraid, neither be thou dismayed: for the LORD thy God is with thee whithersoever thou goest. (Josh. 1:9 KJV)

> And when he had called the people unto him with his disciples also, he said unto them, Whosoever will come after me, let him deny himself, and take up his cross, and follow me. For whosoever will save his life shall lose it; but whosoever shall lose his life for my sake and the gospel's, the same shall save it. (Mark 8:34–35 KJV)

After a morning full of business, Pastor Len G. Broughton of First Baptist Church Jacksonville, Florida, preached the Convention sermon, "The New Way," from Joshua 3:4–5. "Ye have not passed this way heretofore. . . . Sanctify yourselves: for tomorrow the LORD will do wonders among you" (KJV).

In the afternoon, the Convention reassembled in session. Lee Rutland Scarborough, president of Southwestern

Baptist Theological Seminary, brought the final report on the Conservation Commission and the $75 Million Campaign. He concluded with hope for a "more glorious" future through "Southern Baptists' great forward, co-operant movement. . . . We must not lose the things we have already wrought through the mercies and power of God; but we must do our best to bring them to a full reward."[2]

As Scarborough took his seat, C. E. Burts and M. E. Dodd approached the podium. The first annual report of the Future Program Commission was greatly anticipated. Burts's voice cut through the silence of the room as his opening words arrested the missionary spirit of Southern Baptists: "That ours is a critical situation as a denomination all must admit. In presenting this body with our first annual report, therefore, we frankly face the difficulties, but at the same time call attention to certain aspects which should inspire gratitude and give confidence and hope."[3]

Throughout the previous year, many Baptist churches across the South had adopted annual budgeting protocols and were making preparations to include denominational mission funding as part of their annual budgets. The $7,072,234.84 collected in this manner between May 1, 1924, and May 1, 1925, from eighteen states, fell short of the $7,500,000 goal set for it the previous year. But the corpus of those funds still served as "a great stabilized nucleus," a solid foundation on which Baptists were "to build our greater superstructure of financial resources." This new program, Burts insisted, would constitute the "financial hope of our denomination."[4]

Dodd, however, pointed out that although the seven million dollars raised was a good start, it was "inadequate" for the work ahead of Southern Baptists. He argued that ongoing individual appeals from Baptist institutions and unsystematic giving from the churches were choking out the success of the Convention.

The words "demoralization" and "disaster" fell from his tongue, and he characterized this unsystematic giving approach as inefficiently and unnecessarily expensive, wasting Baptist dollars on fundraising rather than maximizing them in the gospel work for which they were given. Fortified by God's revealed direction and emboldened with clarity of purpose, Monroe Elmon Dodd, pastor of First Baptist Church, Shreveport, Louisiana, and chairman of the Future Program Commission, spoke with conviction and courage.[5]

Dodd's report included the provision that upon its adoption, the Future Program be renamed "The Co-Operative Program of Southern Baptists."[6] For a full thirty minutes, he stood for questions from the floor. When the vote was called, no hand opposed; the greatest unified missions-funding mechanism the world has ever known between voluntarily associated autonomous churches was born.[7] The CP of Southern Baptists found its genesis that afternoon, May 13, 1925, in Memphis, the power of the Mighty Mississippi beside it, the Crossroads of the South amidst it, and the command of unanimity behind it. And what would it take for the program to succeed? What was to be the price of innovative, systematic cooperation? What would hold the churches together and thrust them forward in this new season of Great Commission cooperation? "A unity of purpose and consecration never known before."

The need today is as it was then—that we might rediscover and recommit ourselves to a unity of purpose and consecration never known before. The chapters of this book are not merely a testimony to God's faithfulness in CP history; they are also a call to Southern Baptist solidarity in our present and to multiplied sacrifice in our future. Much of our world remains unreached with the gospel, the doors of billions of families' homes darkened by the curse of sin. Apart from Christ they will perish for all eternity, separated from the God who loves them. With all that we have been entrusted and with all the opportunity that lies before us, brothers and sisters, we cannot let it be. We must not. As you read these pages, perhaps your soul will be arrested with the same sense of urgency as ours. Perhaps you will see, as we do, that "the very time has come" for a renewed commitment to joyfully sacrificial investment in our shared mission through the CP.

Chapter 1, by W. Madison Grace II, builds out a compelling biblical doctrine of cooperation. The CP knows a one-hundred-year-old title among Southern Baptists, but it is rooted in a clear biblical theology of intercongregational financial cooperation. First-century churches pooled their resources and relationships together to send missionaries who evangelized the lost and planted churches. The Bible does not prescribe a particular method or organization of missional financial cooperation between churches, but it does record the practice as a regular, celebrated method of Great Commission advance.

In chapter 2, Jason Duesing digs deeply into our Baptist roots to survey the practice of cooperative missions giving. The Baptist movement began in 1609 when John Smyth broke ties with the Puritans and Separatists of his day through credobaptism. The movement fledged as it matured over several decades, but the more churches were gathered, the more they saw the need to work together for church strengthening and missions sending. Cooperation is embedded deeply in Baptist DNA. The Southern Baptist Convention, constituted in 1845, was built upon centuries of mission-minded intercongregational cooperation.

Chapter 3 continues the historical timeline by examining the missions-giving models of the Southern Baptist Convention before 1925. Adam Harwood demonstrates that upon its constitution in 1845, mission efforts of the Southern Baptist Convention were funded through society and associational methods of financial support. Representation in Convention meetings was afforded to members of various mission societies and missions-minded individuals. These society and associational methods of missions-giving and representation in the Southern Baptist movement became more complex as worthy missions organizations multiplied. The need for a unified budget and a strategic giving plan emerged as Southern Baptists' capacity for meaningful missions cooperation multiplied.

Chapter 4, by Taffey Hall, explains the social, political, and cultural context into which the CP was born. The Great War of 1914–1918 awakened American consciousness toward sacrificial cooperation in a common cause. Efficiency became a popular concept in businesses and organizations. Following the war, the roaring twenties saw a post-war concentration on social, economic, and political change. The CP found its genesis in this postwar American context and was, no doubt, influenced by the awakened consciousness of streamlined business practices and organized efficiency.

In chapter 5, Tony Wolfe examines the five years of Convention cooperation immediately before the permanent unified program was approved. Between 1919 and 1924, Southern Baptists launched their most aggressive missions-funding campaign to date: the $75 Million Campaign. While receipts fell woefully short of the goal, the effort can hardly be called a failure. The $75 Million Campaign awakened the Southern Baptist denominational consciousness to its capacity for a great, worldwide movement through sacrificial giving and organized collection. This campaign stimulated the imagination of Southern Baptists and set the stage for the greatest cooperative missions-giving and missions-sending mechanism they have ever known.

Chapter 6 begins the more celebratory, less academic portion of the book with an attempt at concisely defining the CP.

Tony Wolfe proposes the following: "The Cooperative Program is a missions-funding mechanism involving the deliberate and voluntary cooperation of local Baptist churches, state/regional Baptist conventions, and the Southern Baptist Convention through which every contributing Baptist maximizes the Great Commission impact of every dollar given." Churches voluntarily pool their resources together to send missionaries, provide scholarships for seminary students, plant churches, serve communities in crises and disasters, strengthen established churches, encourage church leaders, advocate for biblical values in the public square, and much more. Over the past one hundred years, more than $20 billion has been given through the CP to reach North America and the world with the gospel of Jesus Christ.

Chapter 7, by Leo Endel and Pete Ramirez, reports on one hundred years of CP giving from the perspective of a state convention executive leader. State conventions are the collecting agents of the CP. Each retains a portion of CP giving, as determined by its messengers, to populate the state's budget and reach the states or region with the gospel. For one hundred years, state conventions across America have labored and colabored diligently to plant churches, train church leaders, and propagate the gospel in their communities. God has richly blessed and highly favored the work of Southern Baptist state conventions in these one hundred years of CP organization.

Chapter 8 focuses on the work of the Southern Baptist seminaries as they have been sustained and supported through CP giving. Jamie Dew and Chris Shaffer represent seminary leaders with distinction as they tell the story of the CP from the seminaries' perspective. In 1859, Southern Baptists founded The Southern Baptist Theological Seminary. They founded New Orleans Baptist Theological Seminary in 1917, acquired Southwestern Baptist Theological Seminary in 1925, then founded Golden Gate (now Gateway) in 1944, Southeastern in 1950, and Midwestern in 1957. Since 1925, $1.7 billion of CP funding has been invested in the work of these seminaries resulting in almost 140,000 graduates deployed for missions and for every area of local church leadership.

Chapter 9, by Richard Land and Brent Leatherwood, narrates the story of Southern Baptists' engagement in public policy through the years. While Southern Baptists own a long history in organized public policy engagement, they officially organized the Social Service Commission in 1947, which eventually became the Christian Life Commission (1953) and then the Ethics & Religious Liberty Commission (1997). This organization has advocated tirelessly on behalf of Southern Baptists in Washington on issues of biblical morality and ethicality such as pro-life causes, the sanctity of marriage, biblical gender and sexuality, religious and economic freedom, and more. It has also worked to equip Southern Baptist churches with resources and consultation to engage their local and state governments on issues of biblical morality and ethicality that affect their daily lives in their own backyards.

Chapter 10, from the pens of Kevin Ezell and Mike Ebert, pulls its focus onto one of the first two organizations created by Southern Baptists, the North American Mission Board (previously the Home Mission Board and Domestic Mission Board). The Board has planted churches, mobilized evangelists, and proliferated evangelistic and missional resources in America since 1845. Since the inauguration of the CP in 1925, through their unified funding mechanism, Southern Baptists have continued their legacy of a unified purpose by planting thousands more churches and supporting the work of countless evangelists in an even more unified and systematic way than in their first eighty years. Through NAMB partnerships with state conventions, associations, and local churches, Southern Baptists not only cooperate to reach the nations for Christ but to reach their own neighborhoods as well.

Chapter 11 broadens the focus of Southern Baptist missional engagement as Paul Chitwood, Julie McGowan, and Melanie Clinton celebrate one hundred years of CP giving to the International Mission Board. Since its inception in 1845, "almost 25,000 Southern Baptist international missionaries have shared the gospel, made disciples, planted churches, and planted their lives in 185 countries around the world." Since 1925, this one sacred effort has been made possible by almost $4 billion invested in international missions through CP giving. The chapter follows the record of the Board's historical and concurrent activity and its missionaries' inspiring stories in China, Mexico, Nigeria, Pakistan, Vietnam, and other unreached regions around the world.

Chapter 12 begins the final section of the book by acknowledging present challenges and reaching forward to future opportunities. Since 1925, Southern Baptists have weathered many storms theologically, methodologically, relationally, financially, and organizationally. Challenges are not only behind us but in front of us as well—some new and some tired. But through them all, the persistent spirit of missional unity compels a level of cooperation between the churches with relentless Great Commission focus. Bart Barber acknowledges concurrent theological, sociological, financial, and organizational challenges for Southern Baptists but insists on a present and future hope through the persistent, unifying worldview that is embodied by our cooperative missions-funding program.

In chapter 13, RaShan Frost examines the ethics of cooperation with an eye on next-generation engagement. As the SBC and CP age, we must reproduce denominational understanding and commitment from generation to generation. What is compelling about our Baptist work to millennials and Gen Z? What about our work and our Cooperative Program will capture their hearts and invite them in? Perhaps *how* we engage is as important as *that* we engage.

In chapter 14, Scott McConnell demonstrates how vastly the world has changed since Southern Baptists launched the CP in 1925. The national and worldwide population has exploded. Lostness has increased by number and percentage. Thousands of people groups have been discovered but not yet engaged with the gospel. Technology has awakened our people to greater global awareness. Today the fields are white unto harvest, and the workers are few. The gospel stewardship before us is great, but through the years Southern Baptists have proven their ability to rise to the most extraordinary of challenges with a unity of purpose and prayerful dependence on the Holy Spirit.

Chapter 15 is an invitation to rise to our own time as Southern Baptists, with a unity of purpose and consecration never known before. Daniel Dickard proposes that today we stand at an "intersection" at which we must decide whether we move forward together or leave behind all that we have gained. The future of the Southern Baptist Convention, Dickard writes, will depend on persistent prayer, commitment to the Bible, charity in disagreement over secondary differences, congregational and intercongregational humility, dependence on the Holy Spirit, a refocus on mission and ministry, and renewed sacrificial generosity. "A new generation of Southern Baptist leaders must lean into our cooperative commitments with relentless determination if we are to steward our season successfully to the glory of God."

As you read through the chapters of this book, we hope you feel the urgency of our own day. We hope you hear, through the echoes of our past, the anticipation of our future. *A Unity of Purpose* must be more than a catchy historic quote and a timely book title. It must become the motivation of a newly consecrated people. Our shared mission keeps us together and drives us forward. Today, we must again become that Baptist people who own a unified purpose, a courageous innovation, and an iron resolve to work together for local and global gospel advance.

PART 1

Cooperation—
A Biblical Model

W. Madison Grace II

"Go, therefore, and make disciples of all nations." This was Jesus's final call to his disciples in the Gospel of Matthew. This is the Great Commission. It is the call given to believers by our Lord since the birth of Christianity more than two thousand years ago. It is the call to engage the lost with the truth of the good news that Jesus Christ has conquered sin and death and that salvation is available. This call, however, was never given to just one person. It was not an individual message that we individually accomplish on our own; that would be too enormous a task. Jesus has given *us* this call, his community. Through the people of God, known as the church, is how God has determined that this commission would be fulfilled.

From the book of Acts throughout the rest of the New Testament, we can see that churches are integral to the mission of Christianity. At the church's birth, individual communities gathered together to worship, learn, grow, and pray together (Acts 2).

As they did, the gospel message went outward from Jerusalem, to all Judea and Samaria, and to the ends of the earth (Acts 1). The way it went out, however, was not solely by means of individuals like Paul and Barnabas. The outward-working mission of these local churches occurred in concert with other churches. As Christianity moved to the uttermost, a fellowship existed and developed between believers *and* churches. From the Jerusalem Council in Acts 15 onward, we see churches cooperating with one another for gospel advance for the glory of God. This is why in the short statement on orthodox Christian belief the Nicene Creed makes sure to include the church. In the midst of important credos on the Trinity and Jesus Christ, it also confesses its belief in the "one, holy, catholic and apostolic church."

The universality of this body is integral to its mission. What the church *is* determines what the church *does*—though in modern times we seem to get this backward. Too often we become pragmatic and inwardly focused on what our local churches are doing instead of seeing how we exist alongside other gospel-minded churches. If we are going to be Great Commission churches, we need to accomplish that work as churches working together. Cooperation is essential to the task. Our doctrine of the church depends on it. Cooperation is a necessary part of ecclesiology, and it cannot be ignored.

This is a strong claim. It means individual churches *need* one another—not merely desire, like, tolerate, etc., but *need*. But is this actually the vision of the church we find in the Bible? In answering this question, we find a biblical and historic approach to churches seeking one another. We were not created to be alone, nor are churches intended to be purely independent. We were created to live in community and to work with one another in cooperation for God's kingdom.

As Southern Baptists, we confess a helpful summary of our position on cooperation in *The Baptist Faith and Message 2000*.

> Christ's people should, as occasion requires, organize such associations and conventions as may best secure cooperation for the great objects of the Kingdom of God. Such organizations have no authority over one another or over the churches. They are voluntary and advisory bodies designed to elicit, combine, and direct the energies of our people in the most effective manner. Members of New Testament churches should cooperate with one another in carrying forward the missionary, educational, and benevolent ministries for the extension of Christ's Kingdom. Christian unity in the New Testament sense is spiritual harmony and voluntary cooperation for common ends by various groups of Christ's people. Cooperation is desirable between the various Christian denominations, when the end to be attained is itself justified, and when such cooperation involves no violation of conscience or compromise of loyalty to Christ and His Word as revealed in the New Testament.[1]

In short, what we confess as churches is that we not only need others but that we should seek cooperation with others often and to the best of our abilities as long as we do not compromise our loyalty to Christ and his Word.

In what follows we will engage the doctrine of cooperation by seeing its foundation and function in New Testament churches. We will conclude with a summary of biblical practices necessary for cooperation among churches for kingdom purposes.

Foundations

Before Southern Baptists came together to cooperate for "one sacred effort," there was a long history in Christian tradition of churches working alongside one another. In some traditions this connection is hierarchal and political. For Baptist churches, who are autonomous, this partnership is more implicit but no less present. The need for community—even beyond our local spheres—is as old as New Testament churches themselves. There are many biblical passages in which we could anchor this conversation on the need for cooperation. We could look to creation with Adam and Eve, where we see it is not good for man to be alone. We could look to the creation of Israel as the covenant people of God in the Old Testament. We could see Jesus calling disciples around him and sending them out two by two. But the best place to see cooperation in the Bible is through the redeemed people of God seen in the New Testament: the Great Commission and the church.

In Acts 1:8 Jesus tells his disciples, "But you will receive power when the Holy Spirit has come on you, and you will be my witnesses in Jerusalem, in all Judea and Samaria, and to the ends of the earth." This is the Great Commission in Acts. It is rightly used to remind Christians and churches of our task. This is the gathering of God's people as commanded by Christ before he ascends into heaven. Here we get a commissioning of the people and a promise of their special community, the church. But more is going on in Acts 1 surrounding this commission that is helpful for us to understand its foundation for the church and our cooperation with one another.

Before we look at the nature of cooperation for this new community, I want us to see that even in the best situations we have the opportunity to get things wrong, to read things the way we want them to be read. Cooperation requires that we pay attention to others, not merely looking for our own interests. Twice in this passage we see Jesus's disciples misunderstand what God is doing. First, we notice it in the question they ask: "Are you going to restore the kingdom now?" After all the disciples had been through in the last few years, and especially the last few weeks, they still did not understand. They were looking for the end of their plan and were not in tune with God's plan.

On a basic level, we need to see that cooperation requires us to look beyond ourselves. If we are only pushing our desires and our purposes, we will miss what God is attempting to do in the world around us. I am reminded of churches throughout history who decided they were the only ones who had the right plan, interpretation, or biblical teaching. Many even believed they were the only true Christians. This does not allow for us to look and see what God is doing or to open ourselves up to his will for us.

The second misunderstanding happens after the ascension. Jesus has just given the commission—the action plan—for the people of God, and what do they do in response? They stare into the sky. Sure, they just saw Jesus ascend into heaven. Truly this was a sight to behold, but they had to be rebuked by God's angels. "Why are you staring into heaven? Go do what God told you to do." The ability to complete the commission is halted because of our inactivity. We want to stare and ponder the mysteries, but God has called us to work together to complete his mission.

Actually, we need to complete it with God himself. In the Matthean version of the Great Commission, we have the promise of Jesus Christ saying, "I am with you always, to the end of the age." For those who have come to faith in Jesus Christ, he is with you always; nothing can separate you from the Lord. This is a comforting but powerful thought. We can accomplish the work of God together because of the presence of Christ and the Holy Spirit in our lives.

Shortly after this commission, the church is born. Now there is a people of God gathered around the gospel in the power of God through the Holy Spirit. Authority, power, and divine presence now constitute this people as the church to complete the Great Commission task. These gatherings turn into times of worship, prayer, teaching, and fellowship, but they are never inwardly focused. They are aimed outward, beyond themselves, and as the gospel goes forth, they establish new communities of both Jews and Gentiles. They soon encounter challenges along the way—from within and without. How do we determine right teaching and practice? How do we navigate governmental interference and legal troubles? These and many other problems faced this new community called the church, and they found their help in God through means of other churches. They worked together as they took the gospel to the nations.

The Nature of the Church

Before looking more closely at the way in which the church and the churches in the New Testament cooperated with one another, it is helpful to take a moment to clarify what we mean by "church." A church is not a building. It is not a movement, a political party, or a philosophy. The church is a gathered people, the people of God. It exists as a body (1 Cor. 12), a bride (Eph. 5), a temple (1 Cor. 6). Unlike other gatherings of people in the world, the church is unique because Christ is with it and the Spirit indwells it. Eckhard Schnabel sums up the divine nature of the church as follows: "The Jesus followers were convinced that the one God and the exalted Jesus Messiah were present through the Spirit in their lives and in their congregations. This is arguably the most fundamental conviction of the early church."[2]

Baptism becomes the public identifying marker of this engagement with the Father, Son, and Holy Spirit. This participation in God sets the church and the churches apart from the world, yet it also establishes the rationale for why different churches should cooperate with one another. The same Spirit indwells us. The same Christ unites us. The same commission stands before us. We should want to work together for the kingdom, not work against one another. A call to cooperation is a call to complete God's work.

The nature of the church is intended to be unified. Not a variety of individual churches doing similar work but a group of churches united as the church. Paul speaks about this unity in Ephesians 4:4–6: "There is one body and one Spirit—just as you were called to one hope at your calling—one Lord, one faith, one baptism, one God and Father of all, who is above all and through all and in all." Paul is speaking to the church at Ephesus but is also pointing to the reality that all are unified with one God. Every church that exists does so because of the same Lord, same faith, and same God. We are unified in God, and because of that, we work together toward one end: to make disciples of the nations.

The Cooperation of Churches in the New Testament

When the church was birthed in Acts 2, we find that believers quickly began taking care of one another. In 2:44–45 we see that they "held all things in common" and "sold their possessions and property and distributed the proceeds to all, as any had need." This level of generosity marked the nature of the communion that existed among these believers. From the beginning of Christianity, we see that we are characterized by an inherent need for one another. Great growth accompanied this movement of faithful fellowship, as we see in verse 47: "Every day the Lord added to their number those who were being saved." Then we find that in 5:14, "Believers were added to the Lord in increasing numbers—multitudes of both men and women."

This pattern of mutual care and growth continues throughout the book. In chapter 4 we notice the unity of the church. Verse 32 states, "Now the entire group of those who believed were of one heart and mind, and no one claimed that any of his possessions was his own, but instead they held everything in common." The repetition of this accounting helps the reader see the importance of the nature of the New Testament church as well as the historical growth God was accomplishing within, among, and through them.

We see this growth take new pathways in Acts 8 when the Samaritans now come to faith. The Samaritans were a people akin to the Jews but who practiced their faith differently. Remember Jesus with the women at the well in John 4. The woman points out to Jesus that they worshipped differently—one in Jerusalem and the other on a mountain. However, Jesus's reply to her was a radical statement of what his church would be. In the near future, Samaritans and Jews would worship together "in Spirit and in truth" (John 4:23). That reality is seen in Acts 8 as Samaritans respond to the gospel and receive the Holy Spirit. New communities are created of a variety of people. This is followed by the introduction of the work of Paul, who would become the missionary to the Gentiles and joined with Peter, who, in Acts 10, would come to see that God wants to save the Gentiles as well as the Jews. This group of people, thought of solely as outsiders, now have received the Spirit as well. With the excitement of new churches, comprised of all types of people, come controversies as well. What do we do with Samaritans, let alone other Gentiles? Do they need to become Jews first, or is the gift of the Spirit enough to claim them as fellow believers? How these questions were answered provides the biblical insight into New Testament church cooperation.

Doctrinal Support

In Acts 15 we see a clear example of cooperation that exists between churches as the church in Antioch and the church in Jerusalem work together to solve the issue of Gentile believers. In the midst of a major doctrinal dispute—who can be a church member—Christians sought the assistance of others at another church. This is cooperation. The church at Antioch did not report to the church in Jerusalem; they sought them out to find assistance. If you would allow me to speculate, they likely did not fear that they would lose their local church autonomy or be taken over by the church in Jerusalem. They merely wanted help in discerning a matter that caused great division for them, and a fellow church—a more established one—could help. This is cooperation, and it is found throughout the New Testament.

The activity of churches supporting one another doctrinally and missionally is seen by the sending out of missionaries. These ambassadors for the kingdom of God completed their task by pioneering new areas for gospel advance and leading people to faith in Jesus Christ. They would remain for several months to help establish the new communities of faith and plant churches. We see this most clearly through the variety of letters written by Paul to churches he has been a part of and others he would like to visit. Some of these writings were not meant to be occasional letters only for one individual church. They were intended to be shared. This cooperation for growth in the knowledge of God is prevalent between the churches in the Bible. The New Testament letters were circulated among the churches. Consider Colossians 4:16: "After this letter has been read at your gathering, have it read also in the church of the Laodiceans; and see that you also read the letter from Laodicea." From Acts 15 onward we find that churches cooperate with one another for doctrinal help and teaching.

Prayer Support

We also see that the churches are connected to one another through prayer and gospel work. They are aware of one another and are supportive of one another. From the earliest gathering in Acts, we see that prayer was a major activity of the church. Prayers are offered for those inside the church, but also we find a broader sense of prayer among churches. Consider this example from 1 Thessalonians 1:2–8:

> We always thank God for all of you, making mention of you constantly in our prayers. We recall, in the presence of our God and Father, your work produced by faith, your labor motivated by love, and your endurance inspired by hope in our Lord Jesus Christ. For we know, brothers and sisters loved by God, that he has chosen you, because our gospel did not come to you in word only, but also in power, in the Holy Spirit, and with full assurance. You know how we lived among you for your benefit, and you yourselves became imitators of us and of the Lord when, in spite of severe persecution, you welcomed the message with joy from the Holy Spirit. As a result, you became an example to all

the believers in Macedonia and Achaia. For the
word of the Lord rang out from you, not only in
Macedonia and Achaia, but in every place that
your faith in God has gone out.

In this beautiful passage of prayerful cooperation, we see how different churches are not rivals of one another but are partners in the ministry together. They rejoice in prayers for one another and are encouraged by the way others are imitating them in the gospel. The church has become an example to the broader region of the good news of Jesus. Do not miss the last line: "The word of the Lord rang out from you." This is an effect of the cooperative nature of the churches in the New Testament. They were able to accomplish more (amid suffering) because of the continued cooperation and unity in prayer and support. This is an example of multiple embassies of God's kingdom cooperating with prayerful intentionality.

Financial Support

Not only do we see churches helping one another in matters of faith and prayer, but we also see churches supporting one another financially. As stated earlier, the practice of the church birthed in Jerusalem was to look after the needs of the congregation. Here Christians are sharing all things in common (Acts 2:45; 4:32–35). Although Acts 5 depicts the events of the lies of Ananias and Sapphira, it also shows us that the giving was voluntary (see v. 4). In chapter 6 we see that another need arises in the church in the way in which widows are being taken care of. Not only is a solution for that church found, but the foundation for the office of deacon is established. Clearly voluntary financial assistance is part of the life of a local church.

We also see that different churches are supporting one another. Consider Paul's instructions to the church at Corinth about supporting the church in Jerusalem:

> Now about the collection for the saints: Do the same as I instructed the Galatian churches. On the first day of the week, each of you is to set something aside and save in keeping with how he is prospering, so that no collections will need to be made when I come. When I arrive, I will send with letters those you recommend to carry your gift to Jerusalem. If it is suitable for me to go as well, they will travel with me. (1 Cor. 16:1–4)

A pattern seems evident for how churches are going to financially support one another in the work of the kingdom. We see this in Paul's individual life as churches would send support to him. The Philippian church was an early financial supporter of Paul's missionary enterprise, but eventually other churches joined them in cooperatively funding the work:

> And you Philippians know that in the early days of the gospel, when I left Macedonia, no church shared with me in the matter of giving and receiving except you alone. For even in Thessalonica you sent gifts for my need several times. (Phil. 4:15–16)

> In 2 Corinthians 9 Paul is giving instructions for the way in which a gift is to be given. Paul wanted to ensure that it was not merely zeal that was promised but an actual gift for assistance,

> as the Corinthians had promised. When the gift is given, it should be given from the heart. Paul writes clearly, The point is this: The person who sows sparingly will also reap sparingly, and the person who sows generously will also reap generously. Each person should do as he has decided in his heart—not reluctantly or out of compulsion, since God loves a cheerful giver. (vv. 6–7)

Over and over again in the New Testament, we find a voluntary cooperation of churches to other churches for partnership in the ministry of the gospel.

When we look through the New Testament and see how the different churches interacted with one another, we do not find independent churches who are fortressed off from others or, worse, rivalry among churches. Rather, we find churches that understand their place in propagating the gospel and fulfilling the Great Commission. To do so to the uttermost, these churches operate with the understanding that they *need* one another. The task is too great and too broad for just one church to accomplish. The support in matters of faith, prayer, and financial giving are just some of the ways these churches voluntarily partnered with one another.

Conclusion

So, what does it really look like for autonomous churches to willingly and joyfully cooperate with other autonomous churches for the advancement of the Great Commission? We have seen a variety of examples in the New Testament of what it could look like. However, there is not a prescribed way to cooperate. In

The Baptist Faith and Message 2000, we confess that we should cooperate to "carry forward the missionary, educational, and benevolent ministries for the extension of Christ's Kingdom." For Southern Baptists this means we are able to strengthen and assist one another in these areas. As a national Convention, Southern Baptists have two missions organizations (the International Mission Board and the North American Mission Board), six seminaries that train ministers, and other worthy organizations like Guidestone Financial Resources, Lifeway Christian Resources, and the Ethics & Religious Liberty Commission—all of which exist to assist churches in their kingdom work. These are some examples of cooperation but not the only ways in which a church can participate. In general, cooperation can be seen in three ways: prayer, giving, and support.

Prayer

First and foremost, churches that want to be united to other churches and cooperate for the kingdom need to pray for one another. Again, we see the example of the New Testament where prayers were offered for other churches time and again. Nothing demonstrates unity among churches like prayers offered among them. Just as prayer unites individuals in family units and within each local church, prayer unites the churches with one another. It is good for churches to be aware of other churches in their area and around the world who are engaging in similar missional enterprises. Lift up individual missionaries who are serving globally, and pray for the church down the street. Our end goal is to advance the Great Commission together, and no better method exists to accomplish that goal than praying for the Lord's work in these areas.

Giving

Second, we can give through these ministries. In the New Testament we saw that collections were made for other churches and for individuals who were engaged in gospel work. As local churches collect financial resources for their own ministries, they can take offerings to assist with the kingdom work of other churches and missionaries around the globe as well. In any instance of money in the church, we are just managers of what God has already provided, and we should voluntarily and joyfully distribute the wealth of his provisions in missional ways. A local church should discuss and decide how they will be involved in giving to kingdom work. This could be a percentage of the budget that goes out to missions agencies and community projects, or it could be more granular; but there should be a means through which the church is able to provide resources beyond itself. Might I suggest prayerful consideration of sacrificially funding the entire ecosystem of Baptist Great Commission work through the Southern Baptist Cooperative Program?

Support

Finally, a church can show its cooperation by sending out workers into the harvest. There should be a consistent effort from the church to identify those persons who are to be sent out to do gospel work elsewhere. No church is building its own kingdom but exists as an embassy of the kingdom. When church members give evidence of particular abilities that could help the kingdom, the church should support these persons in sending them forth for gospel advance.

This can look different depending on the person and his or her abilities. Some in a congregation are called out to be missionaries in the world, taking the gospel to places where it is not yet established. Others will be called out to lead as pastors/elders in other congregations. God is calling both types of ministers constantly, and it is dutiful and beautiful for a church to send out these called ones, in cooperation with like-minded churches, to be equipped and to do gospel work. Often these men and women need equipping, training, and assistance. They can find that needed training at our supported Southern Baptist seminaries and a network of mobilization experts in our associations, state conventions, and mission boards.

Though being a pastor or a missionary is often what churches imagine when they talk of sending out the called, there are other ways churches can show their cooperative spirit on a local level. Often, communities need work that churches can provide. Disaster relief, benevolence, and community involvement are all ways that help communities flourish, and churches should send out members to engage in these more localized cooperative missions as well.

These three areas of cooperation (prayer, giving, and support) should be a regular part of church life. However, this at no time comes at the expense of the autonomy of a local church. The ability to cooperate with other churches and ministries is always a voluntary work on the part of the church. No other body has authority over the church, nor does agreeing to cooperate infringe upon that autonomy. Rather, cooperation demonstrates the love, joy, and grace of a church in the way in which it voluntarily joins with broader cooperative works for Great Commission advance.

Personal Testimony

I am a lifelong Southern Baptist and a thorough beneficiary of the CP. When I was born, my parents served in a local Southern Baptist church. When I came to faith, it was in another local Southern Baptist church. There I was taught the Bible through Discipleship Training and Bible drills. I learned about missions as a child in Royal Ambassadors (RAs) as well as from the stateside IMB missionaries who would visit us and tell us about kingdom work around the globe. As a youth I participated in camps—Centrifuge and M-Fuge. I was called to ministry out of a local Baptist church while I was attending a Mississippi Baptist-supported college, Mississippi College. From there I went to a Southern Baptist seminary for two degrees, where I count it my great joy to be able to serve Southern Baptists as I minister and work at Southwestern Baptist Theological Seminary in Fort Worth, Texas. It is hard for me to look back at the decades of my life and not be thankful for the influence of Southern Baptists. That could not have happened without the sacrificial support of Baptist churches giving through the CP.

There are other ways to cooperate for the kingdom, and there are other healthy, Bible-believing denominations one could join, but my life experience has been with Southern Baptists and the CP. We are far from perfect, but so were New Testament churches. What keeps me anchored to the cooperative efforts of Southern Baptists is the overall goal we have in engaging in Great Commission efforts and seeing them accomplished through the thousands of churches and missionaries we are connected to around the world.

2

Cooperation in Baptist Beginnings, 1609–1845

Jason G. Duesing

Why should Southern Baptist churches cooperate? This is one question I ask students taking the required Baptist history class I teach. I ask it because every generation of students asks it, or will ask it, or needs to ask it, and I want them to know how I answer it and have arrived at my answer with cheerful conviction.

While many Protestant and Evangelical churches are like-minded and share the same core convictions about doctrine and missions as the Baptists, for those preparing to serve and lead Baptist churches, my course is designed to help them understand, develop, and defend their convictions about the ecclesial tradition to which their church is connected.

The Baptist movement began in England as small groups of men and women met to establish themselves in churches and then sought fellowship with other churches around common beliefs and practice. This early confessional cooperation grew out of, and centered on, the Reformation program of doctrinal renewal which emerged from the study of the Bible and led to the recovery of the biblical gospel message. As these Baptist churches gained strength, they crossed to the New World and grew into a fleet of churches sailing together, united in doctrine and headed in Great Commission direction.

A Fleet Sailing Together

The picture of churches as ships sailing is fitting for our understanding of the value of intercongregational cooperation as it conveys, first, that they are not the only ships at sea. There are many churches, of course, but not all have set sail, and not all are headed in the direction of global evangelism. Thus, it is helpful for churches to find partners who agree not only in their design and beliefs but also in their shared trajectory. Not all churches aiming to fulfill the Great Commission are Baptist churches, and wherever possible Baptist churches can and should sail with those with whom they can unite in evangelism and missions. Celebrating and encouraging other evangelical churches in this shared task is not something Baptist churches have always done well in their history, but when understood in these terms, they could find value in mutual encouragement. Likewise, as Baptist churches seek to start new churches to add to their fleet, they will find safe harbor and maximized mission when they work with other Baptist churches who not only are sailing in the same direction but also are united on the kinds of churches they are seeking to fund and start together at the ends of the earth.

Second, the picture conveys that these ships do need to tend to their own vessels to maximize speed and stay on course. To stay afloat in the world for gospel proclamation, Baptist churches have found the need to prioritize their own doctrinal and congregational health. These ships will, no doubt, encounter storms without and conflict within. A church that has lost its first love may also lose the Spirit's enabling wind power behind it. Baptist churches at sea need to minimize any hindrance that would pull them off course.

Third, this picture conveys that individuals can serve and live on one ship at a time. While circumstance may dictate the need for believers to change churches, for most the norm is continuing to serve on the ship where one is placed. When a sailor is counting on the buoyancy of his ship for his life and safe travel, he is far more likely to look after the health and heading of the ship. It is the picture of foolishness to see sailors lounging on the top deck complaining about their ship, or envying another ship nearby, when their own is languishing due to their lack of effort. Thus, Baptist churches are more likely to be strengthened, revitalized, and steered back on course when their members are focused on thankfulness for the ship on which they have been placed, the fleet of which they are a part, and using their gifts to help keep that ship, and fleet, on course.

Why should Southern Baptist churches cooperate? This chapter aims to show that from their beginnings, Baptist churches found they needed other churches to maintain their own doctrinal health and to accomplish the shared mission given to all churches. Despite their faults and blind spots, from small groups in seventeenth-century England to the first national Baptist denomination in the United States in the nineteenth century, Baptist churches have persevered to hold intercongregational cooperation in doctrinal confession and missionary endeavor as a key distinctive. As I love to tell my students, this story is worthy of retelling to inspire ongoing renewal of Baptist churches of the present and future as they carry out the same mission. With that intent in view, in this chapter I will tell the story of Baptist beginnings.

A Symphony of History and Theology

Like a coin with two sides, the beginning of the Baptist tradition is a story that must be told in both history and theology. To look only at the historical development minimizes the theological foundation of important pre-Baptist influences. To look only at theological connections minimizes the actual events and people in history who referred to themselves as Baptist by name. As such, it is right to see the theological start of Baptist churches as rooted in the Protestant Reformation, even while the chronicling of churches named Baptist does not appear in history until a century later in England.[1]

Keeping both history and theology in view is what I call a "symphonious approach" to assessing movements in history.[2] Just like a symphony of music, history and theology represent diverse and complementary components; each plays an overlapping part that, when examined together, produces a comprehensive piece. For example, while it is helpful to determine who were the first persons in history to name something or start something, it is also necessary to understand what thoughts influenced their actions and how those thoughts fit into the development of those people and those around them.

In the same way, where it is helpful to examine why churches first adopted the practice of believer's baptism—what they were thinking and how they made their theological argument—it is needed to understand who these people were, how they arrived at their conclusions, and the cultural circumstances that influenced their thinking and actions. A symphonious approach allows the movements of both history and theology to play together and presents both well-ordered history and well-reasoned theology without the distractions of prioritized chronology or doctrine separated from people and churches.

Therefore, as this chapter observes the formation of a fleet of Baptist ships setting sail in a Great Commission direction from 1609 to 1845, it will track the symphony of both their theology and history. To start, I summarize the theological distinctives that grew throughout the history of the Baptist tradition this way:

> (1) A people of the Bible who preach the gospel and have found it helpful to summarize what the Bible says about the Christian life in confessions of faith. (2) The practice of believer's baptism by immersion as the entrance to a (3) believer's church that is (4) free and separate from the state and thus advocates religious freedom for all in society while (5) seeking to share the gospel with all in society and to the ends of the earth in an intentional and organized Great Commission focus on evangelism and missions, all done through (6) biblical cooperation among churches.[3]

This chapter will now survey how these theological distinctives formed in history and, for our purposes, the specific practice of intercongregational cooperation.

Pre-Baptist Cooperation

The Baptist tradition's connection to the Reformation is like that of a tree to its roots. What connects later Baptist churches in England to sixteenth-century doctrinal renewal in Europe is rooted in the Reformation's recovery of the gospel as expressed in the five solas: *Scripture alone, faith alone, grace alone, Christ alone, to the glory of God alone.* Later Baptists demonstrate this connection through their confessions of faith, which sought to maintain connectivity both to the core doctrines of the Christian tradition and to those renewed during the Reformation. The doctrine of the church is where they branched from those roots, following the path started by the Anabaptists—a pre-Baptist wing of the Reformation who championed the separation of church and state as marked by the practice of believer's baptism.[4]

The Anabaptists saw themselves as applying *Scripture alone* to the doctrine of the church—and often at the cost of their lives. This conviction led them to gather with others so minded and adopt a shared confession of faith that focused on ecclesiology, the Schleitheim Confession (1527). The confession reinforced their doctrinal connection to the rest of the Reformers in all areas other than the doctrine of the church. Herein lies an early prototype of Baptist cooperation—churches gathering to define and defend what they believed to accomplish a shared mission. To be sure, there is no historical connection between the Anabaptists and later Baptists, but the Reformation practice of doctrinal renewal based on the Bible and cooperation around church distinctives does serve as principle roots, or a model, of later Baptist intercongregational cooperation.[5]

Seventeenth-Century Baptist Cooperation

The story of Baptist cooperation in England in the seventeenth century is one of survival. Rooted in the English Reformation, these early Baptists were the heirs of a renewal movement that was fueled by access to the Bible in English. Yet, their early movement was illegal, and their existence was threatened by the state church that forbade participation in other worship services. To understand why they persisted, it is helpful to review their beginnings.

Puritans and Separatists

The Reformation of English churches first started with a break from Roman Catholicism for political rather than theological reasons.[6] As such, the Church of England underwent several contentious decades of redefinition until the reign of Elizabeth I. During this era, those leaders who sought a theological Reformation to purify the church from within were termed "Puritans." A more restless subset of the Puritans who desired reformation of the church at all costs found the cost was worth removing themselves from the established ecclesial hierarchy. As a result, historians have classified these churches as Separatists.

The Separatists sought to organize their churches first after biblical instruction instead of tradition. The result was a common belief that each church was autonomous, governed by their congregation.[7] These convictions were recorded by Separatist leaders in A True Confession of Faith (1596), a document that guided their churches and perpetuated the movement, despite opposition. Elizabeth I's "Act against Puritans" (1593) required that anyone not attending their assigned Church of England assembly for one month resulted in imprisonment. Thus, many of the early Separatist leaders faced a decision either to lead their churches from jail or lead them to leave England. One Separatist leader, John Robinson, persevered with his congregation outside London until it grew to a size such that it was bound to attract the attention of the authorities. He and fellow church leader, John Smyth, agreed to divide the congregation for survival. Eventually, they all felt survival meant leaving England.[8]

The General Baptists

John Smyth's congregation, thanks to the financial support of one wealthy member, Thomas Helwys, moved to Holland. There Smyth wrestled with the doctrine of baptism. Because he now viewed the Church of England as a false church, he considered his infant baptism no longer valid. As a result, Smyth became convinced that believer's baptism was biblical, although not necessarily by immersion in water. As there was no other congregation to baptize Smyth and his congregation, he determined it was best to inaugurate the new baptismal practice themselves. Smyth led them by first baptizing himself by affusion, then Helwys, and then the rest of the congregation. Taking place in 1609, this action stands as the first believer's baptism by an English-speaking congregation—though not by immersion and not in England.

Smyth then learned of a local Mennonite congregation and grew fascinated with their practices as well as sampling other theological trends that pervaded Holland. During 1609–1610, he modulated his Puritan theological heritage at several points in favor of the teachings of the Dutch theologian Jacob Arminius. As a result, Smyth regretted his practice of self-baptism and led several church members to apply to join the Mennonites. Helwys and a majority of the congregation, though also influenced by Arminius on some doctrines, especially in a general or universal atonement, maintained their convictions and their practice of baptism and continued to develop their church practice, now separate from Separatism. Convicted that thousands of their countrymen in England were in need of the gospel, Helwys led the congregation to return to London. As they established the first Baptist church in England in 1612, Helwys advocated in print for religious freedom and the end of a state church. This led to his imprisonment and death in 1616, but the congregation persevered, and the English Baptist movement launched. Due to their Dutch-influenced theological convictions in a general atonement, these churches are often called General Baptist churches.[9]

The Particular Baptists

In the decades that followed, another group of Baptist churches in England formed independent of the Helwys church. These churches started from a congregation known by the names of its first three pastors as the Jacob-Lathrop-Jessey (J-L-J) Church. The J-L-J Church met in London as a semi-Separatist congregation, comprised of congregationalist governance while maintaining some connection to the Church of England. Unlike the Smyth Separatist congregation, the J-L-J church maintained its Puritan theological heritage in all areas except ecclesiology.[10] In the 1630s some members, desiring full separation from the Church of England, left after a request for a new baptism was declined. During the next decade, when Henry Jessey served as pastor, many in the church resurfaced the baptism debate, now convinced that biblical baptism is reserved only for believers. This led to some members seeking counsel from other churches.

In 1641, a number of members separated to form a new church that not only practiced believer's baptism but also instituted the mode of baptism as full immersion in water, convinced this mode best follows the New Testament command.[11] By 1644, seven Baptist churches in London cooperated to write a Confession of Faith (1644), sharing a theological and structural foundation with the Separatist's A True Confession (1596). The Baptist Confession provided a cooperative document for Baptist churches to defend themselves from false claims of heresy as well as to define their ecclesiology for other like-minded churches. As the theology of these churches did not waver from their Puritan beginnings, they are often termed Particular Baptist churches, consistent with their belief in a limited or particular atonement.

Confessional Cooperation

This movement of English Baptist churches grew during the 1650s as England entered a decade of religious tolerance due to the absence of the monarchy following a civil war. When the monarchy was restored in the 1660s, persecution for dissenting groups, like the Baptists, increased; and although many were imprisoned, the churches survived. When official religious freedom arrived in England following the Act of Toleration (1689), Baptist leaders Hanserd Knollys and William Kiffen were able to lead these churches to adopt a new confession of faith. Since the first Confession (1644), the English Presbyterians had adopted the Westminster Confession (1646), and the Congregationalists took a revised version of it as their own in the Savoy Confession (1658). To show doctrinal unity with these groups, the Particular Baptists wanted to revise their confessions while updating their ecclesiological distinctives. Drafted first in 1677, the second Baptist Confession of Faith was adopted by these cooperating churches in 1689.

Likewise, the churches that formed from the Helwys church multiplied and began meeting together as an association of churches in what they called the General Assembly. Through the General Assembly, these churches would cooperate to adopt the Standard Confession (1660) also to defend against claims of heresy. For similar reasons as the Particular Baptists, some General Baptist churches wanted to cooperate to adopt another confession to show unity with other non-Baptists while maintaining their Baptist distinctives. They, too, followed the Westminster

Confession (1646), though not as closely, and adopted the Orthodox Creed (1679).

In seventeenth-century England, the intercongregational cooperative effort among the fledging Baptists arose around the need for shared confessions of faith in order to ensure their ecclesiological survival. With religious freedom, the Baptists stabilized and entered the next century with a view toward partnering with one another for expansion and growth, although not without more theological challenges.

Eighteenth-Century Baptist Cooperation

The story of Baptist cooperation in the eighteenth century is one of adolescent growth. Religious freedom in England brought opportunity for growth. Baptist churches could now own property, evangelize, and recruit new members without fear of arrest. However, this freedom also ushered in an opportunity for theological drift.

Doctrinal Decay

Without the refining fire of banding together for the survival of their churches, the adolescent Baptists were distracted by the Age of Reason and the increased questioning of much of what the Reformation recovered. As the Baptists transitioned to a second generation, they inherited a ministerial class that had no formal theological education and no opportunity to receive such. While religious freedom existed, Baptists were not invited to attend English universities. These factors led to doctrinal decay for most of the century. The General Baptists embraced philosophical influences that led them to elevate rational logic as an authority higher than Scripture. They first questioned the full divinity of Christ and then drifted further to a full denial of orthodox

Trinitarianism. The Particular Baptists also pursued logic over Scripture, which led them to adopt theological conclusions about God's work in salvation that immobilized their preaching of the gospel.

The General Baptists

The General Baptists continued in the general assembly of churches for the purpose of doctrinal maintenance and ministry partnership. While some fought to retain biblical orthodoxy, in time they were outnumbered, and by the 1730s the General Baptists denied the Trinity altogether. This drifting coincided with the Great Awakening movement among the Church of England churches, the Congregationalists, and what would become the Methodists. One Anglican who was converted during the Awakening, Daniel Taylor, became a lay preacher and followed his study of the Bible to receive believer's baptism by a General Baptist church in the 1760s. Discouraged by the doctrinal error he found in the Baptist churches, he and others planted a new General Baptist church and sought to form a new assembly based on a return to orthodoxy. The New Connection of General Baptist Churches, formed in 1770, saw a recovery of General Baptist churches and the start of a new cooperative ministry that thrived until Taylor's death in 1816.

The Particular Baptists

The Particular Baptists continued to organize in an association of churches, also for doctrinal maintenance and ministry partnership. They saw doctrinal decline in this era as they adopted a series of theological views commonly called "Hyper-Calvinism." Seeking to uphold the sovereignty of God, they followed Anglican and Nonconformist teachers who made claims of logic that prescribed the restriction of gospel preaching to non-Christians since one does not know whether others were chosen by God for salvation. These conclusions that went beyond the clear commands of Scripture to preach the gospel brought a reduction by half of the total number of Particular Baptist churches in the first half of the eighteenth century.

As the Great Awakening revived many churches in England, the Particular Baptists were awakened from their doctrinal slumber. One Particular Baptist pastor, Andrew Fuller, frozen in his own preaching of the gospel due to the influence of Hyper-Calvinism, started a corrective movement in his church and among other churches in the 1780s. Other than his own reading of the Bible, the chief instrument that led to the thawing of his theology was the writings of the Massachusetts pastor and theologian of the Great Awakening, Jonathan Edwards. Fuller's reading of Edwards convinced him that it is the duty of all people to believe in the gospel; therefore the gospel should be preached to all people. This revival in theology influenced another local pastor, William Carey, and led him to question the long-held interpretation that the Great Commission no longer applied to present-day churches. Convinced that the grand command applied to all Christians, Carey developed a manifesto and a plan to organize Baptist churches to send missionaries to the peoples of the world who did not have the gospel, much less a translation of the Bible. Preaching to pastors at an association meeting of cooperating Baptist churches, Carey challenged them to attempt great things for God, and the association voted to form the Baptist Missionary Society and to send Carey to India. The result of this renewal of theology among cooperating churches was the start of the modern missions movement.

Baptists in America

As Separatists fled England in the seventeenth century for the colonies in North America, Baptists soon followed, establishing churches in Rhode Island—a new colony founded for those seeking religious freedom. As the northern colonies were not conducive for Baptist expansion due to climate and persecution, Pennsylvania emerged as a center for Baptist development in the early eighteenth century. In 1707, five churches started the Philadelphia Baptist Association for the purpose of doctrinal edification and ministerial support. As the churches grew in number and strength, the association served as a connection point for churches to cooperate for the training of ministers with the understanding that they could do more ministry together than any one church could do alone. In 1742, the association adopted a revised version of the London Confession of Faith (1689) to serve as a defining document for churches and for new ministry endeavors. One of those endeavors was the sending of Oliver Hart to aid Baptist churches in South Carolina. Hart pastored a congregation in Charleston and led churches, in 1751, to form the Charleston Baptist Association. Modeled after the Philadelphia Association, Charleston adopted the same confession and ministry program.[12]

Baptist churches, like all church traditions in the colonies, were impacted by the Great Awakening. The revival and conversion of many people in Congregationalist churches sparked conflict among those who were resistant to change. As a result, many of these new Congregationalists became Baptists. Shubal Stearns was one of those new Baptists who, impacted by the Great Awakening, moved to North Carolina to start the Sandy Creek Baptist Church. Soon thereafter, his church planted other churches and, by 1758, established the Sandy Creek Baptist

Association. These "Separate" Baptists adopted their own confession of faith, but the theological differences between these revivalist Baptists and the Philadelphia/Charleston Baptists were slight.[13] These two Baptist groups served different regions and people—the Sandy Creek churches formed among the rural and less educated, while the Philadelphia/Charleston churches served the educated in cities. As a new nation formed in 1776 and the United States grew in territory and people, these associations of Baptist churches would grow closer together for the purpose of shared mission and the advancement of religious liberty, despite cultural and regional differences.[14]

Christianity was slow to take root among enslaved African Americans in the eighteenth century due, in part, to the first representation of Christianity from those that enslaved them. However, once language and cultural barriers were minimized, the gospel spread, and many slaves trusted Christ and joined a new tradition of African American Baptists. George Liele, a slave in Georgia, was converted at Buckhead Creek Baptist Church in 1773, where his owner served as a deacon. After two years, Liele was preaching before the congregation, and his owner granted his freedom. Soon thereafter, he started the first African American Baptist church in America, near Savannah, Georgia. Liele relocated to Jamaica in the aftermath of the Revolutionary War, where he, now functioning as a cross-cultural missionary, started a new church to minister to the slave population. A decade before William Carey organized English Baptists for missions, Liele served as a missionary and helped shape a movement of cooperating churches in Jamaica that reached thousands of enslaved peoples.

In eighteenth-century England, the intercongregational cooperative effort among the adolescent Baptist churches drifted and then recovered around foundational confessions of faith that resulted in the modern missions movement. In America, new traditions of Baptist associations formed with shared doctrine and developing mission, including among enslaved African Americans, despite the culture acceptance and defense of slavery by many Baptists. With a new mission, the Baptists entered the next century with a disposition toward partnership in American-based cooperative missions, for the first time at the national level.

Nineteenth-Century Baptist Cooperation

The story of Baptist cooperation in the early nineteenth century is one of growth for united mission—or, as this volume articulates, as a precursor to the "unity of purpose" they had always shared. As Baptist churches in England sent missionaries through their Baptist Missionary Society, Baptist churches in America were given an opportunity to form their own missionary-sending denomination.

Pioneer Baptist Missionaries

The pioneer Baptist missionaries funded by a national Baptist cooperative effort were sent first by the Congregationalists. Ann and Adoniram Judson were reared in Congregationalist churches in Massachusetts. They met during the years when Adoniram and his fellow seminary students were organizing churches to form a missions society to send them in the footsteps of William Carey. Judson, a bright young man, was converted after college and after years of pursuing his own fame and ambitions. The humbling that came through his faith and trust in Jesus Christ resulted in a willing heart to serve wherever God would lead him. Gathering at Andover Seminary with several like-minded students, Judson consecrated his life to take the gospel to those nations where Christ had not yet been named.

Following their marriage, the Judsons set out for India in 1812, where they planned to meet the now famous William Carey before setting out for Burma. Knowing Carey was a Baptist, Judson set out to study the doctrine of baptism so as to be able to converse (and debate) with him. However, Judson's study of the New Testament in Greek led him, and also Ann, to conclude that believer's baptism by immersion was the biblical expectation. As a result, he and Ann received baptism in India. This decision was a de facto resignation from the missions society he helped form, for he could no longer seek to start Congregationalist churches in Burma. One of the Judsons' comissionaries, Luther Rice, was also convinced and was baptized. Due to Rice's ailing health, the Judsons agreed that Rice should return and work to organize the Baptist churches to form a new society to fund them and other Baptist missionaries.

Luther Rice traveled at length throughout the United States speaking to churches to organize their funding to form a new Baptist missions-sending organization. Rice's zeal proved effective but was not without opposition. Several Baptist churches questioned whether the idea of forming a missions organization was biblical. These were not opposed to the Great Commission or the sending of missionaries but rather remained suspect of the pooling of funds to a new nonchurch entity. Further, there grew among these Anti-Missions Baptists a distrust of Rice and a resistance to his fundraising. While some of the Anti-Missions disagreements were uncharitable and significant, they did not represent the majority of Baptist churches.[15]

The Triennial Convention

In 1814, delegates from churches throughout the country gathered in Philadelphia to form the General Missionary Convention of the Baptist Denomination in the United States of America for Foreign Missions or, in short, the Triennial Convention. For the first time in this country, Baptist churches cooperated to form a national denomination for one overarching purpose: the funding of global missions. Here are their words: "We the delegates from Missionary Societies, and other religious Bodies of the Baptist denomination, in various parts of the United States, met in Convention, in the City of Philadelphia, for the purpose of carrying into effect the benevolent Intentions of our Constituents, by organizing a plan for eliciting, combining, and directing the Energies of the whole Denomination in one sacred effort, for sending the glad tidings of Salvation to the Heathen, and to nations destitute of pure Gospel-light."[16] The primary reason for a national Baptist denomination was the "one sacred effort" of taking the gospel to those nations where Christ had not yet been named.

Conclusion

This survey of the beginnings of Baptist cooperation has the potential to do more than inform. As one author observed, "For every great change, every rebirth or *renaissance* in human culture, has been triggered by the retrieval of something valuable out of the past, making new, creative developments possible."[17] In this chapter, we have seen Baptist churches recover and maintain their confessional commitments in order to preserve their cooperative efforts. We have seen Baptist churches prioritize sacrificial missions mobilization as the primary reason for a national convention. We have seen Baptist churches maintain this priority despite distractions, their own blind spots and sins, economic challenges, restrictions of freedoms, persecutions, and imprisonments.

For centuries, Baptist churches have found that the providential winds of God's kindness and faithfulness propel, sustain, and guide them to the ends of the earth. Why would God do this? While we cannot know in full, we do know that he is certain to receive the glory for the advancement of the gospel that might come from churches cooperating for global evangelism. Thus, surveying the history of Baptist cooperation reminds us of God's plan for his churches and that he aims to use imperfect believers who will cooperate for his glory. This valuable principle, when retrieved from the past, has the potential to ignite the hope and expectation that God will continue to show his faithfulness to future intercongregational cooperation among Baptist churches for the fulfilling of the Great Commission.

Personal Reflection

When I complete my lectures on Baptist church cooperative history in seminary classes, I end by conceding that the Baptist cooperative ship is far from perfect. What is more, there are many other ships from other corners of the Christian tradition committed to the gospel and sailing in a Great Commission direction. What I mean to acknowledge is that no one is required to be a Southern Baptist to be a faithful Christian.

So, then, why am I committed to the Southern Baptist cooperative effort?

I remind the students that for me, as much as it is a matter of joyful conviction about what I understand as biblical ecclesiology, it is also a matter of personal stewardship and testimony. I share with them how God, in his kindness during my college years, called out and saved a spiritually lost, nominal Episcopalian and placed me in a Baptist church sailing with other churches in the Southern Baptist Convention. On that ship, I was discipled, baptized, and loved by a genuine New Testament community of believers.

Over time, that church recognized God's work in my life and sent me to seminary. They, along with thousands of other churches, gave sacrificially in cooperative effort to fund my theological education and, more than that, ensured that the seminary they funded maintained doctrinal integrity. Through that same intercongregational cooperative work, I have visited the mission fields of the world and have seen and contributed to the work of these churches at the ends of the earth. Seeing the end goal of the Great Commission bearing fruit as the result of churches working together has long been what has made me thankful for the Southern Baptist ship on which I first set sail.

To be consistent with my students, I am honest about the sins, faults, and distractions that have beset this Convention of churches and hindered their progress at various points in history. However, I gladly tell them that the end goal is still worthy of pursuit and worth the effort to help all the ships of churches sail in that Great Commission direction. In every sense, I hope I am like the earliest Baptists: thankful for where I have been placed and what I have received, now serving with joy in confessional cooperation, joining with others in Southern Baptist churches to reach the nations for Christ and for the glory of God.

Society and Entity-Based Missions Funding in the SBC, 1845–1925

Adam Harwood

A theologian once observed about the Southern Baptist Convention (SBC), "It is not an exaggeration to say that the Convention has no sufficient reason to exist apart from missions."[1] The statement is slight hyperbole because Southern Baptists engage in other meaningful ministries such as disaster relief, children's homes, and theological education. However, all SBC ministry efforts are rooted in the desire to propagate the message of the gospel of Jesus Christ. Thus, the observation stands: the SBC exists for Southern Baptists to cooperate for missions.

Three eras can characterize Southern Baptist cooperation to fund missions. During the first era, the Triennial Convention (1817–1845), dozens of—perhaps more than one hundred—missionary societies and agencies of various denominations lobbied individual Baptists and Baptist churches for funding. During the second era, the early SBC (1845–1925), Southern

Baptists engaged in foreign and domestic efforts through its two newly organized mission boards. Still, those boards joined other societies and agencies that appealed to the Convention's individuals and churches for funds. During the third era, the SBC Cooperative Program (CP) (1925–present), SBC churches voluntarily cooperated under *The Baptist Faith and Message* (BFM) to pool their money to fund missions and theological education. This chapter concerns this second era of SBC cooperation, from the formation of the convention of churches in 1845 to the establishment of the CP in 1925.

The Triennial Convention (1817–1845)

As a precursor to Southern Baptist missions, it is important to note the missionary efforts of Luther Rice in organizing in 1814 the General Missionary Convention of the Baptist Denomination in the United States for Foreign Missions. Richard Furman presided over the meetings in 1814 and 1817.[2] The meetings became known as the Triennial Convention because they were held every three years. That convention formed the Baptist Board of Foreign Missions. The Triennial Convention and its foreign mission board laid the foundation for the establishment of the SBC in 1845. Two issues divided northern and southern Baptists in the middle of the nineteenth century, slavery and mission funding. First, we'll consider slavery.

A significant—and embarrassing—historical fact concerning the establishment of the SBC is that the division that resulted in its founding concerned whether their mission board would appoint slave owners as missionaries. Southern Baptists separated from northern Baptists because the southerners wrongly affirmed the practice of slavery in the United States as moral and proper.[3] In the second annual meeting of the SBC (1846), special attention was given to Lott Carey (a black Baptist pastor who founded a church in Richmond, Virginia, and later founded a church in western Africa) with the suggestion that black people would be the best missionaries to the people of Africa.[4] While Southern Baptists differed between those who would *not oppose* slavery and those who wanted to *abolish* slavery, they were united in the conviction that black people should be reached with the message of the gospel.

The second issue dividing northern and southern Baptists in the middle of the nineteenth century was mission funding. Although mission funding had been conducted according to the associational method during the second half of the eighteenth century, the beginning of the nineteenth century saw a shift toward adopting the society method. One author estimated that at the beginning of the nineteenth century, sixty-five mission societies north of Philadelphia were dedicated to raising money for missions.[5] It is reasonable to estimate that more than one hundred mission societies across the United States solicited Baptist churches for mission funds. Why were so many societies raising money for missions among Baptists? First, American Baptists (as well as other American Christians, such as Methodists and Presbyterians) were strongly committed to sharing the message of the gospel at home and abroad. Thus, mission funding was a priority. Second, most Southern Baptists had an aversion toward ecclesial bodies or structures that might usurp the autonomy of the local church. Thus, the society method allowed Southern Baptists to fund missions while avoiding the perceived perils of denominational structure.

Associational versus Society Methods of Funding Southern Baptist Missions

In the early nineteenth century in the United States, Baptists funded missions in two ways: the associational method and the society method. The associational method was used primarily in the South from their earliest work to the present, and the society method was used primarily by Baptists in the North until the early twentieth century. This chart illustrates the differences between the two methods:[6]

Associational Method	Society Method
Denominational—interests of the denomination considered when establishing a program	**Independent**—a society was autonomous and made decisions based solely on its work
Geographic basis—support was based on the association's commitment to a geographic area	**Financial basis**—support was based on giving to the society's particular work
Typically involved in **many** benevolent activities	Involved in a **single** benevolent activity (whether home missions, foreign missions, publishing, etc.)
Individuals participated in missionary programs only as members of **associated** churches	Participation in missionary programs required **no relationship** between churches and societies
Interdependent and **connectional** relationships between churches to accomplish mission work	Mission work was accomplished by independent churches with **no formal relationship**

In the early decades of the nineteenth century, Baptist churches in the south shifted to a society method, in which various mission agencies and societies lobbied churches and individuals for support. Francis Wayland had advocated the society method, and the rationale was to safeguard the autonomy of local churches against denominational control while churches engaged with and funded individual mission societies. Brand and Hankins observe, "This rejection of the associational model would be one of the sparks that would ignite the separation between Baptists North and South less than two decades later."[7]

Funding Missions in the Early SBC (1845–1925)

At the founding of the SBC in 1845, William B. Johnson proposed an associational model in which two mission boards were formed—the Foreign Mission Board (FMB) and the Domestic Mission Board (DMB).[8] Both mission boards would fund their mission work through the society method. Though the SBC was organized as associational because churches were cooperating voluntarily with one another in mission work, the SBC nevertheless employed the method of individual societies—including these two boards and many other organizations—soliciting churches to fund their work.

Today, Southern Baptists enjoy the benefits of the streamlined system of SBC churches pooling their financial contributions through the CP to fund evangelism, missions, and theological education. Churches are better together because they can accomplish more through cooperative efforts. However, Southern Baptist churches were funding evangelism, missions, and theological education before the development of the CP in 1925. How did they accomplish this task? Rather than pooling their funds through one central pot of money distributed to fund their efforts, multiple mission societies, missionaries, and theological institutes appealed to churches and individuals for funding. A historian described mission funding at the beginning of the SBC: "Contributions were made by individuals and Baptist bodies of any character to each organization according to the interest of the contributors."[9]

It is difficult for Southern Baptists today to imagine multiple mission societies and agencies soliciting churches for funds to engage in their work. At the birth of the SBC, the significant question facing Southern Baptist churches was: How will we fund missions? In their 1846 annual meeting, an offering was collected for foreign and domestic missions. However, how would funds be collected among SBC churches in the months between annual meetings and among the churches not represented at the annual meetings? The FMB appointed its first missionary within six months of being constituted, and several other missionaries were in the process of being approved for service. It seemed that God was raising up individuals to serve as missionaries; now, it was time to consider how to fund their work.

The FMB appointed agents "who would spend varying amounts of time in designated areas, promoting foreign missions and soliciting funds for the work."[10] Some agents were officially elected, and others volunteered their services. In exchange for keeping a portion of the collected funds, the agents would publicize and raise funds for particular mission work. Near the end of the nineteenth century, agents collecting funds for the FMB kept up to 25 percent of the money they collected. Though the percentage might seem steep, expenses for their travel and communication were also high, so using agents to collect funds from churches seemed to be the best arrangement at the time.[11] The DMB faced even greater struggles. In the years following the

Civil War, finding agents to collect funds for domestic missions was difficult. In 1876, $19,000 was collected for domestic missions, and 44 percent was kept for administrative costs, most of which funded the fundraising agents' salaries and expenses.[12]

There were other problems in addition to the high cost of using agents. First, there was the problem of the frequency of agent visits. In the absence of central coordination, some churches received infrequent visits. Also, bad weather sometimes prohibited an agent from keeping an appointment for a scheduled visit with a church or might keep the congregation from attending if the agent made it to the meeting. Churches would not know if an agent might visit twice per year or only once every two years. Conversely, urban and wealthier churches sometimes received too many visits by agents. Multiple agents of various societies would visit, each presenting a compelling case for why their mission in that region or their effort to fund the publication of a book or establish a theological school was worthy of the congregation taking up a special offering. How many special offerings can a congregation afford to take up in a year before they become tired of the many appeals for money and begin to withhold funds or even resent the requests? Shortly after the agency system began, Southern Baptists grew weary of it. The DMB reported to the Convention in the 1859 annual meeting that it had only two agents in the field, and the mission agent work had "agitated" the SBC and was "extremely annoying." Even so, agents were crucial to raising funds. The report provided an example. An agent of the FMB collected almost $400 in an Alabama association in less than one month; the previous year, without the agent collecting funds, the churches in the association contributed only $4. If the agent system was to be abandoned, the report explained, another system must be in place for raising funds.[13]

Next, we'll consider the history of the FMB in the early SBC (1845–1925).

The Foreign Mission Board in the Early SBC (1845–1925)

James B. Taylor served from 1846 to 1871 as the first corresponding secretary of the FMB.[14] He led initial missionary work in China, then moved into Africa and Italy. Taylor led the mission-funding effort during the Civil War, when money and attention were diverted during our nation's bloody internal conflict. Taylor also countered the opposition of Landmarkism, led by J. R. Graves, which opposed missionary boards because the Landmarkists believed the boards were assuming a role that should only be filled by local churches. Taylor was able to fold those concerns into the development of the mission-sending structure that would respect congregational autonomy and the New Testament's authorization of local churches to the missionary-sending role.

The second corresponding secretary was Henry A. Tupper (1872–1893).[15] Tupper opened new work in Japan, Mexico, and Brazil. He also led the deployment of single female missionaries, including Southern Baptists' most famous missionary, Lottie Moon. Also, during Tupper's tenure, the Woman's Missionary Union established an annual Christmas offering for missions, which would later be named after the diminutive missionary to China, the Lottie Moon Christmas Offering. The FMB's work in Brazil was the second largest investment, and William and Ann Bagby led the efforts. The couple was appointed in 1881, and subsequent generations of the Bagby family invested their lives in the propagation of the gospel among the people of Brazil. Tupper also navigated theological disputes, which resulted in rescinding the appointments of two former students of The Southern Baptist Theological Seminary (SBTS) professor Crawford Toy. The problem was they adopted the higher-critical view that Scripture contains errors. Also, Tupper dealt with conflict over concerns about mission-funding methods raised by T. P. Crawford that would continue to be debated during the next secretary's tenure.

Like his two predecessors, the third corresponding secretary, R. J. Willingham (1893–1914) served a lengthy tenure in the role.[16] The longevity of leadership provided stability and continuity for the FMB. Missionary work had already been established in six regions: China, Japan, Africa, Italy, Brazil, and Mexico. Willingham focused most of the effort during his tenure on China, and he expanded work into Argentina and Uruguay. He was forced to address the Crawford controversy, which had continued from the previous secretary's administration. The controversy concerned whether to fund mission churches. Willingham's solution was to cite the principle that mission churches should be self-supporting. The FMB slowly transitioned from providing support to local churches on the foreign field to reducing external support so that local churches could be self-supporting.

The fourth corresponding secretary, J. Franklin Love (1915–1928), oversaw the FMB during a period of global tumult and structural change in the SBC.[17] Love's administration began during the Great War and continued during the adoption of the BF&M, which unites Southern Baptists around a statement of faith to cooperate for evangelism and missions. The BF&M, essentially an update of the New Hampshire Confession of 1833, was constructed and adopted in light of the modernist-fundamentalist controversy.

Next, we'll consider one individual's contribution to SBC foreign missions.

Lottie Moon

Charlotte Digges "Lottie" Moon (1840–1912) is probably the most famous SBC missionary. The Convention's annual Christmas Offering for International Missions bears her name. Though she stood only four feet three inches tall, she was a tour de force in her mission field service and letter writing to raise funds for foreign mission work.[18] Moon was a highly educated woman for her day, earning a bachelor's degree from the Virginian Female Seminary and a master of arts degree from Albemarle Female Institute. She was a schoolteacher before she departed for service on the mission field in China in 1873, where she invested the remainder of her life. An editor of her collected writings observes that her changing views of the Chinese people can be seen in her letters. Earlier letters reflected a sense of her superiority and their inferiority, referring to the people as "John Chinaman" and "heathens." Nevertheless, God shaped her heart and attitudes, replacing her ethnocentrism with a selflessness to serve the needs of the Chinese people, especially women and children. She endured the same hardships the Chinese people faced in the austere environment, and she became known for her service of making delicious cookies.[19]

Moon's appeal for more foreign missionaries is stated in her first letter to FMB secretary Henry Tupper shortly after she arrived in China. She explained, "What we need in China is more workers. The harvest is *very* great, the laborers, oh! *so few*. Why does the Southern Baptist church lag behind in this great work?" Moon wrote, "Our Presbyterian brethren are putting us to shame." While commending the strength of the Presbyterians' work in China, she was concerned that Southern Baptist work would end if the seasoned missionaries were not replaced with a younger generation.[20] She addressed financial matters. In an early letter, she volunteered to receive a lower annual salary than was offered by the FMB, $650, rather than the $800 that the FMB had approved.[21] Her letters concerned balancing missionary efforts on the field, noting twelve missionaries from multiple Christian denominations in one city (Soochow). Still, there was no mission work in Hwang Hsien, a city twenty miles from her location.[22] She apprised the secretary of the FMB of significant developments and needs on the field, and she continually appealed for prayer to the Lord of the harvest to raise up more workers.

Moon was bold and unafraid to write hard truths. For example, she commended a Presbyterian man who filled the local pulpit in her Chinese city twice per month until he returned to the U.S. She lamented that after his departure, there was no minister available to administer Communion or baptism. She expressed wonder that one million Southern Baptists could provide only three men to serve in China. Although there are five hundred preachers in Virginia, her church in China must rely on a Presbyterian to fill the pulpit. She remarked, "But then we Baptists are a great people as we never tire of saying at our associations and Conventions."[23]

Moon's article in the *Foreign Mission Journal* educated SBC readers about Chinese culture and mission work. Her 1887 articles titled "An Earnest Plea for Helpers" and "From Miss Lottie Moon" provided the foundation for the later establishment of the annual Christmas Offering that bears her name.[24] In the former article, Moon pleads, "It is certain that women can be found willing and glad to come and work for God in China. The lack is not of women who would come, but of money to send and sustain them."[25]

Moon's tireless work to organize, advocate for, and procure funding for mission work in China is a legacy that continues to aid in funding the sending and sustaining of missionaries worldwide. In the latter article, she builds on the model of Methodist women missionaries by recommending that focused prayer and giving for missions should occur the week before Christmas. She closes her appeal by asking how many women "imagine that because 'Jesus paid it all,' they need pay nothing, forgetting that the prime object of their salvation was that they should follow in the footsteps of Jesus Christ in bringing back a lost world to God, and so aid in bringing the answer to the petition our Lord taught his disciples, 'Thy kingdom come.'"[26]

Next, we'll consider the history of the DMB in the early SBC (1845–1925).

The Domestic Mission Board in the Early SBC (1845–1925)

The first issue facing the new DMB, located in Marion, Alabama, was to find a corresponding secretary. The first person elected to the position, J. L. Reynolds, declined. The second person elected to the position, D. P. Bestor, assumed the role but resigned before the end of 1845. Bestor concluded that churches preferred to fulfill their domestic mission work through local associations and state conventions. At the end of 1845, Russell Holman assumed the role.[27]

During its first year, the DMB deployed six domestic missionaries (one each in Virginia, Florida, Alabama, and Louisiana, and two in Texas). In its first Convention report, the Board identified the fourteen U.S. states and eight million people within its field of ministry.[28] The missionary task ahead of the DMB was significant. A salesman from the American Tract Society reported to the DMB secretary that he met people in Alabama who had neither heard a sermon nor seen a Christian minister.[29] John Tucker, a DMB missionary in Florida, reported that although he was not an ordained minister, he traveled a 450-mile route every two months preaching the gospel and ministering to families. He planted five churches in that region and baptized more than fifty people, but he received almost no financial support for over one year.[30] The needs were great, and God raised up Southern Baptists who were faithful witnesses of Jesus Christ.

In 1855, the DMB merged with the Indian Mission Association to become the Domestic and Indian Mission Board. The Board began mission work among internationals who lived in the U.S., such as the Chinese in California and Germans in Maryland and Missouri.[31] Domestic mission work was difficult. Most of the population lived in rural areas, so because of the limited rail lines at the time, most regions were accessible only by horseback over rough terrain. A Bible salesman's report for Louisiana illustrates the difficulties. "On Sunday last I attended a meeting at a school-house, where brother Franklin . . . has been preaching about a year. It was a large house, and well filled with an attentive congregation. Many of them came from a distance across the river,—among them a woman, to whom I sent a Bible, who lives ten miles from the church, and has no way of getting there, except to walk and carry a child in her arms. I was informed she had not been to church before in ten years."[32]

Despite the challenges in conducting domestic missions, Southern Baptists saw the need as well as the interdependence of foreign and domestic missions. The DMB's initial report to the Convention declared that "the ultimate prosperity of the *foreign* mission enterprise depends much on the successful operation of the *domestic* department."[33] Nevertheless, the funding of domestic missions often fell short. For example, in 1849, the DMB asked Southern Baptists to raise $20,000 for domestic missions.

Though the amount was close to the average amount collected between 1845 and 1859 ($19,025 per year), only $12,176 was collected in 1850. Missionaries were funded by actual contributions rather than promised ones, so collecting those contributions was an important task. J. B. Lawrence observed about DMB reports to the Convention from this era, "It was suggested, again and again, that the churches should have a systematic method for raising money for missions."[34] But it would be many years before God raised up the CP as a solution.

The American Civil War devastated domestic mission work. In 1860, the DMB had 166 missionaries. By 1862, one year into the war, they had only six missionaries. Work was shut down among the white population, among the black population, and among Native Americans. The DMB lacked the money to continue their work, and broken lines of communication west of the Mississippi River made any work impossible.[35] Healthy men, including pastors, enlisted in the military. Southern Baptists capitalized on this movement of men to the military, endorsing 137 missionaries among the Confederate soldiers, including statesmen such as Russell Holman, W. C. Buck, and John Broadus. The difficult years of Reconstruction following the Civil War were followed by the economic depression of 1873. Nevertheless, the people of God who called themselves Southern Baptists trusted God with their finances and cooperated with one another to commission and support missionaries throughout the growing nation.

Formal Theological Education in the Early SBC (1845–1925)

Though much could be written about the development of Southern Baptist colleges and universities during the era of the early SBC, I will limit this section to a brief survey of the establishment of the first three Southern Baptist seminaries. During this era, Southern Baptists were—and they are today—people of the Bible. Thus, we value pastors who know and can rightly preach and teach the Scriptures. Formal theological education is not a requirement for godliness and is no substitute for the anointing of God's Spirit. One historian observed that "Baptists had grown by means of lay preaching" during this period.[36] Formal theological education was not available to most Baptist ministers during this era. Thus, A. T. Robertson observed that most ministers were self-educated, often aided by their wives.[37] Despite its scarcity, Southern Baptists valued formal theological training so their pastors could be called workmen who don't "need to be ashamed, correctly teaching the word of truth" (2 Tim. 2:15). Toward that end, Southern Baptists founded three seminaries during this early period to train pastors and missionaries in Christian ministry.

James P. Boyce challenged South Carolina Baptists in their 1856 annual meeting to establish a seminary by using $30,000 from Furman University as seed money to grow the amount to $100,000, on the promise that the seminary would be located in Greenville, South Carolina, and that other state conventions would contribute to the cause.[38] Boyce traveled the state to raise money, and other states contributed. The Southern Baptist Theological Seminary (SBTS) was established and met for its first semester in Greenville in the fall of 1859 with twenty-six students. It would move to Louisville, Kentucky, in 1877. Although conflict over Walter Whitsitt's (SBTS's third president) claims about baptism resulted in Southern Baptists nearly severing ties with the seminary, the president's resignation satisfied the aggrieved state conventions. E. Y. Mullins provided stable leadership for the seminary, published several significant theological works, and raised (through agents) a $1.8 million endowment for the SBTS Twentieth Century Endowment Campaign. As Duke McCall described this early period, SBTS "rose not on the shoulders of the denomination but on the personal sacrifices of many individual donors."[39]

Southwestern Baptist Theological Seminary (SWBTS) was established as Baylor Theological Seminary in 1905 by B. H. Carroll, who began fundraising to establish a new seminary due to his vision for theological education in the Southwest while riding a train through the panhandle of Texas. He knew of schools in the Southwest dedicated to training doctors, nurses, lawyers, and farmers but none for training Baptist preachers.[40] Carroll was already regarded by this time as a Southern Baptist statesman due to his skillful preaching, many commentaries, and published sermons, and twenty-eight years of fruitful ministry at First Baptist Church of Waco. He raised $30,000, which he estimated would fund faculty salaries for three years. Also, he wrote letters to one hundred friends, asking for annual gifts of $100 as an emergency fund for the seminary, raising another $20,000 in cash and pledges.[41] SWBTS was chartered in 1908. Two years later, it relocated to Fort Worth when Carroll secured $100,000 in promised funds from city leaders. Classes began in the fall of 1910 with 126 students. In 1925, SWBTS was transferred to the SBC.[42]

New Orleans Baptist Theological Seminary (NOBTS) was the first seminary founded by the SBC (because the Convention had adopted the previous two seminaries after their founding). In contrast, NOBTS was founded by messengers to the SBC annual meeting in 1917. It was originally named the Baptist Bible Institute (BBI).[43] The city of New Orleans had been explicitly mentioned in several SBC annual meeting reports, beginning with the first one, when the DMB was instructed "to direct its effective attention to aid the present effort, to establish the Baptist cause in the city of New Orleans."[44] Baptists in Mississippi and Louisiana worked for several years, pledging and raising funds to begin BBI. In 1917, the board of directors, chosen by the SBC, selected Byron Hoover DeMent as its first president, and they also secured the purchase of the campus of a local women's college for $100,000. Within one year, DeMent had raised one-quarter of the funds necessary to purchase the campus.[45] The fundraising efforts required eleven thousand miles of travel by train and the delivery of 133 sermons and speeches. By the next year, three more state conventions—Florida, Texas, and Tennessee—agreed to cooperate in founding the school.[46] Classes began in 1918, and Louisiana Baptists pledged $164,000 to BBI in 1919. In 1925, the state conventions and board of directors gave up total ownership of BBI to the SBC.

Conclusion

The assertion made at the beginning of this chapter bears repeating: the SBC exists so churches can cooperate for missions. During the era of the Triennial Convention (1817–1845), the issues of slavery and mission funding resulted in the separation of mission work between northern and southern Baptists. During the early years of the SBC (1845–1925), Baptist churches attempted to fund mission work and theological education through the society method in which various mission boards and societies solicited churches for funding. The society method faced the challenge of properly coordinating those efforts among the churches. It faced the challenge of using agents who consumed large percentages of the funds. And it faced the theological concern of Baptists working through a denominational structure that may possibly threaten the autonomy of local churches in their mission-sending efforts.

Despite these challenges, Southern Baptists cooperated at their founding meeting in 1845 to establish the mission boards, which later became the IMB and NAMB. The SBC was unified in its mission to spread the message of the gospel throughout the United States and to the ends of the earth. The corresponding secretaries of the FMB worked to balance theological concerns that emerged while also funding the sending and sustaining of missionaries to other nations. Lottie Moon's faithful ministry among the people of China and advocacy for global missions served as a point of unity in the SBC for establishing cooperation among SBC churches to fund international missions.

Similar effort was exerted in domestic missions. The challenges were significant—between the U.S. Civil War and subsequent economic hardship—SBC leaders and churches worked from their founding day to fund domestic missions so that every person in the nation might hear the message of the gospel. In addition, three SBC seminaries were founded during this period. Each seminary was born out of a need to train ministers of the gospel, and each institution was nearly closed due to similar issues that threatened the work of the FMB and DMB. Thankfully, SBC churches cooperated for missions and theological education during this early period, though the efforts were stifled by a lack of centralized cooperation and inefficiencies in their efforts. Providentially, the period of the early SBC would conclude with the formation of cooperative efforts, resulting in what we know today as the Cooperative Program.

Personal Reflection

I have been both a contributor to and beneficiary of CP funds my entire life. My dad received his theological training from SWBTS while I was a toddler. I was raised in Southern Baptist churches, listened to SBC preachers, and was educated under its programs, including Sunday school, Training Union, Royal Ambassadors, children and youth choirs, Vacation Bible School, and Centrifuge summer camps. The materials for those programs were developed and distributed by SBC entities. Those churches contributed to the CP, and the pastors serving in those churches were educated at SBC seminaries, which the CP funded. In college, I continued to worship, learn, and serve in SBC churches, and I was also active in the ministries of the Baptist Student Union. I also served as a summer missionary through the Home Mission Board. In my early twenties, I began eleven years of master's and doctoral studies at SWBTS—all of which were heavily subsidized by CP funds because I served in local SBC churches during my time in seminary.

I have participated in international mission trips to Europe, Asia, and Africa, all in partnership with IMB personnel (whose salaries and work are funded by the CP). The SBC churches which I served on ministry staff in Oklahoma and Texas for twelve years contributed to the CP, and the SBC church in Georgia, where my family worshipped and served, was also a CP contributor. Since 2013, I have worshipped and served at First Baptist Church of New Orleans, which gives to the CP, and I have served on faculty at NOBTS, whose institutional funding depends on the CP. Since 2017, I have served as a NAMB-endorsed chaplain in the Louisiana Army National Guard. I'm aware of and thank God for using other mission structures and partnerships to advance his kingdom. Even so, God has used the

CP throughout my life as both a conduit for a portion of my missional giving and a source of funding for my small contribution toward God's work in his world.

4

War and Roar: 1910s and 1920s American Context Influencing the Development of the Southern Baptist Convention Cooperative Program

Taffey Hall

The 1910s and 1920s were rife with a varying assortment of challenges and opportunities in the United States. The Great War of 1914–1918 awakened American mindfulness toward sacrificial cooperation in a common cause. Efficiency became a popular concept in businesses and organizations. Paralleling these premises rested a national consciousness aimed at providing uplift and social betterment for the desolate and needy through a plethora of new and expanded benevolence programs. Additionally, the elevated status of women, exemplified through ratification of the Nineteenth Amendment and the tireless labors of women's work through temperance, Anti-saloon Leagues, and charitable endeavors cast an important spotlight on the vital role of female contributions to society and family life. Indeed, the 1910s and the Roaring Twenties witnessed a concentration on social, economic, and political change on a grand scale. The Cooperative Program of Southern Baptists (CP) found its genesis in this American context and was, no doubt, influenced by the awakened consciousness of streamlined business practices and organizational efficiency, expanded charitable concern and ministry opportunities, and the steadfast assistance of women in organizing and promoting sacrificial giving for missions causes.

Unifying, Mobilizing, and Centralizing during the First World War

The First World War, though devastating for Europe, unified United States citizens in the 1910s. Divisions of the Civil War, which had not really healed in the latter decades of the nineteenth century, found more solid grounding as together Americans observed increasingly unstable events unfolding on the European continent. Then America entered the Great War and a spirit of solemn American togetherness abounded.[1]

Early in the European conflict, like most Americans, most Southern Baptists backed President Woodrow Wilson's policy on neutrality. Editors of Southern Baptist newspapers used denominational publications to voice views of peace and neutrality. The Southern Baptist heritage of striving to live an honorable life, believing the Bible is God's literal Word, and strong emphasis on evangelism and missions shaped those views. Also at the turn of the century, most Southern Baptist mission work with immigrants and ethnic groups on American soil remained in its infancy, and this fact also likely contributed to a somewhat detached feeling from events happening across the pond.[2]

Still, as the war in Europe progressed, any ambivalences Southern Baptists felt about America's involvement in the war were soon to change. The sinking of Allied ships by German forces—especially the British vessel *Lusitania* on May 7, 1915, which killed more than one hundred American citizens—greatly disappointed Southern Baptists.[3] Later, on April 6, 1917, when the United States Senate declared war on Germany, most Southern Baptists, like most Americans, pivoted their dispositions and supported the war cause as their "attitudes of neutrality shifted to an attitude of national patriotism."[4] At the Southern Baptist Convention annual meeting in New Orleans, Louisiana, in May 1917, the Report of the Committee on the Present Crisis addressed the war and proclaimed: "Deeply as all of us deplore war, ardently as we longed and labored to avert or avoid it, we may be cheered and heartened in remembering that we are moved in entering it, neither by lust nor hate, but by the love of humanity."[5]

The war had given Southern Baptists a chance to reflect on the needs of a hurting world in ways they had not previously considered.[6] The nation as a whole had come together, and the American heartbeat was strong and in sync, patriotic and proud. Southern Baptists were a part of that national united opus. They shared in the new opportunities and general feeling of "jubilant optimism" infiltrating the nation for America's role of molding a world that was safe for democracy following the First World War.[7]

There were practical applications to the unification that swept the nation as well. Southern Baptists, like most Americans, watched as the sale of government bonds during the war provided an efficient and effective template for uniting Americans through fundraising. Leaders of many religious denominations in America witnessed the success of the sale of these bonds in uniting large groups of people to raise large amounts of money in fairly short order for a good cause. As a result, many religious groups, including the Southern Baptist Convention, launched major fundraising campaigns during the 1910s aimed at informing and inspiring large numbers of their members to systematically consolidate financial resources to the good causes of their respective denominations.[8]

The Southern Baptist 75 Million Campaign, initiated in 1919 and predecessor to the CP, was a product of this context. In 1920, L. R. Scarborough, president of Southwestern Baptist Theological Seminary and director of the campaign, emphasized the impact of the Great War on the campaign's fruition when he proudly proclaimed, "It set us to thinking in terms of millions and billions. The sacrifices of the war taught us new lessons in self-surrender and self-denial. The glories of a successful life were put in the hearts of people everywhere."[9] As historian William Leach has observed, America's entry into the First World War birthed a moment in which the United States "mobilized and centralized its resources to an unheard-of degree, greatly accelerating economic productivity and the concentration of economic power."[10]

American Business Expansion and Corporate Consolidation

At the turn of the twentieth century, business expansion and corporate consolidation marched lockstep in metronomic rhythm pacing Americans to want and accomplish more and more. Many of the services, amenities, and modes of operation that became commonplace to most Americans by the end of the century incubated during this time. Innovative commercial institutions such as department stores, dine-in restaurants, hotels, movie theaters, investment banks, and national corporations burst on the scene and began transforming American culture. Prepackaged, mass-produced, and multiple-option ready-to-use choices were becoming the new norm as Americans shifted their purchasing practices from using local mom-and-pop general stores to acquiring books, clothing, furniture, groceries, hardware, meats, and pharmaceutical products from local chain stores. Items previously considered luxuries, such as cosmetics; clocks and watches; electrical appliances including dishwashers, fans, refrigerators, stoves, and vacuum cleaners; toys; and products for pets gradually infiltrated more and more American homes and businesses and changed the way Americans lived, worked, and played. A focus on improved and expanded infrastructure in the form of new highways and bridges and cars and trucks to transport goods and commodities ensured that Americans of every cluster could be closer and closer to more and more stuff.[11]

As these goods and services and the stores that sold the items continued to expand, institutional consolidation became the name of the game by the end of the 1920s.[12] Americans searched for better, more efficient, and less complicated ways to operate and sustain an ever-enlarging goods and services economy and way of life. Just as they had gleaned inspiration from the sale of war bonds during the First World War in formulating denominational fundraising campaigns in the 1910s, in similar vein religious groups in America adapted and responded to the new business and consumer culture by which they were encircled. Walter Johnson, chaplain at Wake Forest Baptist College in North Carolina, urged in 1914, "There is a 'speeding up' in every line of human activity. Religion must catch the pace or be left behind."[13] Southern Baptists, like most Americans, were engaging the hustle and bustle of the dawn of the new century with eager anticipation. Baptist historian Leon McBeth put it simply and succinctly: "Consolidation was in the air in the early twentieth century, and Baptists breathed that air."[14]

Southern Baptist Expansion and the Need for Denominational Efficiency

The Southern Baptist Convention was growing by leaps and bounds in the early 1900s as more members, more churches, more missionaries, and more denominational benevolent programs and services entered the fold. In 1900, the Convention included 18,963 churches, 1,608,413 members, and registered 646 messengers to its annual Convention meeting. By 1920, those numbers had increased to 25,303 churches, 2,961,348 members, and 1,641 messengers at the annual meeting. Missionaries, both at home and abroad, multiplied as well. In 1900, the Home Mission Board supported 671 missionaries, but by 1920 the number of home missionaries had increased to 1,641. The Foreign Mission Board supported 227 missionaries in 1900, and by 1920, the number had swelled to 1,320—an increase of nearly 600 percent.

By the 1920s, the Convention's Home and Foreign Mission Boards, Sunday School Board, Relief and Annuity Board, and Education Board, were joined by a kaleidoscope of other special committees and commissions including those on chaplains, the denominational press, Executive Committee, hospitals, Laymen's Movement, Southern Baptist Sanitorium, temperance, Woman's Missionary Union, and Commission on American Baptist Seminary (a joint opportunity with the National Baptist Convention for training African American Baptist ministers in

Nashville, Tennessee). The number of benevolent institutions climbed as well. In 1900, Baptists in the South operated two hospitals, but by 1920, they owned seventeen. In 1900, the Home Mission Board had few Mountain Mission Schools, but by 1920, reported sixty-one schools with 312 teachers and 9,321 students. Expansion of educational institutions was no less impressive. In 1900, Southern Baptists operated sixty-five schools (thirty-nine for men or as coeducational institutions and twenty-six for women only). These senior colleges, junior colleges, high school academies, and Bible and theological schools enrolled 11,130 students in 1900, and by 1920 enrollment had surged to 31,196.[15]

In expanding these and similar benevolent ministries, Southern Baptists were applying their understandings of a larger Social Gospel movement present in the nation in the early decades of the twentieth century. The Social Gospel sought to assign Christian values to a plethora of social problems. Among its most prominent advocates was northern Baptist preacher Walter Rauschenbusch. Due to the mostly rural economy of the South, most Southerners generally faced different social issues than those experienced by their neighbors in the North. Mountain mission schools, orphanages, and rural uplift became some of the best examples of avenues through which social Christianity manifested in the South.[16]

The growing social consciousness of Southern Baptists, combined with the growing number of people, churches, and denominational apparatuses, necessitated a better, more efficiently organized system. The cauldron was starting to boil, and something had to be done. "If efficiency in religious work is ever to have an opportunity, now is the time," one Baptist seminary student proclaimed in 1925.[17] There had to be a more effective method.

Quest for Southern Baptist Efficiency / Inefficiency of the Agent Method

For decades at Southern Baptist Convention annual meetings, Convention messengers had pursued various attempts for denominational efficiency. In a bit of roller-coaster fashion, on several occasions from the 1840s through the 1910s, messengers to annual SBC meetings recognized the need for both improved coordination and efficient modes of Convention operations, and stable and sustainable funding processes for missions and evangelistic endeavors. Messengers appointed committees to address efficiency, and they heard reports from corresponding secretaries of SBC boards and institutions bemoaning the lack of an organized, efficient, and simple strategy for collecting funds to support missions and denominational programs.[18]

On the committee side of the equation, the Committee on Systematic Giving (1873), Committee on More Generous Giving (1879), Committee on Plan of Systematic Benevolence (1884), Committee on Tithing (1895), Committee on Changes in Financial Plans (1908), and Committee in Regularity in Missionary Contributions (1913) represented attempts to coalesce Southern Baptist giving in a unified manner.[19] While succeeding in keeping the need for an efficient funding operation front and center on Southern Baptists' minds, committees such as these were ultimately unsuccessful in the later decades of the nineteenth century and the first decade and a half of the twentieth in producing a plan for unified systematic giving.[20] The Landmark influence of the late nineteenth and early twentieth centuries contributed to the lack of success of these committees.[21] An up-and-down cycle of acknowledging the necessity for financial efficiency but falling short of accomplishing the goal remained the reality.

Efficiency across the SBC gained stronger footing in the 1910s. Several state Baptist conventions structured more efficient organizations.[22] Additionally, at its annual meeting in 1913, in St. Louis, Missouri, the SBC appointed the Committee on Efficiency to "secure the highest efficiency of our forces" and commence a "thorough examination of the organization, plans, and methods of this body."[23] The committee was also asked to address budgeting and to encourage churches to give regularly to Convention causes.[24] Recommendations from the Efficiency Committee to the following year's SBC annual meeting would ultimately stumble for the next couple of years until finally resulting in 1917 with creation of the Executive Committee of the Southern Baptist Convention, at last a structure through which the Convention could conduct business between annual meetings.[25]

While formation of the Executive Committee marked an important milestone in the Convention's path toward efficiency, it still did not alleviate the cascade of irritations many throughout the Convention experienced related to funding institutions and ministries. Much of the frustration on this front expressed at SBC annual meetings for the Convention's first seventy-five years of existence rested with the agency system of funding Southern Baptist missions and ministries.[26] This system, a carryover to the SBC from the earliest days of Baptist organization in America and both friend and foe (more often the latter) to denominational executives, was a method through which Southern Baptist mission boards, state conventions, and later educational and benevolent enterprises solicited funds for particular causes through the use of representative agents. These agents traveled to local Baptist churches across the hinterlands and made appeals for money. They received both financial compensation from the boards and a portion of the special offerings they collected.[27]

From its earliest use in the SBC, the agency system was at best adequate but more often burdensome. Corresponding secretaries of the Convention boards, especially the Foreign and Home Mission Boards, on multiple occasions, used their reports to the annual Convention meetings to illuminate challenges with employing agents.[28] In his report to the 1849 SBC annual meeting in Charleston, South Carolina, James B. Taylor, corresponding secretary of the Foreign Mission Board lamented "extreme difficulty in procuring men of suitable qualifications for the agency work."[29]

Isaac Taylor Tichenor, who served as corresponding secretary of the Home Mission Board from 1882 to 1899 and was instrumental in significant growth and expansion of moral outreach ministries at the Board, voiced a myriad of concerns during his tenure about difficulties in perpetual reliance on the agency system. In his 1884 report to the Southern Baptist Convention in Baltimore, Maryland, Tichenor, becoming increasingly exhausted with the system, implored, "These spasmodic efforts and passionate appeals upon which we have relied must be abandoned, and our people must be taught to give by system. They must be shown that when each performs his part, how easy it would be to supply all that is needed for the spread of the gospel, and how small a contribution from every one will hush the cries of destitution, and fill our own and distant lands with songs of joy."[30]

B. H. DeMent was on the job for less than two months as president of the Baptist Bible Institute (now New Orleans Baptist Theological Seminary) when he experienced firsthand the spasmodic fundraising efforts Tichenor described. In early December 1917, DeMent wrote to I. J. Van Ness of the Sunday School Board recounting the immediate and laborious toil he was already facing in securing funds for the newly formed school.

"We launched a campaign here last Sunday to secure $20,000.00 to pay for the Institute plant," he wrote. "Since coming to New Orleans I spoke in every Baptist church from two to half a dozen times. Last Sunday I spoke in all six of our Churches. I took in two at the Sunday School hour, two at 11:00 a.m. and two at the night hour."[31] It was a heavy load for certain and an all-too-common occurrence for Convention boards and institutions prior to formation of the CP.

Denominational executives were not alone in their discouragement with the agency-funding system. Often the irritations they felt paled in comparison to those felt by pastors and attendees of local Southern Baptist churches. At the local church level, agitations with the agency system were amplified as pastors and church members experienced the repetitious appeals of agent after agent for worthy cause after worthy cause Sunday after Sunday.[32]

The system was laden with problems. In an exhausting rat race, agents hopscotched the Southland thwarting both internal forces including agents from other denominational boards, state Baptist conventions, sundry benevolent programs, and external factors of unpredictable weather, unpredictable roads, and varied modes of transportation.[33] Agents who reached a church first and gave the most captivating, heartwarming appeal often reaped the highest offerings.[34] The agency method was so disruptive, "confusing," and "overwhelming" for one early twentieth-century pastor he admitted that if he had allowed every agent who appealed to his church time to speak to his congregation, "he could have occupied his pulpit only twice in the last year."[35] James Sullivan, president of the Sunday School Board of the Southern Baptist Convention from 1953 to 1975, was alive during the waning years of the agency system and recalled similar experiences at the church where he grew up in Tylertown, Mississippi. "We had so many solicitors coming from so many agencies and so many Sundays during the year that we felt we were robbed of the marvelous preaching of our own pastor," he explained.[36] James Dillard, director of promotion for the newly formed Executive Committee clarified that it was from multiple accounts of church experiences like these that the CP was birthed. Local Baptist churches "almost demanded some more equitable, economical, Christian plan for carrying out the work."[37]

Southern Baptist Rural Church Survey and Local Church Efficiency

Fortunately, relief was on the way. Southern Baptist churches, yearning for greater efficiency within their local congregations, were requesting guidance from Convention leaders, and their leaders were responding.[38] In 1922, the Department of Survey, Statistics, and Information at the SBC Sunday School Board, under the leadership of E. P. Alldredge, conducted a massive survey on the status and needs of Southern Baptist country churches. Results of the survey were printed in the Board's *Southern Baptist Handbook* in 1923. This 190-page survey, one of the largest of its type produced in the early twentieth century, recorded data for 22,043 white rural Baptist churches and around 3,225,000 Baptist church members in the South. These 22,043 churches represented 88.5 percent of Southern Baptist churches in 1922, and most (79.3%) had less than 150 members. The survey shed light on problems experienced by rural Southern Baptist churches and served as a wake-up call to Convention leaders of challenges confronting the majority of their members. Among the study's more alarming findings included poverty, high rates of illiteracy, difficulty of rural churches to obtain trained pastors, low pastor salaries, average pastor tenure of only twenty-seven months, lack of fire insurance for church buildings, and few modern church buildings as houses of worship.[39]

According to the Rural Church Survey, the majority of Southern Baptists at the turn of the twentieth century were rural, poor, and white. Most (80.7%) were farmers. The survey also found the majority of Southern Baptists were living in an economic environment that was changing in the South. The South's economy, devastated by the Civil War and Reconstruction, was finally stabilizing, and both the quantity and value of goods and commodities were increasing significantly as new industries such as coal mining and textile mills multiplied across the South and Appalachia at the turn of the new century.[40]

Given what they were learning about operations in their majority rural churches, turn-of-the-century Convention leaders garnered avenues through which they could offer the churches practical assistance in their journey to become more organized and efficient. In 1920, Gaines Dobbins introduced a course on church efficiency at The Southern Baptist Theological Seminary that resolved "to train pastors, missionaries, and other church workers in the most vital and practical phases of modern religious activities" with detailed analysis "of the Southern Baptist Convention and its Boards, of the State Mission Boards, and of the District Associations, all with the view of increased efficiency."[41] Additionally, Convention leaders, through Sunday School Board publications, produced two particularly illustrative examples of books for local church efficiency around 1920.[42] The first, *Church Obligation and Methods: A Manual for Baptist Churches* (1917), had been authorized by messengers to the 1916 SBC annual meeting in Asheville, North Carolina. The purpose of the manual was to offer feasible suggestions to churches in areas such as enlistment, uniformity, effectiveness, oneness, efficiency, church finances, and standardizing church organizations and methods. Its authors proposed that "the key to every Baptist denominational problem is the front door key of our Baptist churches."[43] The second book, *The Efficient Church* (1923), aimed to address a local Baptist church's "growing demand for a better correlation of its activities and a thorough utilization of its resources."[44]

Efficiency, indeed, permeated the consciousness of all areas of Baptist life in the early 1900s. In addition to publishing books on efficiency for local Baptist churches, the Sunday School Board also sought to help churches become more organized in two other important areas. The first rested in an ever-expanding array of church programs. Formed in 1891, the Board, by the early 1900s, had amassed a herculean ensemble of innovative practitioners who were promoting more church programs and more church efficiency to local Baptist churches. These areas of work included graded Sunday school lessons, Baptist Young People's Union, Vacation Bible School, church architecture, research and survey work, church administration, and publication of church music resources. With all the new church programs of the early 1900s, local church administration was becoming akin to executive administration in the business world, and a new platform of efficiency tools was needed to meet the challenge.[45] Second, as Baptist historian Robert Baker observed, the Board learned quickly at the turn of the century that instituting sound business practices into their operations was vital to their ability to stay afloat in the religious publishing industry.[46] Under the astute leadership of J. M. Frost, the Sunday School Board demonstrated organization, efficiency, and streamlined business practices—all of which proved instrumental in the Board's ability to expand its church ministry enterprises. In turn, as Southern Baptists gazed upon the Board's rapid expansion of church programs and accompanying potpourri of products and services, they thought, *We need to become more efficient too.*

To that end, keen business leaders within the Convention mimicked the Board's strategies. The Southern Baptist Laymen's Missionary Movement, formed in 1907, provides a case study of this process.[47] The Laymen's Movement was, according to Frank Grissom, the "first widespread attempt to educate Southern Baptists about the responsibilities of Christian stewardship."[48] Baptist laymen, many of them business leaders, assigned heavy merit on the importance of local church members giving regularly to their church and to tithing.[49] They proposed an "every member canvass" through which churches would set a time to personally visit each member of their congregation and explain the importance of financial support for local church and Convention ministries.[50] "The causes are many and the needs are great, and we have adopted a program so large that it is going to take the utmost resources of all our givers to maintain the high standards which we have adopted," explained E. Y. Mullins, president of The Southern Baptist Theological Seminary, in an SBC Laymen's Missionary Movement publication.[51]

Women's Work: Precision and Grace in Efficient Convention Assistance

Equally as eager to contribute their "utmost resources" to the Southern Baptist Convention's efforts in navigating the path toward a more organized and efficient Convention at the turn of the twentieth century were Southern Baptist women. New opportunities were opening for women in the United States in the early 1900s, and Baptist women in the South, while generally remaining more conservative than their sisters in the North, embraced the era's new conveniences.[52] In 1921, the Sunday

School Board of the SBC (what would later become Lifeway Christian Resources) applauded the recent advancements of women in America and Southern Baptist society, and proclaimed, "The last twenty years have brought more privileges to women than in any previous period. Practically every occupation and service that men enjoy may now be filled by women. Hence the women have accepted not only the occasion for a larger life but the obligation for adequate preparation to measure up to the new opportunities."[53]

Expanding avenues for women's contributions to the American social fabric outside the home at the turn of the twentieth century included support for the Women's Christian Temperance Union (WCTU) and Anti-Saloon Leagues and their crusades against consumption of alcoholic beverages (an ill many Southern Baptists viewed as causing a huge number of problems), impacts of the women's suffrage movement, participation in women's missionary societies, and women's literature publications including those supporting missions.[54] Southern Baptist women accepted the emerging responsibilities in the civic and social arenas of American life at the time.

Baptist women in the South, for example, were particularly adamant in their opposition to the distribution and consumption of alcohol.[55] In 1891, only three years after its founding, the Woman's Missionary Union passed a resolution opposing alcohol, and members of the WCTU were speakers to both the national and state Baptist convention WMU annual meetings.[56] The issue of women's suffrage included Southern Baptists who both opposed and supported the measure, with the latter group often connecting women's voting rights with opposition to alcohol.[57] While interestingly only a small number of Southern Baptist women spoke candidly in favor of women obtaining the right to vote, the reserved voices of women Baptist leaders in the

South changed on this issue after ratification of the Nineteenth Amendment as leaders of the WMU stressed the value of women's influence on moral issues at the ballot box.[58]

Chief among the ways early twentieth-century women, including Southern Baptist women, responded to moral concerns rested with their participation in women's missionary societies. In the later decades of the nineteenth century, many Protestant groups in America formed women's associations for promoting and supporting the missionary efforts of their respective denominations.[59] These societies gave women a chance to cooperate and lead in areas of missions advocacy and benevolent causes. The Southern Baptist Convention's Woman's Missionary Union, formed in 1888, was a product of this movement. By the early 1900s, the WMU, which included a host of state Baptist conventions, local associations, and local Baptist church societies, proved itself an excellent example of how the layered system in Southern Baptist life worked and how women worked that system efficiently.[60] In terms of fundraising, for example, the proficiency and trust incorporated into the SBC women's missionary societies at all levels ultimately meant that the "societies were more willing to accept direction from the national WMU than the autonomous-driven local churches were from the SBC."[61] The fact that the WMU exceeded its pledge to the Southern Baptist 75 Million Campaign provides a prime example of the dexterity of the fundraising efforts of Baptist women in the South in the early 1900s.[62]

During the campaign, Baptist women leaders including Kathleen Mallory (WMU corresponding secretary "who lifted women in the churches and made them working handmaidens of missions"), Minnie James, Isa Neal, Janie Cree Bose, and others traveled extensively across the South promoting systematic giving to Baptist women.[63] WMU leaders encouraged women to give regularly (even small sums of money counted) and to tithe.[64] At the conclusion of the campaign, "a new day of influence and recognition had dawned" for leaders of the Woman's Missionary Union as Southern Baptist women had demonstrated to the SBC a powerful example of how to get things done and make people feel more involved.[65]

Another contribution of Southern Baptist women to the overall arch of efficiency in the early 1900s involved distribution of information through women's publications. Southern Baptist women first published missionary journals such as the *Heathen Helper* and *Baptist Basket* (both from Kentucky) in the 1880s; *Our Mission Fields* (renamed *Royal Service* in 1914), the flagship WMU publication, appeared in 1906.[66] Publications such as these educated Southern Baptist women about missions and missionaries as well as social and moral issues important to women like orphans, mountain mission schools, and care for the sick and desolate. The impact of women's publications on missions was vital to the crusade to make the Southern Baptist missions movement both abroad and at home better.[67]

Conclusion

At the turn of the twentieth century, Southern Baptists were struggling to make things work better. The malleable world in which they lived before the Great War segued to an era of optimism and opportunities after the war. For Southern Baptists, it was a time of reflection—a chance to evaluate and take measurable action on how to do better the ministries they most cared about. These motivating factors included missions around the world, caring for children and the elderly, helping the sick and the poor, providing young men and women with educational training, and evangelism for African American and immigrant communities. The journey included incorporating efficiency concepts from the American business world into streamlined giving practices for Southern Baptist causes. The process required assistance from all accords of Southern Baptist life. At times, the trek toward development of the CP was bumpy. But in the end, at this remarkable moment in time, Southern Baptists determined that in order to meet people's needs, they had to do better than they had done before. And the only way to do better was together.

Personal Reflection

The Cooperative Program allows Southern Baptists of all stripes the chance to participate in a broad array of worthy missions and ministry opportunities and to accomplish those endeavors better together. In my research on the beginnings of the CP, I was struck by how difficult the task was for those early pioneers not only to develop the mechanics for the Cooperative Program but also to convince Southern Baptists that it was the best way to do ministry. Because of that, the Cooperative Program has provided services that have changed millions of people's lives across the world.

Personally, I am grateful that one of the CP-supported ministry services, where I have served for more than two decades, is the Southern Baptist Historical Library and Archives. Receiving less than one-fourth of 1 percent of the CP allocation budget, the SBHLA is the largest, most diverse, and most accessible collection of Baptist historical materials in the world. It is the central depository and archive of SBC records; serves as a research center for the study of the life and history of Baptists; collects, preserves, and makes available for use a wide range of materials that document Baptist history; and assists local Southern Baptist churches, local Baptist associations, state Baptist conventions, and SBC agencies in the location and preservation of historical records. The collection's resources include archival records and manuscripts, annuals of Baptist associations and conventions, thousands of books, comprehensive files of Baptist newspapers, audio and video recordings, photographs, pamphlets, microfilm reels of Baptist historical materials, and an environmentally controlled rare book room featuring a collection of rare Bibles dating from the early 1600s. I am thankful Southern Baptists invest in this vital ministry and special collection, with the charge of stewarding the many events, people, and institutions that document the Southern Baptist Convention throughout its history.

5

Setting the Stage: The $75 Million Campaign as Precursor to the Cooperative Program

Tony Wolfe

Lee Rutland Scarborough, early twentieth-century denominational pioneer and champion of Southern Baptist missional cooperation, saw in the New Testament a clearly taught "doctrine of cooperation" which "extends from the individual of a local church to the co-operation of churches of like faith and practice with each other in carrying out the Gospel program of Christ in world-wide redemption."[1] For Scarborough, a church's financial cooperation with others of like faith and practice was a biblical expectation both taught and modeled in the New Testament.[2] More recently, Scott Hildreth has suggested, "To cooperate is to be Southern Baptist."[3] This spirit, this theology of cooperation, became the heartbeat behind an organized system-shift that would pump vitality through the veins of Southern

Baptist cooperative missiology for generations to come. The dawning of the twentieth century shed light on new business practices in organizational financial management. Southern Baptists who were committed to cooperative missions at the local, state, and national levels acknowledged the prudence of a unified budget. They also acknowledged their need to restructure their overall missions-funding strategy which led them, in 1919, to launch their Southern Baptist $75 Million Campaign.

From the day of their constitution in 1845 until 1919, Southern Baptists employed what was later called a "society model" of cooperative missions funding. Their various mission and education agencies (Domestic Mission Board, Foreign Mission Board, The Southern Baptist Theological Seminary, etc.) employed fundraising personnel to travel the states seeking financial contributions from individuals, churches, associations, and other Baptist-minded groups and individuals.[4]

During the second decade of the new century, God prompted Southern Baptists to rethink their strategy. The Southern Baptist $75 Million Campaign was the short-term missions-funding strategy that inspired one of the greatest missions-funding movements in the history of evangelicalism—the Cooperative Program of Southern Baptists. L. R. Scarborough's influence on this new model of intercongregational financial cooperation for missions is not to be underestimated. As the general director of the 1919–1924 campaign, Scarborough was "the spearhead of an innovative ideology"; his work and the spirit it inspired became the "model and forerunner" of the CP, which has served as the primary missions-funding strategy for the Southern Baptist Convention since the program's genesis in 1925.[5] Through the lenses of the campaign's failures and successes, this chapter will offer a brief historical survey of the Southern Baptist $75 Million Campaign as the "model and forerunner" of the CP.

Historical Background

The Southern Baptist $75 Million Campaign was born into the postwar cradle of American patriotism, cooperation, and bureaucracy. "Efficiency," "centralization," and "economic organization" were the trends of the day.[6] President Woodrow Wilson reflected on that season of American life during which the trials of urgent need were adjudicated in the cooperative spirit of American volunteerism: "America was never so beautiful as in the spring, summer, and autumn of 1917 when people were stirred by a passion in common, forgot themselves and political differences in an urge to put all they had, all they were, to use in a great purpose."[7]

Within only two years after America entered the Great War, an army numbering millions was drafted, thousands of new government bureaucracies were formed, and "farmers and factory workers and millionaires alike" enlisted in the financial program to fund the war.[8] Every American could do something to play his or her part and become involved in the cooperative effort. As a result, as historical biographer Scott Berg notes, the economic growth and financial commitments of the American economy during and immediately following the war years were unparalleled—the gross domestic product more than doubling to $76.8 billion by the fall of 1918 while the gross public debt almost tripled to $14.6 billion.[9] President Calvin Coolidge later reflected on the war years as a great unifying period in American life. He acknowledged the "missionary spirit" of Christians in that day and commented, "The whole nation seemed to be endowed with a new spirit, unified and solidified and willing to make any sacrifice. . . . The entire nation awoke to a new life."[10]

At their 1919 annual meeting in Atlanta, Georgia, Southern Baptists reflected on the successes of the war efforts, the renewed spirit of American patriotism, the efficiency of unified budgets and businesslike practices, and the new opportunities of global evangelism and missions in the postwar era.[11] President J. B. Gambrell, in his Convention address, exhorted the churches to collectively "go afield all over the world with the sword of truth flashing in the sunlight and piercing to the heart of everything that exalts itself against the sovereignty of Jesus in the realm of the soul. . . . Let us gird up our loins and go forward."[12] He closed his message with an appeal for Southern Baptists "to adopt a program for work commensurate with the reasonable demands on us and summon ourselves and our people to a new demonstration of the value of orthodoxy in free action."[13]

Agreeing with the spirit of Gambrell's exhortation, J. T. Henderson, general secretary of the Executive Committee of the Laymen's Missionary Movement of the Southern Baptist Convention, acknowledged "the thorough methods of organization that have come from our experiences within the World War . . . the lessons of this new day." Henderson continued to press the Convention for "a period of simultaneous education and enlistment, to be followed by a simultaneous drive throughout the South in the interest of all the enterprises of the denomination, both general and local."[14] His report was adopted unanimously. Initially, the five-year campaign was proposed at $50 million, then was officially recommended at $75 million.[15] It was organized after efficient businesslike practices but within the boundaries of voluntary cooperation necessitated by the Baptist doctrine of local church autonomy. The program was to be a willing partnership between local churches, state conventions, and the national Convention in all its agencies and boards. Lee Rutland Scarborough, president of Southwestern Baptist Theological Seminary, was chosen as general director for what was named the $75 Million Campaign.

In the first year, campaign pledges were recorded at over $90 million. Scarborough pointed to a ten-year period of the development of a certain "missionary conscience" and an "enlargement of the missionary vision" of Southern Baptists, having "gripped our people, as never before. . . . The call of Christ in all the world has been sounding the soul of Southern Baptists in a mighty fashion for ten years, getting them ready for the great task of the Seventy-five Million Campaign."[16]

During the 1919 convention, Scarborough insisted, the impetus toward this campaign was not the work of a few Convention leaders. Rather, it "seemed to come out of the very soul of the messengers."[17] An enlarged, cooperative mission vision had taken hold among Southern Baptists, and the $75 Million Campaign was the mission-funding strategy they needed to underwrite their God-given vision.

A brief review of denominational media both leading up to and following the campaign reveals that expectations were high and pressure was great for the success of the overall program. In his written report to the 1919 convention, Foreign Mission Board Corresponding Secretary J. F. Love foreshadowed the severity of possible failure:

> If Southern Baptists fail in this the Seventy-fifth year of their history to make a program for Foreign Missions which will take care of that with which they are solemnly charged, they will prove themselves unfaithful stewards and unwise statesmen in the Kingdom of God. . . . Will the Convention now make a financial program which will enable the Board and the missionaries to execute on the field the denominational program which has been

made for them? Or will we, failing to do this, place our missionaries in a false light and shame them before those who would delight to see our denominational program break down?[18]

As Scarborough concluded his 1919 pamphlet *Evangelism, Enlistment, Enlightenment*, which set out the great needs and opportunities of the campaign, he argued that the campaign itself would be a defining moment for Southern Baptists toward a future of either "meager endeavor" or "great victories."[19] For better or worse, before a single pledge was committed on Victory Week in 1919, Southern Baptists tied the success of their cooperative missions to the successes of the $75 Million Campaign.

The 1920–1921 depression adversely affected the American economy and, by extension, the collection of pledged funds. As one historian records, "ruinous inflation" "ravaged" the American economy between 1919 and 1920, toward a comprehensive economic collapse that peaked in May 1920.[20] By November 1919, the cost of living had increased 82.2 percent above the 1914 level; by July 1920, it had peaked at 104.5 percent over 1914.[21] While the economy mostly recovered by early 1923, Southern Baptists had not caught up on financial installments toward their pledges to the campaign.

In its final days, serious pledge-collection shortfalls became evident. Several denominational leaders employed language of failure to describe the shortage. In April 1925, F. S. Groner, executive director of the Baptist General Convention of Texas, wrote an article published on the front page of the *Baptist Standard* pleading with Texas churches to fulfill their commitments in the final hours of the campaign: "If we fail . . . it will be regarded as a sure token that the budget plan is a failure."[22] In the same month, Tennessee Baptists also felt this sense of dire consequence upon the inevitable shortfall of pledge collection: "Baptists are in a mighty struggle. . . . The battle is on. The next few days will record for eternity the efficiency or inefficiency of Tennessee Baptists in this battle. . . . Every interest of Christ's kingdom is imperiled."[23] At the beginning and end of the $75 Million Campaign, failure to collect on pledged funds would be deemed unworthy of Christ and unworthy of the great missionary task taken up by the convention.

The Hard Lessons of the Southern Baptist $75 Million Campaign

The $75 Million Campaign was the first comprehensive, streamlined missions-funding strategy undertaken by Southern Baptists. It called for a unified budget to be promoted and maintained over its five-year period by a unique, functional cooperation between local churches, state agencies, and national agencies.[24] With a goal of $75 million, its overall objectives primarily concerned "worldwide evangelization . . . [and] the financial aspects of our work as a Convention."[25] Scott Hildreth declares the campaign a "watershed in Southern Baptist history."[26] But to the disappointment of many, the campaign ended in a dispiriting shortfall, the commission collecting only 78 percent of its published goal, a mere 63 percent of its pledges.[27]

Collection Shortage

By the end of 1919, pledges to the $75 Million Campaign were recorded at $92,630,923. Campaign director L. R. Scarborough was rightfully encouraged and invigorated by Southern Baptists' response to the campaign's launch.[28] But when the campaign was completed, actual receipts fell short of the goal by almost $16.5 million, with a total collection of $58,591,713.69. Some disagreed with the campaign's philosophy altogether and argued it was doomed for failure before it began. J. Frank Norris, Scarborough's greatest opposition through the campaign and in the years that followed, referred to the initiative as "unscriptural and ill fated."[29] Louis Entzminger, Norris's thirty-four-year friend and partner in the ministry, agreed with the Fort Worth pastor that the campaign was "ill-fated" from the start, comparing its leadership and collection methodology to "Roman governors," the "Sanhedrin when they stoned Stephen," and a "conscienceless, heartless denominational machine" destined for obvious and embarrassing failure.[30]

Despite the vocal opposition, the Conservation Commission was appointed at the 1920 annual meeting to carry through to completion the work the Campaign Commission began in 1919. For reporting purposes, initial subscriptions were divided by state according to the pledged five-year amounts recorded during Victory Week.[31] By the end of 1919, total pledges came to $92,630,923. Figure 1 presents a state-by-state comparison between pledged and collected campaign funds.[32]

State	Amount pledged in 1919	Amount collected by 1925
Alabama	$4,200,000	$2,717,464.62
Arkansas	$3,114,407	$2,319,654.72
District of Columbia	$250,000	$301,848.81
Florida	$1,375,000	$1,009,416.89
Georgia	$10,100,000	$5,282,493.24
Illinois	$912,362	$691,245.89
Kentucky	$7,454,387	$6,414,159.87

Louisiana	$3,002,163	$1,681,438.52
Maryland	$900,000	$729,440.82
Mississippi	$4,209,585	$3,107,040.36
Missouri	$981,756	$2,438,561.24
New Mexico	$732,260	$708,124.80
North Carolina	$7,250,000	$5,174,865.61
Oklahoma	$3,144,682	$1,462,030.34
South Carolina	$7,600,000	$4,773,889.11
Tennessee	$4,540,003	$3,950,655.49
Texas	$16,560,000	$8,720,161.50
Virginia	$8,100,318	$6,657,778.86
Other	$8,231,346	$451,443.00
TOTAL	**$92,630,923**[33]	**$58,591,713.69**

Figure 1. $75 Million Campaign Pledges and Collection Comparison by State.

In the Conservation Commission's final report to the body of messengers in 1925, the committee acknowledged an overall disappointment in collections and corresponding distributions.[34] Because of the drastic shortfall of collected funds, the campaign's distributions to the various boards and agencies were significantly less than anticipated in 1919. Figure 2 summarizes the discrepancy between promised and actual distributions according to campaign allocations:[35]

Recipient of distributed funds	Projected $75 million distribution amount in 1919	Actual total distribution by January 1925
Foreign Missions	$20,000,000	$11,615,327.91
Home Missions	$12,000,000	$6,622,725.55
State & Associated Missions	$11,000,000	$9,900,785.93
Christian Education	$20,000,000	$16,087,942.07
Orphanages	$4,700,000	$5,134,522.10
Hospitals	$2,125,000	$2,975,380.07
Ministerial Relief	$5,000,000	$1,786,676.30
Other/Miscellaneous	$175,000	$4,468,362.76
TOTAL	**$75,000,000**	**$58,591,713.69**[36]

Figure 2. $75 Million Campaign Projected and Actual Distribution Comparison.

If the success of the $75 Million Campaign is to be measured by the collection of pledged funds alone, the effort stands vulnerable to being labeled a failure. As a missions-funding strategy, the campaign promised to fund specific cooperative mission efforts on behalf of Southern Baptist churches. It did not completely deliver on that promise. "The prospect that the campaign would end in failure was a devastating thought," Chad Owen Brand and David E. Hankins suggested in their 2005 book *One Sacred Effort*. "Yet fail it did."[37] But does a shortfall of collection rightfully qualify the entire campaign as a failed effort?

Institutional Indebtedness

As Andrew Smith notes, general expectations, other than from early dissenters such as J. Frank Norris, were that Southern Baptists would come through with the funds; such overconfidence by campaign and institutional leaders in Southern Baptists' ability and willingness to make good on their campaign pledges, Smith notes, led to "a rash of spending that threatened to bury Southern Baptist denominational work underneath a mountain of debt."[38] O. S. Hawkins further explains, "Baptist mission boards and institutions planned and spent according to the promised amount pledged rather than the actual receipts," resulting in seemingly insurmountable debt.[39] Southern Baptist institutional indebtedness rose quickly and steeply during the years of the campaign. The various boards of the Convention "had borrowed money for capital improvements" among other things, but due to the drastic shortfall in collected and distributed funds "basic functions of the boards were dramatically impacted."[40]

For example, "In a state of enthusiasm and high expectancy" toward the beginning of the campaign, the Foreign Mission Board was ordered by the convention "to advance in the scope and care of its work" and "to loan money to three theological schools which are within the bounds of the Convention."[41] The leaders of the Board estimated they would receive a minimum of four million dollars per year during the campaign, but because of the shortfall in receipts, the Board's allotment amounted to merely $2.1 million in 1920, $2.4 million in 1921, $1.8 million in 1922, and commensurate amounts in 1923–1924.[42] The financial shortfall created "consequent embarrassment" to the Foreign Mission Board "and peril to its work."[43]

Between 1920 and 1924, the Board cut $3.5 million from its promised missions-funding expenditures and still ended the campaign with "enormous debt" totaling more than $700,000, the interest on which totaled more than $70,000 in 1923 alone.[44] Corresponding secretary J. F. Love noted that the financial shortfall and corresponding indebtedness effected resident missionaries, colleges and seminaries, hospital buildings and medical equipment, and other needs "for every one of our mission fields. This wholesale denial to the missionaries of material equipment for their work will be a sad historical incident in the annals of this work."[45] In the face of mounting debt and unfulfilled financial promises, Love frankly laid out the options before the convention: "retirement from some fields and retrenchment in all, or else increased contributions by Southern Baptists to their foreign mission work."[46]

Similarly, the Home Mission Board mounted institutional indebtedness during the early years of the campaign, but by its 1924 convention report began to see reduction in its debt, albeit due to "drastic retrenchments in our operations."[47] The debt incurred was "heavy and burdensome" as receipts diminished year over year during the campaign, leaving the Board "handicapped" in its work.[48] Total indebtedness for the Home Mission Board climbed to $822,183.60 in 1924, not including $53,724.58 promised yet unpaid in individual church gifts.[49]

Prior to 1919, the Convention's newly formed Education Board launched a $15 million campaign to benefit denominational educational institutions, but this effort was rolled into the larger $75 Million Campaign upon its commencement with the promise of 4 percent allocation, or an expected total distribution amount of $3 million. However, in the Board's 1924 convention report, corresponding secretary W. C. James lamented that only 53.8 percent of the Board's promised allocations had been collected. "This means a severe handicap," he regretted, "since only a little more than one-half of the expected funds have been received upon which to administer and carry forward the work."[50] The Education Commission promised Illinois, New Mexico, Arkansas, Louisiana, and Florida a total of $500,000 ($100,000 each) to strengthen educational institutions in their respective states, promises upon which these institutions made plans and investments; however by 1924, only between $8,000 and $40,000 had been dispersed to each.[51] The inability of the Education Board to invest the promised funding in these schools due to the failure of Southern Baptists to make good on their campaign pledges, together with the plans the schools enacted based on the expectation of those receipts, was seen not only as an imperilment to the future of the educational institutions but also as a great embarrassment to the states in which they were planted.[52] Additionally, three Southern Baptist seminaries—The Southern Baptist Theological Seminary, Southwestern Baptist Theological Seminary, and New Orleans Baptist Bible Institute—had been granted advance loan funds totaling $330,413.11, but the financial shortfall of the campaign made it "manifestly impossible" for the Education Commission to follow through with the loan funding it had promised and which the respective seminaries had already begun to spend.[53]

John Mark Terry and J. D. Payne in *Developing a Strategy of Missions* suggest strategic financial planning for missions. They warn missionaries of the dangers of "foolishness with resources" which does "not result in the Lord's blessings, whether resources are few or many."[54] When financial resources do not come through as expected, the authors suggest "it is more likely that the strategy was in need of revision and that God's calling had not changed" than that "God was not involved in the strategy" or that the strategy itself is without value.[55] Perhaps, for the

Southern Baptist $75 Million Campaign, the disappointing discrepancy between total pledged and total collected amounts does not tell the complete story of the missions-funding strategy's overall success or failure.

The Successes of the Southern Baptist $75 Million Campaign

Great institutional debt and shortfall of collection on pledges wounded the convention's campaign outlook, but it simultaneously invigorated its cooperative spirit. An overarching sense of "malaise" and borderline "depression" was palpable in the convention at times; however, in other ways the $75 Million Campaign "was a remarkable success."[56] In 1942 H. E. Dana, L. R. Scarborough's first biographer, labeled the campaign "the most significant forward movement ever launched by the Southern Baptist Convention."[57] Scarborough himself argued early in the campaign's life cycle, "The money to be realized from the Campaign is of far less consequence than the spiritual energy aroused and the demonstration of spiritual unity which has been made."[58] Southern Baptist historian H. Leon McBeth argues that the campaign "represents a great leap forward in Southern Baptist stewardship, promotion, and denominational self-identity."[59] The successes of the movement can be captured in at least three categories: financing ongoing cooperative mission works, stimulating cooperative evangelistic zeal, and awakening greater denominational missions cooperation.

Financing Ongoing Cooperative Mission Works

In their final report to the convention in 1925, the Conservation Commission highlighted the following advancements made in the funding of ongoing cooperative mission works.[60] In the area of ministerial relief, the five-year campaign did more for the one thousand supported retired preachers and their families than Southern Baptists had done for them in their combined seventy-five-year history. The number of Baptist hospitals doubled from twelve to twenty-four, and the value of their properties tripled. From 1919 to 1925, Southern Baptists added two orphanages, invested almost as much money in colleges and seminaries as the combined value of their property, and enlarged their missionary force by 100 percent. Local churches baptized 225,000 people, increased membership by 375,000, and planted twelve hundred new congregations.

The Foreign Mission Board, in the same 1924 annual report that lamented the campaign's financial shortfall and the corresponding enormous debt it provoked, reported the following net gains from 1919 to 1924: missionaries, 216 (66% increase); native workers, 1,867 (298% increase); churches, 590 (117% increase); members, 62,213 (125% increase); self-supporting churches, 165 (115% increase); contributions, $271,296 (156% increase); baptisms, 7,221 (128% increase).[61] In the same breath as his disappointment over the campaign's financial shortfall, Love celebrated that "the Spirit of God has in these recent marvelous years created an atmosphere, mellowed human hearts, ripened mission fields, quickened Christian aspiration, nurtured the graces of the Spirit, removed religious prejudice and created hospitality for the truth on all our mission fields."[62]

The Home Mission Board reported a field-wide exponential increase in baptisms, funds raised, and church leaders trained in schools and seminaries over 1919 numbers.[63] Hildreth notes an 84 percent increase in per capita giving among Southern Baptists from 1914–1918 to 1919–1924 followed by another significant average increase in 1925–1929 totaling more than a 100 percent per capita increase in giving among Southern Baptists as a result of the campaign years.[64] While the opportunities of the $75 Million Campaign were tremendous, those that lay ahead of Southern Baptists were even more so. Notably, the sacrificial and cooperative spirit born in the five-year campaign not only financed concurrent mission works but also stimulated Southern Baptists for the unified, strategic funding of ongoing mission works as well. "The ends of the world, with their growing need for Gospel remedy, have come in upon the soul of the South," Scarborough noted in 1920, "and the missionary impulse has been quickened a thousand-fold."[65]

Stimulating Cooperative Evangelistic Zeal

The entire campaign was marked by an evangelistic zeal woven through every aspect of the movement. McBeth argues that the impact of the campaign's "unified effort upon evangelism" is evidence of its overall success, despite its financial shortfall.[66] Following Victory Week in late 1919, Scarborough noticed unanticipated "doors of opportunity" opened to "evangelism and missions" as well as an overall "new dignity for the power of redemption over the lives of men."[67] He continued, "One of the most meaningful and heaven-honed by-products of the Campaign is to be found in the deepening of the evangelistic and compassion and hunger for the salvation of a lost world. . . . Everywhere a revival spirit was started. A new zeal . . . the kindling of new spiritual fires for soul-winning have started the revival hope everywhere throughout the South."[68]

In the Home Mission Board's 1924 convention report, corresponding secretary B. D. Gray acknowledged the "financial depression of the past three years," a "necessary retrenchment in our forces," and the drastic shortfall in collections on pledge funds, but still reported "the unwonted favor of God upon the labors of our missionaries and evangelists."[69] He reported advancement in historically difficult fields of labor, "thousands" having been brought to Christ, and an overall season of "great harvest" during the years of the campaign: "The success of our workers—evangelists and missionaries—has been so great as to create needs never before dreamed of."[70] He noted that the five-year campaign strengthened Southern Baptist churches in self-support and awakened them to new fields of cooperative evangelism and missions: "Our people have been brought to a consciousness of responsibility and opportunity in their Christian lives. . . . The spirit of evangelism and the activity of our evangelists and missionaries have penetrated unexpected fields which in turn have responded to the gospel message and are sending out pleas for help."[71]

Gray believed the $75 Million Campaign's legacy would be more than a shortfall in receipts or incurred institutional debt. He noted a certain, identifiable, permeant "success" in evangelistic and missionary zeal and effectiveness in the field of labor.

Six months into the campaign, Scarborough reported witnessing "the mightiest spiritual awakening among Southern Baptists . . . known in all Baptist history."[72] "Everywhere revivals broke out. Hundreds of souls were saved."[73] From its inception, the program was to be inaugurated and carried forth in "the most glorious spirit of evangelism."[74] It was. During the campaign years, local churches baptized 225,000 people, increased membership by 375,000, and planted twelve hundred new congregations.[75] As a missions-funding strategy, the finances themselves were not the vision but, rather, one goal of many. The vision was the rekindling of the Southern Baptist spirit of missions and evangelism, inflamed and carried along by new measures of efficiency to unify and mobilize the churches for the Great Commission. According to Terry and Payne, "missionary strategy" makes use of goals, but those goals are not an end unto themselves; rather, they are "accomplishments on the journey toward the achievement of the vision."[76] If the $75 Million Campaign enumerated the goal, the advancement of evangelistic and missional cooperation among Southern Baptists was the vision. In this regard, the $75 Million Campaign knew colossal success.

Awakening Greater Denominational Missions Cooperation

Campaign and commission chairman L. R. Scarborough ended his final report to the 1925 convention with language of great expectation: "The 75 Million Campaign has left Southern Baptists a great heritage, which is more precious than life or gold . . . a great spirit of co-operation and liberality. . . . If Southern Baptists are to take care of what the 75 Million Campaign has left them every one of us must make a holy covenant to do his dead level best in the highest possible standards and claims of New Testament cooperation, sacrificial liberality and prayerful, aggressive, co-operant, constructive kingdom-building evangelism."[77] On the same page of the 1925 annual report, the Future Program Commission offered its first annual report that would begin the Cooperative Program of Southern Baptists.

On behalf of the Home Mission Board, B. D. Gray wrote in 1924,

> So marvelous have been God's favors upon our people in the last few years, and especially during the five-year Campaign, that we are ready by virtue of our forces and resources to seize the present situation and make Southern Baptists the greatest single religious force in the South and throughout our nation and the whole world. . . . May God help our people in this great day of opportunity.[78]

In the creation of a future campaign, the Board advocated for "terms and agreements" that would take into account lessons learned from the $75 Million Campaign and that in the future work there be "conference and cooperation" between state and the national agencies.[79] It formally recommended to the 1924 messenger body "Cooperative Missions—with their unifying influence among Southern Baptists," and "Evangelism and Enlistment—without which the Kingdom of our Lord cannot progress or our denomination succeed."[80] Within this newly formed denominational consciousness, the CP was born.

The $75 Million Campaign showed Southern Baptists "the power of cooperation, a unified budget, and a denominational stewardship plan."[81] Barnes credits the five-year campaign with revealing to Southern Baptists "the desirability and the possibility of enlisting the whole membership of the churches in the work of the Convention."[82] The Southern Baptist Convention entered the twentieth century with a laser-sharp focus on world evangelism, and the $75 Million Campaign showed them they had the means and the mechanism to carry out that big vision. The five-year campaign served as a prototype and inspiration for the Southern Baptist CP, which became their permanent, unified missions-giving strategy for the future.[83]

H. E. Dana reflected on the $75 Million Campaign and the years that followed it: "The Seventy-five Million Campaign did not attain its objective, but it was by no means a failure. . . . There developed a new consciousness of corporate capacity and co-operative possibilities."[84] Theirs was a corporate capacity Scarborough called "a new denominationalism. . . . The consciousness of world power . . . the bonds of denominational life have been strengthened."[85] The $75 Million Campaign awakened Southern Baptists to a new season of cooperative missions. It funded and expanded ongoing Southern Baptist mission initiatives, inspired renewed cooperative evangelistic and missional zeal, and galvanized a new and more efficient missions-funding strategy for the future. The successes of the five-year campaign are to be found in the fruits of the cooperation rather than the funds of the ledger. It truly solidified within Southern Baptists a unity of purpose.

Conclusion

Upon the consummation of their remarkable quinquennial missions-funding strategy, acknowledging the gravity of the task still before them and the denominational solidarity undergirding them, in 1925 the leaders of the $75 Million Campaign reflected on their work with expectant wonder: "Not until the Heavenly record is unfolded will we know the mighty meaning of these days to the glory of Christ and the salvation of men."[86] While financial shortfall and institutional indebtedness loomed over their heads, an inspired awe of the immeasurable good that God had done warmed their hearts. None who cooperated would be convinced the campaign was an overall failure; its successes were too great and the Convention's evangelistic and cooperative missional fervor was too palpable.

Some may suppose that to evaluate success in a missions-funding strategy is to look primarily, if not only, at the financial projections and receipts. If finances alone may measure success in such an effort, then the Southern Baptist $75 Million Campaign should be recorded as a failure in the annals of history. However, if success is to be determined by the evangelistic and missional outcomes of the overall program which the missions-funding strategy promotes, fuels, and supports, then the $75 Million Campaign should be known for all posterity as one of the most resounding successes in Southern Baptist history.

In the Southern Baptist Convention's eightieth year, the CP began as a perennial extension of the new unified missions-funding mechanism they discovered in the five-year program that preceded its inauguration. As Hildreth suggested, the campaign was a "watershed in Southern Baptist history."[87] During the years of the $75 Million Campaign, through both its successes and its failures, Southern Baptists developed a reformed denominational consciousness, a renewed commitment to inter-congregational cooperation, and a rigorous organizational model that set the stage for a more effective paradigm for cooperative Baptist missions—the Cooperative Program.

PART 2

6

What Is the Cooperative Program?

Tony Wolfe

"What is it?" she asked. I placed the oddly shaped, primitively constructed Amazonian object in her hand and replied, "It's an ocarina." The confusion in her eyes told me that didn't help much. After only a second or two, the precious four-year-old East Texas sweetheart, with a Pineywood drawl in her voice and a cheerful scrunch in her nose, came back at me: "Yeah, but, what *is* it?" Apparently, to name something is not to define it.

I continued, "It came from South America where my brother was a missionary. Natives have handcrafted these and sold them in local markets for centuries. My brother picked one up for me when he was returning to the States and gave it to me as a souvenir. I keep it on my shelf to remind me of his missionary work and of the people he was reaching, whom God loves very much and who are worthy of our greatest efforts to go and share the gospel of Jesus Christ." Again, with childlike innocence her inquiry persisted, "Yeah, but what *is* it?" Apparently, to historize or memorialize something is not to define it either.

So I explained that while it looks like a toucan, it's actually a musical instrument. You put your lips over the extended tail, position your fingers over the holes on the bird's body, and blow. If you lift your fingers one at a time, or in groups of two or three, the pitch changes. If you know how to play this, it can make beautiful music. Her curiosity was sparked, but she hesitated. She held it in her hand and looked at it more intently now, but she still didn't engage. I suppose to explain something also is not to define it.

I extended my hand and asked, "May I?" She entrusted it back to me for a moment. I positioned my fingers over the holes and brought the instrument up to my mouth, then gave it my best shot. Now, I'm no professional ocarinist, but hearing its music was the final piece of inspiration she needed. She abruptly snatched the toucan-shaped ocarina from my hand, put it to her mouth, and exhaled. She was hooked. My sweet little friend carried that bird around the church the entire day, telling everyone what it was and demonstrating its musical genius. I suppose to define something is, at least on some level, to demonstrate it. Things have words. They have stories. They require explanation. But in the demonstration of things we often find the inspiration and invitation we need to meaningfully engage.

I hope you might consider this chapter a prelude to the rest of the book. These pages contain a definition of the thing. Here the thing is named, historicized, and explained. But the demonstration and invitation you're looking for are to be found in the following chapters. The thing I'd like to place into your hand right now is the Cooperative Program of the Southern Baptist Convention (CP). Come in closely and observe this thing. Ask,

"What *is* it?" Bear with me as its story is briefly unfolded; then join me in contemplating the explanation of the thing.

To be Southern Baptist is to cooperate missionally. The Southern Baptist Convention is, most simply, an annual convening of messengers from invested Baptist churches. To be "part of" the Convention is to be a contributing and cooperating church. A church can be Baptist without cooperating with the Southern Baptist Convention. A local association or state convention can be Baptist without cooperating with the Southern Baptist Convention. But to be *Southern* Baptist is to be part of, and invested in, the Southern Baptist effort—to cooperate with the work of the Southern Baptist Convention.

After eighty years of unsystematic funding, the Southern Baptist Convention came to what one researcher has called "a watershed moment in Southern Baptist history."[1] On May 13, 1925, messengers to the Southern Baptist Convention gathered in Memphis, Tennessee, inside the ten-thousand-seat hall of the newly constructed Ellis Auditorium on the corner of Front Street and Poplar Avenue. Awakened to a new denominational consciousness for cooperative financial efficiency through the $75 Million Campaign, there Southern Baptists embraced a methodological pivot point in intercongregational financial cooperation. They affirmed a unified budget plan for their ongoing missional efforts, calling it "The Cooperative Program of Southern Baptists."[2] The program effort formally began with a weeklong emphasis throughout the South, November 30 through December 7, 1924. By May 1, 1925, CP receipts totaled $1,888,506.05 passing through eighteen state conventions. Twelve-month (May 1, 1924–May 1, 1925) receipts of $7,072,234.84 were also reported to demonstrate the potential in this transition from the $75 Million Campaign to the new CP.[3]

The CP was designed to eliminate the perpetual competition of Southern Baptist causes by direct funding appeals to churches and individuals. As the Southern Baptist work grew and expanded, it necessitated more financial resources. Developing opportunities for Southern Baptist entities gave way to increased fundraising efforts by each. Increased fundraising efforts required these entities to hire agency fundraisers, expending significant financial resources on the work of promotion and collection. Southern Baptist funding methodology was at a critical moment. It suffered from a lack of unified strategy, created competition among autonomous Southern Baptist entities, and wasted precious resources on promotion and fundraising. "MAY GOD HELP OUR PEOPLE TO SEE IT!" M. E. Dodd, chairman of the Future Program Commission, reported with urgency:

> We have reached a stage in the financial development of our denomination which provides by systematic giving the magnificent sum of $7,000,000 or $8,000,000 a year. Are we going to think and speak disparagingly of this splendid dependable resource . . . with the hope of meeting the pressing needs of some single activity by indiscriminate and non-co-operative appeals and efforts? Your Commission believes that the very time has come when this entire Convention should commit itself, with a unity of purpose and consecration never known before, to the common task of the enlistment of our people and the working out of this plan. We need to see that any other course means only chaos and ruin.[4]

So, with "unity of purpose and consecration never known before," the Cooperative Program was born.

But what, exactly, is it? During my tenure in Southern Baptist servant leadership, I have heard the CP explained countless times. Sometimes it is explained correctly and sometimes incorrectly. Sometimes it is explained compellingly and sometimes stodgily. Often, it is expressed in terms of history or functionality. It has been explained and described. It has been storied and flowcharted. But explanations and descriptions notwithstanding, what *is* the Cooperative Program? What *is* it?

Defining the Cooperative Program

Consider some working definitions of the CP offered by Convention leaders and influencers of the past and present:

- During convention proceedings in 1939, leadership called the CP "the budget plan" of the Convention: "the greatest step forward in Kingdom finance Southern Baptists have ever taken. . . . The Cooperative Program should be looked upon as the budget plan for using the contributions of our people in financing the affairs of our denomination. . . . To thoroughly understand the plan is to love it, to love it is to work at it."[5]
- The 1958 *Encyclopedia of Southern Baptists* defines the CP according to its organizational relationship between the state and national conventions: "A unified appeal for all denominational causes, state and Convention-wide, a program of

co-operation, not among state conventions nor among churches, but between the Southern Baptist Convention as an organization and each separate state convention as an organization. This co-operation involves three things, all related to the question of money: the soliciting, the securing, and the dividing of funds."[6]
- In 2005, Chad Brand and David Hankins wrote *One Sacred Effort* in which they defined the CP, in the simplest of terms, as "a unified budget for the Convention . . . a missions-funding process."[7]
- Scott Hildreth's 2018 *Together on God's Mission* defined it as "the major funding mechanism" of the Southern Baptist Convention, "structured as the means by which local churches cooperate in the mission of the convention."[8]
- In their 2018 book *SBC FAQs*, Keith Harper and Amy Whitfield also defined the program primarily in terms of its functionality: "The Cooperative Program is the Southern Baptist Convention's giving plan . . . a way of distributing undesignated funds among the ministries of the SBC."[9]
- In their 2019 book *Better Together*, Robert Matz and John Yeats favored more missiological terminology: "It is the most powerful tool at our disposal to effectively accomplish the broader calling our churches have to reach the lost for Christ. . . . Through

the Cooperative Program a church can reach their community, their state, North America, and the nations with the gospel."[10] They further captured the program's identity in terms of process and functionality: "The Cooperative Program (CP) is the process we use to support these ministries. It funds all that Southern Baptists do."[11]

While all these definitions are helpful, I offer the following definition as more concise and conclusive: The Cooperative Program is a missions-funding mechanism involving the deliberate and voluntary cooperation of local Baptist churches, state/regional Baptist conventions, and the Southern Baptist Convention through which every contributing Baptist maximizes the Great Commission impact of every dollar given.

To define the thing is not only to name it, historize it, or explain it, but to demonstrate it in a way that is both accurate and compelling. Perhaps embracing the above definition will assist Southern Baptists in more comprehensively and more compellingly communicating the value of our unified budget program to our people for generations to come.

The Cooperative Program is a missions-funding mechanism...

God is on a mission. He is sovereignly working through the timeline of human history to redeem for himself a sanctified people. People from every nation and tongue who repent from sin and place their faith in Jesus Christ—those who are born again of the will of God (John 1:13)—are cleansed from sin and sealed by the Holy Spirit for the purpose of enjoying God's glory with him forever in heaven. God's mission is to save his people from their sins and prepare them for heaven. He has made ultimate provision for this mission through the life, death, burial, and resurrection of his Son Jesus Christ. He has instituted his church as the primary messenger and vehicle of his mission in our age, and he has invited every follower of Jesus to join him in this mission by plugging into and working through his church. "Our mission," Kevin DeYoung and Greg Gilbert explain, "is to go into the world and make disciples by declaring the gospel of Jesus Christ in the power of the Spirit and gathering these disciples into churches, that they might worship the Lord and obey his commands now and in eternity to the glory of God the Father."[12] Local churches find their place in God's mission when they sacrificially invest themselves in gospel witness within their local communities and partner with like-minded churches to advance the gospel regionally, nationally, and internationally. The CP is, in its simplest form, a "plan of finance,"[13] a strategic mechanism through which like-minded Baptist churches can accomplish their shared mission together with God regionally, nationally, and internationally.

It must be said, however, that God does not need our money. Perhaps a more accurate statement is that God already owns all our money. As he unfolds his mission in our time, God has in his possession and at his disposal "the earth and everything in it" (Ps. 24:1). Every dollar given through the CP is a practical expression of God channeling his own financial resources through the hands of faithfully sacrificial stewards. So, first and foremost, the CP is a practical invitation to find our place in God's mission by sacrificially reinvesting his financial resources into his mission as a matter of faithful, biblical stewardship. It may be appropriate at this point to clarify, as others have through the years, that churches give *through* not *to* the CP.[14] The CP is not an end in itself. It is a mechanism. A program. Machinery.

The CP is a conduit for sacrificial giving through which local churches strategically invest in God's mission. We give *to* God's kingdom work; we give *through* the CP. The mechanism of the CP is a unified budget plan to unite the efforts of God's people in God's mission. So the CP is a missions-funding mechanism.

The Cooperative Program is a missions-funding mechanism involving the deliberate and voluntary cooperation of local Baptist churches...

If the CP is predicated on missions-funding cooperation, then who are the agents of cooperation? Who are the cooperants? Individual Baptists give to God's mission work through their local churches, but individual giving is not the CP. The missions-funding program of Southern Baptists is found in the voluntary financial interdependency of local Baptist churches. Baptist churches, each autonomous from the others, choose their own levels of participation with the larger work of Southern Baptists. Most regularly invested churches give between 5 and 10 percent of their undesignated receipts through the CP. Some give less. Some give as much as 15–20 percent. Each church decides its level of participation in the larger missions-funding program, and each can change its level of commitment whenever it chooses, for whatever reason.

Hildreth is wise to emphasize that the "Cooperative Program, even though it funds a global organization, is a local church program. . . . The Cooperative Program is for, and by, the local church."[15] A local Baptist church's participation in the CP is deliberate in that a church thoughtfully and methodically decides its own level of financial commitment. Encouragement toward the 10 percent mark has been considered a bit of a gold standard through the years. Initiatives for 1 percent more or extra end-of-year CP giving from churches have come periodically over the past one hundred years. But when all is considered, each church determines its own level of participation. The deliberation belongs to each Baptist church. The program is, therefore, "for, and by, the local church."

Financial cooperation is not only deliberate but also voluntary. No denominational hierarchy exists to require churches to give through the CP. There are no annual dues or fees because there is no perpetual club of which churches can be a member. No Southern Baptist leader, entity, or sister church can command or force a church to participate. The CP is a voluntary interdependence among local churches. So the success of the CP is dependent on the degree to which local churches understand its value and participate in its mechanism. As Brand and Hankins once suggested, "The fundamental key to the success of the Cooperative Program and all Convention ministries is *the local church*."[16]

Through the CP, local churches partner with one another in the ongoing Great Commission work of the Convention. They are not cooperating with entities, boards, committees, or leaders. The churches are cooperating with one another. In this way, the CP involves the deliberate and voluntary cooperation of local Baptist churches with one another. If churches refuse to financially partner together through this mechanism, they will have no CP.

The Cooperative Program is a missions-funding mechanism involving the deliberate and voluntary cooperation of local Baptist churches, state/regional Baptist conventions...

If the churches are pooling their funds through intercongregational missions giving, who (or what) is the collection agency? Where do the churches send those funds in their unified missions-giving mechanism? The answer is state/regional conventions. Local Baptist churches pool their resources through the CP when they send a portion of their undesignated receipts to their state/regional Baptist convention. Since 1925, conventions of churches (by state or region) have been the collection agents for CP giving. Just as members of cooperating churches decide their church's level of participation in the CP, messengers to each state/regional convention decide their convention's allocation for state/regional and national distribution.

Autonomy is a Baptist hallmark at every level of cooperation, so state/regional conventions must decide what percentage of collected funds to keep for mission and ministry in their spheres of influence and what percentage to pass on through the Southern Baptist Convention for national and international mission work. Brand and Hankins explain, "The Cooperative Program is primarily a partnership between the Southern Baptist Convention and the various state conventions for serving Southern Baptist churches in their mission enterprises . . . a way for state conventions of Southern Baptists and the national Southern Baptist Convention to have a unified approach with the churches for funding missions."[17]

In *Better Together*, Matz and Yeats champion this as "the best part of this plan" in that "it starts at home. Cooperative Program giving flows *through* our state and regional conventions. . . . For congregations, this means our ability to support and uphold our work throughout the world starts right in our own backyards."[18] In 1925, eighteen state conventions participated in the CP. In 2024, that number was forty-one.

Just as the churches partner together in CP giving, it is the joy of their state/regional conventions also to partner with one another for the advancement of the gospel by allocating a percentage of undesignated receipts to the national and international causes of the Southern Baptist Convention. Through the

CP mechanism, local Baptist churches support statewide and regional mission work to reach their neighbors and communities with the gospel while they also extend substantial financial resources through these state/regional conventions to fund the larger work of Southern Baptists.

The Cooperative Program is a missions-funding mechanism involving the deliberate and voluntary cooperation of local Baptist churches, state/regional Baptist conventions, and the Southern Baptist Convention...

The CP is unique to Southern Baptists. You will not find its equal in any other denominational structure or funding mechanism. The lynchpin is voluntary cooperation decided and governed by messengers from invested churches. Annually, messengers from invested churches gather to either reaffirm or redecide the allocation of funds toward their shared mission. Messengers to the annual Southern Baptist Convention have full control over the approval or amendment of the budget presented to them in annual session. In 2022, for example, messengers to the Southern Baptist Convention chose to allocate 50.41 percent of CP receipts to the IMB, 22.79 percent to NAMB, 21.92 percent to the six seminaries, 2.99 percent to the SBC operating budget, 1.65 percent to the ERLC, and 0.24 percent to the Southern Baptist Historical Library and Archives. Messengers' participation in this budget approval, on behalf of their local Baptist churches, reflects a commitment to invest their financial resources in the missions-funding mechanism over the course of the next year. Throughout the year, CP funds are collected and distributed according to the allocation set by the messengers the previous year.

In the following pages, you will see centennial reports and celebrations from Southern Baptist entities which are funded through

CP giving. Since 1925, Baptists have invested more than $20 billion in the ministries of these institutions through CP giving. Each of them, other than the state conventions and their entities, is a distinctively Southern Baptist institution; they belong to and are governed by their relationship to the Southern Baptist Convention. Lifeway Christian Resources and GuideStone Financial Services are also Southern Baptist entities, but they do not receive direct funding through the CP. The Woman's Missionary Union is an auxiliary to the Southern Baptist Convention, working alongside Southern Baptists to raise awareness about, and additional funds for, our cooperative missional endeavors.

For one hundred years, churches giving faithfully and sacrificially through the CP have funded our shared mission as Southern Baptists by making provision to evangelize communities, train and resource church leaders, plant churches, send missionaries, advocate for biblical values in the public square, and so much more. They have done so because they believe in and are sacrificially invested in their shared work as Southern Baptists. The mission belongs to God. The work belongs to the churches. The mechanism they have created and sustained for their cooperative engagement is distinctively Southern Baptist. The CP is the missions-funding mechanism of the Southern Baptist Convention.

The Cooperative Program is a missions-funding mechanism involving the deliberate and voluntary cooperation of local Baptist churches, state/regional Baptist conventions, and the Southern Baptist Convention through which every contributing Baptist maximizes the Great Commission impact of every dollar given.

"You will receive power when the Holy Spirit has come on you," Jesus told his disciples the day of his ascension, "and you will be my witnesses in Jerusalem, in all Judea and Samaria, and to the ends of the earth" (Acts 1:8). Since you are reading a book on the CP, there is likely nothing I could tell you about the Great Commission that you do not already know. In Matthew's Gospel the same commission is bookended by the power and presence of Christ himself: "All authority has been given to me in heaven and on earth. . . . I am with you always, to the end of the age" (Matt. 28:18–20). Christ commissions every born-again Christian to "go . . . and make disciples"—to "be my witnesses" locally, regionally, and globally. Our commission is great. Our time is short. "The Great Commission is for the whole church," DeYoung and Gilbert emphasize, and that means you: "We go, we proclaim, we baptize, and we teach, all to the end of making lifelong, die-hard disciples of Jesus Christ who obey everything he commanded."[19] Through redemption in Jesus's blood, every individual Christian has received the invitation and command of God to join him in his mission, under the guiding presence and commanding authority of Christ himself. We participate in God's mission by fulfilling the Great Commission.

Ultimately, the CP begins right there, with individual Christ followers sold out for the Great Commission. United by essential Baptist doctrines and gathered in Baptist churches, they invest in Great Commission advance through their local churches and advocate for those churches to participate sacrificially in the shared missions-giving mechanism of the Convention. The CP starts here. It "originates with the undesignated gift of the individual Baptist to his church's general budget."[20] Brand and Hankins emphasize that the ability of the CP to thrive is entirely predicated upon individual Baptists practicing biblical stewardship.[21] Another has written, "The Cooperative Program begins with individuals and ends with ministries."[22]

When the CP was born, budgeting was a fairly new concept for churches. Educating on and championing biblical financial stewardship for individuals and churches was as much of an "enlistment" activity by Convention leaders as was CP enrollment.[23] The CP thrives when individual Baptists give faithfully and sacrificially to God's kingdom work through their local Baptist churches, and those churches extend that faithful and sacrificial stewardship through the Convention's missions-giving mechanism. Through the CP today, fourteen million individual Baptists are funding the Great Commission. The program minimizes unnecessary duplication and financial waste, maximizing the effectiveness of every dollar given. Every dollar given through the CP extends gospel witness locally, regionally, nationally, and globally. The CP is not the only way to fund the larger Great Commission work, but since 1925 it has been, without equivocation, one of the most comprehensive and efficient. Through the CP, every contributing Baptist maximizes the Great Commission impact of every dollar given.

"Certainly the task ahead for Southern Baptists is greater, more meaningful and resultful than the task already accomplished," Lee Rutland Scarborough, director of the $75 Million Campaign, envisaged in faith while the heroic spirit of Southern Baptists began to form into a unified funding strategy for their shared Great Commission work. "We have merely begun in a more intensive and a more completely organized, co-operative way, our work of unifying, mobilizing, organizing, informing, instructing, enlisting, and marshalling our forces for the forward working of Christ's Kingdom. . . . Our program as mentioned above must have great, stirring, enthusiastic, and wisely-wrought-out plans for the future."[24] As the CP developed and enlarged, Scarborough saw his conceptual, unified missions-funding mechanism explode with Great Commission success.

The program strengthened and gave new expression to the unity of purpose Southern Baptists had shared since their earliest days.

Perhaps one hundred years and $20 billion later we too "have merely begun." As we await the end of the age, we pour our lives out for the fulfillment of the Great Commission, together. We evangelize. We disciple. We equip. We train. We mobilize. We give. Baptists are a sacrificial people. To facilitate our sacrificial Great Commission cooperation, we have partnered in the gospel these past one hundred years through the genius of the CP. But I believe the work ahead of us is even greater than the work behind us. I believe we have only just begun.

The CP is a missions-funding mechanism involving the deliberate and voluntary cooperation of local Baptist churches, state/regional Baptist conventions, and the Southern Baptist Convention through which every contributing Baptist maximizes the Great Commission impact of every dollar given. Hold it in your hands. Observe it. Examine it. Think about the hundreds of millions of souls across the globe who have heard the gospel of Jesus Christ because of Baptist churches working together in this missions-funding mechanism. And think of the billions more right now who stand in urgent need of the same. As you read the following pages, I invite you to put the CP to your own lips and share its beautiful music with the world. The CP is just an instrument. But in the right hands and on the right lips, it facilitates the advancement of the Great Commission in a biblical, exponential way. Look closely, and you'll see.

Personal Reflection

For forty-three years I personally have been blessed by churches who gave faithfully and sacrificially through the CP. Raised and saved in a Baptist church, discipled through associational and state children's and youth programs, encouraged and sharpened by Baptist pastor networks in three state conventions, educated in two Southern Baptist seminaries, regularly assisted by the ERLC in legislative and political engagement, and continually mobilized on short-term mission all over the world with NAMB and IMB, my journey in ministry would have been impossible without the CP. Now, as a state convention executive director-treasurer, I have the daily joy of facilitating those same blessings for hundreds of thousands more Baptists every day. The names of current and future generations of Southern Baptist pastors, church leaders, professors, church planters, and missionaries cross my desk daily. Occasionally I stop to reflect on how our family of Baptists, in all its autonomous organizations, joyfully and sacrificially invests in each one of those individuals. I'm filled with gratitude and burdened by the gravity of it all. Ours is a great entrustment.

To those churches who give faithfully and sacrificially through the CP, thank you. Thank you for investing in my salvation, my discipleship, my education, my ministry, and my leadership. Thank you for allowing me the daily joy of facilitating these same CP investments on behalf of current and future generations of our Baptist people. With the apostle Paul, "I give thanks to my God for every remembrance of you, always praying with joy for all of you in my every prayer, because of your partnership in the gospel from the first day until now" (Phil. 1:3–5). May Christ see through to completion this good work he has begun in us, until he comes again.

7

What Has God Done in the States?

Leo Endel and Pete Ramirez

Southern Baptists typically think of the North American Mission Board (NAMB) or the International Mission Board (IMB) when they think of the Cooperative Program (CP); however, the CP begins to fuel missions through the forty-one state conventions that cooperate with the Southern Baptist Convention (SBC). While the pinnacle of SBC life is at the local church, the state conventions and associations provide the mechanism and relationship connections to link the two hundred churches within Minnesota-Wisconsin and the twenty-three hundred churches within California, for example, and missionally link them to the approximately forty-seven thousand SBC churches in North America.

What has God done in the state conventions through the CP? You will be amazed! He has done great things!

The Historical Background of State Convention Development

Going back to Baptists' earliest roots in England, Baptists, though independent and autonomous, have frequently sought to connect and cooperate. The first Baptist association in America was established in Philadelphia in 1707. Southern Baptist work began in Charleston, South Carolina, in 1672, and by 1751 four churches established the Charleston Baptist Association under the leadership of Oliver Hart, from the Philadelphia Baptist Association.[1] Seven years later, the Sandy Creek Association was founded in Sandy Creek, North Carolina.

McBeth notes the importance of this early association in Baptist Life: "One could hardly overestimate the importance of this association to Baptists in the South. It provided their major forum for discussion of issues, ventures in church extension and home missions, efforts in ministerial education, and served as a clearing house for churches and pastors seeking settlement. Like the Philadelphia Association, it dealt with issues which troubled the churches, often offering assistance in matters of discipline."[2]

State conventions began to appear in the 1820s with the first convention being the South Carolina Baptist Convention founded in 1821. Associations had begun to outgrow their geographic boundaries with greater mission opportunities.[3] One of the South Carolina convention's chief tasks was to "sponsor home mission work throughout the state."[4] The constitution "named its 'grand objects' the promotion of missions and education."[5] Other new state conventions were soon started with the same and expanded intent. Tasks that once seemed impossible or too large for a single church or association could be done when many churches (and associations) joined together. So state conventions began as Baptists and Baptist churches, already associating locally, saw the need to organize for mission regionally. Each association could organize and affect a local missions strategy. But churches from multiple associations could organize and effect a statewide or region-wide strategy.

The unified budget strategy of the $75 Million Campaign (see chapter 5) was the stimulus for the CP, officially adopted by the SBC in 1925. Since then, state conventions have worked together through the CP as collecting agents to provide a unified mission-funding strategy for the Convention and all its missions and ministries. They keep a percentage of CP receipts, as determined by their messengers, for their state's missions and ministries. The rest of a state convention's CP receipts are then forwarded for larger and broader mission causes through the SBC. For one hundred years, we have diligently labored together to plant churches, to train church leaders, to share the gospel in every corner of our states, and to join others in the national and international cause. God has graciously used the CP to fuel his work to the ends of the earth.

In recent years, we have seen a decline in the average percentage of missions giving through the CP (from over 11% per participating church in 1978 to under 5% today).[6] Missions giving through Lottie Moon and Annie Armstrong have also declined when adjusted for inflation and as a percentage of local church giving. The CP has sustained and supported both the infrastructure and the foundation of all that Southern Baptists do together. With the decline, some of our seminaries and state conventions have struggled to support the foundation of SBC missions. Like playing a game of Jenga, our work rests on the voluntary interconnected support of one another. Be careful! Pull out the sustaining blocks of our work, and the tower will collapse.

What Has God Done in the States through the Cooperative Program?

God has used the CP to build strong networks of cooperative work in every state in the U.S. While it does take money to reach the world for Christ, the CP is much more than money. It is the "rope of sand," as James L. Sullivan once explained, that has held us together as autonomous Baptists cooperating together for the cause of Christ. It has focused our energies on gospel advance; it has provided us the means to pull together our various giftedness; it has held us together when lesser causes than the gospel would pull us apart. It has fueled the advancement of the Great Commission at home among an increasingly multiethnic nation and abroad.

The blessings and benefits of the CP to state convention work are innumerable and incalculable. However, in the pages that follow ten are identified.

1. The Cooperative Program funds missions and ministries strategically and efficiently.

The funding of cooperative Baptist missions and ministry before 1925 was haphazard and inefficient (see chapters 3 and 4). The adoption of the CP removed much of the competition, inequity, and inefficiency. It allowed state conventions and the SBC to become more strategic and effective in their work. The benefits for both the state conventions and the SBC are clear. We are able to receive ongoing and predictable support with a minimum investment in fundraising salaries and promotional materials. This allows more money to be spent on ministry impact and less on running the funding mechanism.

Because the giving stream is predictable, state conventions can prioritize their strategies, and church messengers can choose to fund the strategies deemed most valuable through the budget approval at the state convention's annual meeting. This allows state conventions to be directly accountable and responsive to the people and churches of their convention. In turn, people typically give more sacrificially to causes they can see and direct.

I (Pete) have seen how churches of the California Southern Baptist Convention value the ministry of their state convention. They value the ministries focused on reaching the greatest mission fields with the most diverse and the biggest population in the nation. The churches recognize the urgent need to fund in-state evangelistic and church-strengthening efforts, and that need is reflected in their CP allocation.

2. The Cooperative Program funds the network connections that keep us working together and sharing resources.

Early in my (Leo) ministry, I pastored in a small Missouri town where the city's water pipes were coming to the end of their lifespan. For years, they had been properly repaired and maintained, but as the community declined, they were neglected. As a result, my shirts were orange, not white. Quickly, we learned we could no longer assume the clean, clear delivery of water; we also learned that what we had taken for granted could not easily be replaced. When churches work together for the sake of the gospel, they stay connected. When churches begin to take one another for granted, the system of cooperation begins to fail. Baptists understand that the mission matters most. Missions was the foundational cause for which the SBC was organized. The need to cover the cost of the mission is why churches have given billions over the past one hundred years. As the system worked efficiently, it drew us together for the common cause of the gospel. Because we were connected, we found synergistic ways to cooperate for missions impact locally, nationally, and globally.

Networks are built on complex relationships. It is challenging enough to relate well within your local church. Add to that complexity the challenge of connecting forty-seven thousand autonomous churches and fourteen million people. It is impossible without some level of intermediary relationships. One national organization cannot connect with the people of every town and village. Associations and state conventions are intermediaries to connect and resource the challenges of ministry. They are much closer relationally and geographically to where the "rubber hits the road," as the saying goes.

Before serving in the state convention, I (Pete) knew of the Great Commission work we accomplished together because it was taught and modeled to us at First Bilingual Baptist Church in Pico Rivera, where I grew up. Our senior pastor Joe De Leon, who served there in my early years, moved to serve elsewhere. He served with the IMB for almost a decade, followed by a second move to the California state convention as the church planting leader. He was offered that ministry position by a former pastor of that same church who had served with the Home Mission Board and had been elected as the executive director of the California Southern Baptist Convention.

When I first became a pastor and encountered problems, I did not seek the support from folks from national agencies. I did not know them. I did not seek the support of my associational director because I really did not have a relationship with him either. However, I knew pastor De Leon and Dr. Whittaker (executive director at the time), and they knew me. I was able to receive guidance and ministry from them during some difficult seasons in ministry. I knew I could count on them. These men had been my spiritual mentors, my pastors, and, more importantly, my friends. Our culture competes for attention with screen time and celebrity preachers and leaders. We need intentional, personal relationships to mentor, sustain, train, collaborate, and encourage. The closer we are to the local church, the more effectively we can work together.

The CP sustains the work of the state conventions and allows them to serve as networkers who can connect pastors and churches to others who have expertise, human resource, and strategies that might help a sister church. "You should talk with Pastor Jim about what they are doing in Sioux City." Or, "NAMB has an evangelism tool that might be useful to you." These kinds of connections are invaluable to the kingdom and help us stay connected and effective.

The larger Southern Baptist identity is primarily an identity brokered at the state convention level. Most pastors and laypersons will rarely or never attend a national SBC meeting. Travel distances and expenses exclude the vast number of Southern Baptists. But such limitations are dramatically reduced when the state convention meeting is only three hours away. In these meetings, many Baptists find their connection and identification within the larger SBC family. They connect with national leaders who both share the vision of the larger SBC and hear the local vision and passion from the field.

3. *The Cooperative Program helps fund intentional church planting.*

A great many things need to happen for a church to be started. The CP has provided seminary education, church planter assessment, leadership pipeline development, expertise, and funding to start churches across North America. Can church planting take place without CP funds? Of course, but arguably not as effectively or as efficiently. Some of the resources and assistance can most efficiently come from experienced experts outside the local mission field (NAMB), but it also takes the knowledge and contextual experience of those in the local mission field to successfully launch a new church. We do this best when we work together at the associational and state levels.

While associations are not directly included in the CP allocation, many receive stipends from state conventions and national entities for various ministry projects, especially in church planting partnerships. The importance of their involvement in church planting (among other mission and ministry areas) cannot be overstated. Associations of churches provide immediate local pastor connections for encouragement, strategic insight, real-estate assistance, training hubs, and more to church planters. Most state conventions work directly with associational leaders in church planting assessment, strategy, training, and networking. Many state conventions work in concert with the North American Mission Board for assessment, funding, and training as well. The CP provides that necessary financial stream that flows from local churches across the state, through the state convention, then back to associations, sponsor churches, and the North American Mission Board, so that every church planter is best set up for success. The CP brokers an extensive network of cooperative relationships for Great Commission advance. For example, in California, the state convention strategically uses its financial resources and ministry teams to work in partnership with NAMB as Send Network California. I (Pete) believe we are the strongest church planting movement in California. When firing on all cylinders, perhaps the value of statewide Baptist cooperation is nowhere more evident than in church planting efforts.

4. The Cooperative Program funds a great diversity of gifted and experienced leaders who serve the churches of our conventions.

Most associations are too small to fund a full range of leaders to assist the churches in specialized ministries. Because the state convention draws resources from many churches, we can frequently fund specialists to assist churches with discipleship development, youth and children's leadership, evangelism, leadership development, church fundraising and construction, legal expertise, stewardship development, ministry coaching, strategic planning, sexual abuse, and more. There are economies of scale at the state convention level that make it possible to pool expertise and experience to rise to almost any ministry challenge. Associational leaders often know best where the challenges and opportunities exist in their areas. For some state conventions, the associations are considered as the tip of the spear in accomplishing their mission. When the relationship is healthy, associational leaders can see state convention staff as their own unpaid staff of consultants to assist the churches.

5. The Cooperative Program funds creation of and ministry to/through Baptist colleges and universities, hospitals, children's homes, retirement homes, outreach centers, and crisis pregnancy clinics.

Union University in Jackson, Tennessee, was founded in 1823 by Baptists in the South—twenty-two years before the Southern Baptist Convention was constituted. Since that time, state conventions have started and/or sustained fifty colleges or universities.[7] These universities sustain a Christian (Baptist) worldview and train lay leaders, pastors, and missionaries for the advancement of Christ's kingdom. In addition, Baptist collegiate ministries, sponsored primarily through state conventions, have been established on 768 campuses and involve more than 70,472 students in their ministries.[8] These college students have regularly served to extend missions and ministry through summer missions and semester missions opportunities in cooperation with NAMB's GenSend program, the IMB's Journeyman program, and state convention missions-sending efforts, all of which are fueled by CP giving. God has used these internships to expose young people to a greater vision for life on mission. On the West Coast, California Baptist University is the most impactful student ministry for the state convention and beyond, leading students to live their purpose and graduating more than three thousand students each year. If it were not for sacrificial giving through the CP, California Baptist University would have never made it into the 1990s. More than 10 percent of California Baptist CP giving has been allocated each year, for decades, to allow this school to keep its doors open and succeed in its mission. Only heaven knows the number of men and women God has called to ministry and mobilized on mission through these efforts.

State conventions have established and funded various kinds of ministry centers in cooperation with local associations and churches. As of today, an estimated ten thousand children are cared for in twenty-three state convention-supported Baptist children's homes, for example.[9] Scores of hospitals, migrant ministries, retirement homes, and crisis pregnancy centers have their roots in Baptist state conventions' vision and ongoing support. For one hundred years, CP giving has fueled not only church planting and mission-sending at home and abroad but also the meeting of human needs all over the country and the world, coupled with evangelistic witness and strategic Christian discipleship.

6. The Cooperative Program provides the network necessary for the development of Baptist foundations.

Many people are unlearned in the concept of community banking which funds the advancement of community development by pooling and holding the resources of a community so that those resources can be lent to local businesses and projects that will benefit the local community at large. Baptist foundations provide a similar service for Baptist causes within state conventions. By managing finances for shared causes, these organizations draw funds that would have gone outside gospel purposes but are now invested and accumulating for the advancement of the gospel. It is no stretch to say that our Baptist people have accumulated much wealth over these past one hundred years. Much of those financial assets are held by secular for-profit institutions whose benefactors are their own executive leaders, stakeholders, and other corporations that do not embody biblical values. When those financial assets are held in state Baptist foundations, however, the interest earnings cover minimal administrative overhead, and the rest is deployed in the form of gifts to various Baptist causes, invested in businesses that share the values and vision of Southern Baptists, or used to lend small churches or church plants the monies they need for facility purchases or repairs (a ministry which many secular banks will not fund at all and which others may take advantage of for capital gain).

State convention Baptist foundations are making an incredible difference in funding evangelism endeavors, church building projects, property acquisitions, funding for education positions at colleges, universities, and seminaries, intern development programs, college ministries, and almost any worthy ministry one can imagine. These pools of financial resources are making an incredible difference in the local church as well as in shared ministries throughout our states. As I (Pete) attend board meetings of California Baptist institutions and partner organizations, I see their budgets and how they are benefiting from the faithful work of the Baptist foundations that have been built on the back of the CP.

7. The Cooperative Program trains and funds disaster relief ministries.

The CP helps fund the training, equipping, and deployment of thousands of Baptist volunteers to minister and share Jesus during times of disaster. Disaster relief ministries help people who are hurting, and they have proven to be valuable opportunities to share Jesus in times of great need. The organization, training, and networking of the state conventions in partnership with NAMB has made it possible for Southern Baptists to be the third largest nongovernmental relief agency in the United States, exceeded by only the Salvation Army and the American Red Cross. In the 2022 SBC Annual Report, SBC Disaster Relief volunteers logged 93,248 days of service, served 966,735 meals, and shared the gospel with 7,617 people.[10] When kindhearted, generous individuals give directly to many of the most popular disaster-relief and human needs nonprofit organizations, a large percentage of those gifts is used for salaries and overhead costs. But because the CP covers most of the administrative and overhead costs for state convention disaster relief programs, when those same individuals give freewill offerings to a particular disaster relief effort through their state convention, an overwhelming percentage of that gift goes directly to the crisis relief for which it was given.

If you have never experienced the need for relief due to a natural disaster, you may not have personally felt the blessing this ministry provides. During those situations Southern Baptists, thanks to the CP, are able to sustain multiple state conventions' disaster relief teams deploying men and women to be the hands and feet of Jesus. They bring help, hope, and healing during a time of loss. They share the hope of the gospel usually accompanied with a cup of water, food, clean clothes, a shovel to remove ash or mud and recover personal items, and a Bible. It is a clear demonstration of unselfish love, coupled to gospel readiness, to the least of these.

8. *The Cooperative Program provides leadership training and opportunities.*

The state conventions have long served as the liaisons to the larger SBC family. This connection makes it possible for the churches to know what resources have been developed nationally and regionally to effectively raise up and equip leaders. The CP enables state convention staff to bring the best of NAMB and Lifeway resources, for example, closer to the churches and to make them culturally effective for the states.

Additionally, state conventions often employ some of the most intelligent, most experienced, and most missionally minded staff in the country. They produce resources that are often tailored to their own state's contextual needs. For one hundred years, the CP, channeled through state conventions, has allowed associations and local churches regularly to take advantage of workshops, seminars, and printed and digital resources from their state convention staff—resources that are specific to their ministry context and are connected with a statewide evangelism and/or discipleship strategy.

Southern Baptists hold a shared history and a shared missional methodology. The state convention has been an important ministry partner in maintaining the relational connections necessary for ongoing missional cooperation and Baptist identity.

9. The Cooperative Program provides seminary education for pastors and church planters to engage in our states.

New work areas could not build and fund seminaries without the help of the larger family of churches. When the CP was originally designed, our ancestors were wise to include an intentional plan for seminary education at a reduced cost. They knew pastors and missionaries would be hindered from receiving a costly education and, by extension, might be prevented from going to mission fields where the work would be hard and the finances difficult. With inflation and high living costs in states like California, if not for the CP support given to members of Baptist churches, it would not be possible for most pastors and church leaders to attend seminary. Additionally, the CP has made it possible for gifted and educated pastors and missionaries to go to the hard places.

Chapter 8 in this book provides more details into the historic work of Southern Baptist seminaries and celebrates more explicitly the advantage of the CP in their efforts. Even states that own and/or support Baptist state colleges and universities understand the value of formal seminary education and champion SBC seminaries as part of the larger academic and practical ministerial preparation that helps pastors prepare for a lifetime of ministry.

10. The Cooperative Program makes it possible for small churches to do full spectrum Acts 1:8 missions beyond their community and to the ends of the earth.

Pooling the giving of small churches makes it possible for those churches to maintain their passion and involvement in world missions where they might be tempted to think their involvement is of little significance. I (Leo) remember as a boy sitting in the sanctuary of Moose Creek Baptist Church outside of Fairbanks, Alaska, placing my nickel in the offering plate—a tithe of 20 percent on my rare allowance. I remember the joy of thinking that part of my nickel was going to pay for the church's heater (important when it was 40 degrees below zero outside), a part would help pay our pastor (whom I loved), a part would go toward the work of the regional missionary who was helping us start a new church, and a part of it would go to Africa to help a foreign missionary tell someone about Jesus. By my sixth-grade year, I had a big vision even though I was a little boy in a little church. That's the vision for cooperation I was taught by state convention appointed and supported directors of mission and state convention missions leaders. It is the vision of the CP I joyfully embraced so many years ago and that I still joyfully embrace today. Through the CP, for one hundred years, every Baptist, in every pew, in every cooperating church has been part of an international Great Commission movement. Portions of their faithful and sacrificial giving have played a crucial role in the evangelization of hundreds of millions across the globe. Because of the CP, no gift is too small to make a big difference.

Conclusion

Herman Ostry of Bruno, Nebraska, needed to relocate his barn because the creek had eroded part of the foundation making the barn unstable. His only apparent option was to tear it down and rebuild at the new site, but after some deliberation with his son, Mike, and some of his neighbors, they came up with a crazy idea—let's invite the folks of Bruno to help us pick up the barn and move it! Initially, they thought the idea was ridiculous, even impossible (kind of like the Great Commission being shared with people who had never been more than a hundred miles from home). But on July 30, 1988, using hydraulic jacks to get the barn off the ground, 328 of Herman's friends and neighbors picked up the twenty-thousand-pound barn and carried it 115 feet to the new location. Herman estimates that each person lifted and carried only fifty to sixty pounds.[11]

Many challenges are impossible for us to do alone, like reaching eleven million Minnesota and Wisconsinites with only two hundred churches or reaching forty million Californians with only twenty-three hundred churches. But when we work together, God does far more than we could ever do alone. In California, for the past three years our theme has been "Better Together." We are seeking to make sure we work with every Baptist partner and every Baptist church to accomplish the mission and be pleasing to our Lord by living out the unity he desires. That's why we are Southern Baptist, and that's why I believe in the CP.

Personal Testimonies

Both of us have long said that we are products of the CP. Our family lives have been dramatically changed by the CP; we both heard the gospel because of the CP. We were both nurtured by the mission passion of the CP. We were prepared for ministry by the CP, and our ministries have been driven by the missionary purpose behind the CP. It was not an accident that we both even wrote our doctoral dissertations on the CP.

When I (Leo) was seven years old, my mom, a nominal Catholic, reluctantly agreed to go to a new Southern Baptist church plant in Grand Island, Nebraska. What happened in that church changed my life and my future. First, my mom came to Jesus, and our homelife realigned around God, the church, and the Great Commission. Within a year, I, too, became a believer. Immanuel Baptist Church nurtured us and taught us for almost three years. Though I didn't yet understand it, my mom and dad became passionate about missions and about how the CP made it possible for our church to be planted and our family to be reached with the gospel.

What happened next began a pattern for our family that ultimately led to a calling for me. My dad, an enlisted airman, received orders for Billings, Montana. Being from Texas, he always wanted to go south, but God obviously wanted us to go north. For the rest of my youth, we were stationed in non-evangelical areas of the country: Anchorage, Alaska; Billings, Montana; Tonopah, Nevada; Fairbanks, Alaska; and Sault Saint Marie, Michigan. Everywhere we went there was a new SBC church plant funded by the CP. When I was in high school, we spent two years in Angeles City, Philippines, and belonged to an SBC church started by the Foreign Mission Board (now the IMB). In this church I came to fully understand the amazing power of the CP.

When God called me into the ministry, I was educated at an SBC seminary funded by the CP. When God took me to Northern Iowa and then to Minnesota, I knew God had prepared me for the new work areas of the SBC. His fingerprints were all over my preparation, and the funding of Southern Baptists had made it all possible. When we started planting churches in Iowa, the CP provided most of the financial resources for the church planters. Later, when the Lord led us to Minnesota-Wisconsin, I had the unique privilege of seeing the big picture of Southern Baptists' almost fifty-year investment into this new area. In these last twenty years, we have grown from approximately 135 churches to just under 200.

I (Pete) saw my parents come to faith in a Southern Baptist Church in East Los Angeles that was funded through the CP. My parents were also Catholics and lost without hope until they were invited to church by people who were committed to the Great Commission. They became members in that church and raised me to know Christ, and their faith impacted my life. Now my children know and follow the Lord. My seminary education was affordable due to the CP funds and the scholarships made possible by the state convention. I have served the California churches for the past seven years and for the past three as the executive director. I am committed to continuing to promote the CP that allows so many of us Baptists to serve as missionaries to strengthen the churches in order to fulfill the Great Commission.

Our lives would not be what they are if it were not for Southern Baptists' missions giving through the CP. The eternal destination of countless lives continues to be impacted by the faithful, sacrificial giving of so many Baptists. To God be the glory for what he has done and will do through his church.

8

What Has God Done in the Seminaries of the Southern Baptist Convention?

Jamie K. Dew Jr. and Chris Shaffer

We are both products of the education Southern Baptists have provided through the seminaries of the Southern Baptist Convention (SBC). Today we share the common bond of having been called to be a part of the training and equipping of pastors, church leaders, missionaries, counselors, and other leaders the churches of the SBC send to the seminaries. Our students are being sent by a church with an affirmation of their calling to service in vocational ministry. We are glad to train these men and women and send them back out to those churches and ministries more prepared.

Even before the founding of the first seminary by a group of Southern Baptists, Southern Seminary in 1859, Baptists recognized that theological education and training helped pastors and church leaders to be better equipped for service in the local church. James Boyce, in an address to the trustees of Furman University in 1856, noted that "Baptists are unmistakably the friends of education and the advocates of an educated ministry."[1] There has always been a commitment from Southern Baptists to support and encourage an educated clergy. While our polity does not require pastors or church leaders to be formally trained in a seminary context, thousands of churches in the SBC have sent men and women called by God to be trained through seminary education.

The men and women who founded the six Southern Baptists seminaries recognized the need for theological education, but we cannot imagine that they considered the long-lasting impact their work might have on Southern Baptists and the kingdom of God at large. Three of the seminaries predate the creation of the CP,[2] but today the students of all six Southern Baptist seminaries are beneficiaries of the sacrifices men and women make every Sunday in churches across our Convention. When they place their tithes and offerings in the passing plate, and when their churches give faithfully and sacrificially through the CP, the financial gifts of millions of Baptists help financially support seminary students preparing for ministry.

Today, Southern Baptists support six strong and healthy seminaries. From the beginning of the Convention, seminary education has been at the forefront of the work of Southern Baptists. Our seminaries are training thousands of men and women each year on their campuses and across the world.

The Southern Baptist Theological Seminary was founded in 1859 (now in Louisville, Kentucky). In 1917, Southern Baptists voted to create a seminary in New Orleans, Louisiana—originally, Baptist Bible Institute and now New Orleans Baptist Theological Seminary. In 1925, the Convention acquired Southwestern

Baptist Theological Seminary (in Fort Worth, Texas); the seminary had originally been founded in 1908 by Texas Baptists. Golden Gate (now Gateway Seminary) was founded in 1944 (originally in Mill Valley, California, but now in Southern California in the Los Angeles area). Southeastern's founding followed in 1950 (located in Wake Forest, North Carolina). Then Midwestern followed in 1957 (located in Kansas City, Missouri). Each of these institutions has served our Convention of churches faithfully through the decades, and by God's grace they will continue to do so.

Due to unique geographic locations and the various personalities that have led within these institutions, each seminary has its own characteristics and emphases. However, what unites the six seminaries is the shared task of training the men and women the churches of the SBC send to each. Many of our counterparts in the Association of Theological Schools[3] are selective in their acceptance of students and often decline to accept individuals making application. Our six seminaries accept all students, with a few exceptions, the churches of the SBC send to us each semester. We are committed to serving you, and when you communicate to us that this is a student you approve, we are glad to receive him or her as a student. Our goal is to welcome the students, train them with excellence, then send them back out to the field of ministry as soon as possible.

As institutions of the Southern Baptist Convention, we have a particular theological commitment that is in keeping with what Southern Baptists believe. Throughout most of the history of our institutions, we have worked to maintain that doctrinal commitment. There have certainly been moments in the history of some seminaries where those commitments have been slack, but the seminaries today strive to be faithful to the Word of God and teach in keeping with *The Baptist Faith and Message 2000*.

The final words of B. H. Carroll, the founder and first president of Southwestern Baptist Theological Seminary, to L. R. Scarborough were a charge to keep the seminary lashed to the cross.[4] At the 1997 annual meeting in Dallas, Texas, the presidents of the six seminaries recommitted themselves and their respective institutions to the churches of the SBC. In front of the messengers, each taking his turn in the chair of B. H. Carroll, the presidents signed a covenant titled "One Faith, One Task, One Sacred Trust" that served as a commitment of unity among the presidents to communicate to Southern Baptists that the seminaries serve the churches of the Convention. At the time, Dr. Al Mohler, president of The Southern Baptist Theological Seminary, stated, "This sacred covenant anchors the six seminaries of the Southern Baptist Convention to the solid rock of biblical conviction. . . . [It is] a mature and timely statement from six seminary presidents who stand together before the convention at a time of unprecedented unity."[5]

The current six presidents continue this faithful legacy before the Convention: "Our schools are not generic institutions for religious studies. We are the six theological seminaries serving the Southern Baptist Convention. We belong to you; we belong to the churches of this Convention. We are proud to carry your charge, and we declare our fidelity to you as a sacred trust. In this trust we stand before the Southern Baptist Convention, and we stand together."[6]

Each year at the annual meeting of the SBC, our seminary presidents give a report to the Convention. That report rarely fails to mention our gratitude for the generosity of Southern Baptists through the CP. In every context where we are engaging with Southern Baptists, we as the seminary presidents express our deep appreciation for the financial support we receive because Southern Baptists give faithfully each week. Ultimately those resources make their way to the entities of the SBC, including the six seminaries. The impact of the CP cannot be overstated.

The SBC has given the six seminaries the ministry assignment to prepare God-called men and women for vocational service in Baptist churches and in other Christian ministries throughout the world through programs of spiritual development, theological studies, and practical preparation in ministry.

Too often in the history of Christianity, denominations have become untethered from Scripture. They have compromised on the understanding of Scripture as having "God for its author, salvation for its ends, and truth, without any mixture of error, for its matter . . . [making it] totally true and trustworthy."[7] One of the emphases of the Conservative Resurgence was to ensure that the seminaries of the SBC remained steadfast and committed to the authority of Scripture. Today, Southern Baptists support six seminaries that are biblically grounded, committed to the inerrancy of God's Word, theologically conservative, and striving to fulfill the task of training God-called men and women for service in the local church.

The impact of the seminaries on the communities around them is profound. The students who live on our campuses serve the churches in our communities in a variety of capacities. Many of our seminary students are training and studying each day in the classroom and then serving in local churches in a volunteer or staff position. They study the concepts and ideas of ministry each day in class and then immediately put them into practice in the churches they are serving while in seminary. When Southern Baptists created the school in New Orleans, they determined that the students would have an important impact on New Orleans, South Louisiana, and the Gulf South. At its founding, the Convention determined that the training school "established in the city of New Orleans . . . should have for its primary purpose the object of Missionary propaganda."[8]

Due to our service here, we are most familiar with the story of NOBTS and the impact of Southern Baptists on this region. When the Baptist Bible Institute (the original name for the New Orleans Baptist Theological Seminary) was founded, there were approximately thirteen hundred members of six Southern Baptist churches in the region within a city of more than three hundred thousand residents. In the first twenty-five years of the Baptist Bible Institute, those numbers grew to twenty-seven churches with just under nine thousand members. Today, there are 130 churches in the New Orleans Baptist Association, and there are tens of thousands of Southern Baptists in the region of South Louisiana. According to data collected by the New Orleans Baptist Association and NOBTS, of the 130 Southern Baptist churches in the area, 120 of them have a current seminary student, current or retired faculty member, or alumni on the church staff.

Jeff Iorg, former president of Gateway Seminary, described the founding of Golden Gate (now Gateway Seminary) as an institution focused on prayer that led to an institution that is "a beacon of biblical scholarship with missional intentionality shaping leaders who expand God's kingdom."[9] Each of the seminaries has encouraged its students to actively participate in ministry while in seminary. The leaders of the seminaries have actively served in ministry roles before or during their tenure as seminary administrators. For example, Adam Groza, president of Gateway Seminary, has served as interim pastor while also serving at Gateway Seminary. Jason Allen, president of Midwestern, has served as an interim pastor while also serving as head of the institution. Jamie Dew served several churches as pastor while serving on the faculty and administration of Southeastern and has been an interim pastor while also leading NOBTS as president. Hershael York, currently the dean of the School of Theology at Southern Seminary, served as a pastor for twenty years while also serving on the faculty of Southern Seminary.[10]

Twenty-five years after its founding, leaders of the Baptist Bible Institute described the impact of the school on New Orleans and the surrounding community in this way: "Turn loose . . . eager devoted young preachers and missionaries into any mission field and you will have results. This stream of young life has vitalized every church activity in New Orleans."[11] Still today, you could insert the name of the cities where our seminaries are located, and the quote would be an apt description of the impact the seminary community has on the surrounding areas.

The most recent snapshot report of the seminaries shows that our SBC seminaries are training 24,322 students.[12] Of those, 13,471 are students in graduate programs.[13] Based on data compiled from reports of the Association of Theological Schools,[14] of the 270 ATS accredited schools, all the seminaries of the SBC rank in the top ten of the largest seminaries in North America.[15] This is a testimony to the commitment of the SBC to theological education and the training of leaders for service in the local church.

Since its inception in 1925, the CP has helped to fund the ministries of the Convention. The churches of the SBC have tasked the various entities with this work and directed, in particular, the seminaries to provide theological education and training to the men and women those churches send to their seminaries. The number of resources placed under the stewardship of the seminaries through the CP is staggering. Since 1925, when there were only three seminaries, until today (with six SBC seminaries), the churches have forwarded $1.7 billion through the CP to their theological training institutions. When you consider the enormity of that gift to the six seminaries over the course of one century, it is a humbling figure. This is a weighty stewardship that has been given to the seminaries of the SBC. Our task today is to steward these financial resources well and to maintain the trust given to the seminaries to ensure that the men and women are returned to places of ministry better prepared to accomplish their God-given task.

In the one-hundred-year existence of the CP, the six SBC seminaries (three of which did not exist until 1944, 1950, 1957), have sent nearly 140,000 graduates into their fields of service.[16] This is a profound force of ministry leaders who have been trained following a similar curriculum that is grounded in the Word of God. These servants of the Lord have gone to small rural churches, mercy ministries, large urban contexts, remote parts of the world, and places that many of us have never heard of and will never visit. They have answered this call, sent out by the local church and equipped for ministry by the seminaries, in order to be obedient before God. Their impact on the kingdom will not be known until the new creation comes and their work is revealed by God.

Conclusion

Today, our seminaries are training thousands of students to take the gospel wherever God calls them. We will graduate students who will serve as the only staff member of a smaller membership bivocational church, as pastors and ministers on large church staffs, as missionaries in countries that cannot be named, as worship leaders, youth ministers, counselors, professors, Sunday school teachers, associational leaders, and more. Thousands of men and women and their families will leave our campuses in order to obediently follow Christ. Our stewardship of the financial and human resources provides us the ability to do this task faithfully before God on behalf of the churches of the SBC. Today, in our seminaries, more than one hundred nationalities are represented among our student bodies. We have students training in faraway countries, getting up at all hours of the day and night to participate in classes through online delivery methods. These faithful students are training in preparation for service exactly where God has called them to serve. Each year we also serve thousands of residential students in hundreds of buildings and on thousands of acres across the United States. These residential learning communities provide current and future church leaders with the opportunity to grow and be sharpened together, striving to be prepared to share and defend the faith once for all delivered to the saints.

Personal Testimony

When I (Dew) was a college student planning to continue in seminary education, I briefly entertained the idea of going outside the SBC seminaries for my training. I looked at Trinity Evangelical Divinity, Gordon-Conwell, Alliance Theological Seminary, and a few others. These were in fact great schools. But once I compared them to the six SBC schools, my choice was easy! Our SBC schools were among the best seminaries in the country, and they were way more affordable. Furthermore, the SBC schools were clearly the best option for anyone called to serve in a Baptist context. And so I enrolled at Southeastern Baptist Theological Seminary in the fall of 2000 and went on to earn my MDiv and PhD. Not only did I receive a world-class education, but because of the CP, I also finished these degrees completely debt free. In fact, after various other scholarships I received, I actually cleared several thousand dollars each year above tuition that I could use for living expenses. I would not be where I am today without this great blessing.

A seminary education would have been nearly impossible for me (Shaffer) without CP support. I have received a phenomenal education that has prepared me for the task God has called me to fulfill. That education came with lower costs because of the ways in which Southern Baptists have sacrificed each week as they place their tithes and offerings into the passing plate. The CP enabled me to pursue a seminary education at a Southern Baptist seminary where I studied under professors faithfully committed to the inerrancy of God's Word, alongside men and women who were seeking obedience before the Lord. These men and women have become lifelong friends and ministry partners because of these unique learning communities supported by the CP. I am a better follower of Jesus because of my time in seminary, made possible only because of the Cooperative Program.

9

What Has God Done in the Public Square?

Richard Land and Brent Leatherwood

The Ethics & Religious Liberty Commission (ERLC) plays a small but vital role in the life of the Southern Baptist Convention (SBC), representing the Convention and its members in the public square. Its existence tells a story about who Southern Baptists are, what they care about, and how they see their role in the world. Throughout its more than century-long history, the organization that became the ERLC has been a part of some of the most important cultural and policy conversations in our nation's history. While not perfect, the history of the ERLC reflects a Baptist focus on the local church, the love of neighbor, and a desire to bring gospel influence to the public square.

What came to be known to Southern Baptists as the Christian Life Commission (1953–1997) began life as the Committee on Temperance (1908–1913) and morphed into the Social Service Commission (1913–1947). Then a second version of the Social

Service Commission (1947–1952) later culminated in the Ethics & Religious Liberty Commission (1997–present).

During the first half of the twentieth century, Southern Baptists faced moral issues inspired and informed by their commitment to Jesus and his gospel command to be salt and light in society (Matt. 5:13–14). Significant numbers of Southern Baptists supported the Prohibition movement's attempts to outlaw alcoholic beverages in the United States, which were at alarmingly high consumption rates.[1] They also took stands against gambling (especially state-sponsored proposals for lotteries). While still an overwhelmingly racially segregated denomination, the Social Service Commission and the Christian Life Commission called on Southern Baptists to oppose violence against African Americans and to treat all human beings with Christian charity.[2]

Of course, in all its various institutional forms, what became the Christian Life Commission defended religious freedom (the right of churches to operate according to their beliefs) and the separation of church and state as outlined in *The Baptist Faith and Message* (1925). Much of the work of religious liberty and church-state relations was carried out in conjunction with the Baptist Joint Committee on Public Affairs (BJCPA), an alliance of Baptist denominations headquartered in Washington, DC, dedicated to defending religious freedom for all citizens.

When A. J. Barton, who had led the Social Service Commission (SSC) since 1913, died in 1942, the Commission selected J. B. Weatherspoon as his replacement. Weatherspoon was a longtime professor of homiletics at The Southern Baptist Theological Seminary in Louisville, Kentucky. In 1944, Witherspoon emphasized race, peace, and alcohol in his address to the convention. He declared that the Commission's purpose was to call "Christians to relate themselves in a Christian way to our common social life." Further, he urged Southern Baptists to always remember "that the baseline of all social judgments and proposals is Christian moral teachings." He also reminded convention messengers that "the social function of this Convention is not to promote social action as a substitute for evangelism and education, but rather to combine and coordinate . . . evangelism, education, and action."[3]

According to one writer, where Barton had been a "crusader," Weatherspoon was more characteristically a "planner" who set "in motion the methodology that would be embraced for decades."[4] For Weatherspoon, the role of the Commission was to state clearly the facts of "social practices as they related to Christian ideals and standards."[5] This included the creation of regular pamphlets, resources, and national gatherings so as to provide Christians with the information necessary "to see where the lines of Christian morality and social practices meet."[6] One of the final addresses Weatherspoon would give in his role as chair of the Commission was for the "Special Committee on Race Relations," which he persuaded the Convention to create in 1946. As part of the Committee recommendation, it put forward a number of principles and commitments shaped by faith and biblical teaching about the dignity and worth of all people and called for the application of these Christian and Baptist principles to "the necessary consequences in racial attitudes."[7]

After World War II, the Southern Baptist Convention took steps to make the Social Service Commission a full-fledged institution or "entity" of the Southern Baptist Convention with trustees elected by the messengers at the annual meeting and with an allocation from the Cooperative Program (CP).[8] During this same time, it gave the primary responsibility of speaking to religious freedom issues to the newly created BJCPA.

In 1947, Hugh Brimm was elected to replace Weatherspoon to head the Commission. His brief tenure included attacks on racial segregation as well as a host of other issues. At the 1950 Southern Baptist Convention, Brimm, who was committed to racial reconciliation, quoted E. M. Poteat of North Carolina stating, "If segregation is not un-Christian we must advocate it; if it is un-Christian, we must protest against it."[9] There was no question where Brimm and the Commission stood. Other topics included a denouncement of militarism and war during the Korean conflict in his 1952 address.[10]

Following Brimm's resignation, Acker C. Miller was elected the executive secretary-treasurer of the newly renamed Christian Life Commission in 1953. Miller had previously served as the director of the Baptist General Convention of Texas's Christian Life Commission. In his 1954 address, his first before the convention as the CLC director, Miller spoke to the recent *Brown v. Board of Education* decision in which the U.S. Supreme Court unanimously declared that the "separate, but equal" doctrine in public education was unconstitutional. The *Brown* decision was handed down on May 17, 1954, and the convention met the first week of June. The case had roiled much of the nation, most particularly the South, and Southern Baptists were no exception.

Miller acted boldly (some would say prophetically) by bypassing the Resolutions Committee and going straight to the messengers, presenting a recommendation to the Convention itself. Miller called on messengers to commend the court's decision and for "all Christians" to "conduct themselves . . . in the spirit of Christ."[11]

After considerable and heated debate—which included J. B. Weatherspoon's thundering reminder that "if we withdraw this from our consideration tonight, we are saying to the United States of America, 'Count Baptists out in the matter of equal justice, and I do not believe we want to do that'"—the convention voted to approve Miller's recommendation.[12] Future generations of Southern Baptists should be grateful to our heavenly Father that at a pivotal point in the nation's, and the Convention's, history, the Christian Life Commission was used by the Holy Spirit to do the right thing, the "Christian" thing.

Miller announced his retirement in the fall of 1959. By March the following year, Foy Valentine (Miller's first choice) had been elected as the new executive secretary of the Christian Life Commission at the age of thirty-seven.

Valentine, like Miller, came to the CLC from the Baptist General Convention of Texas's Christian Life Commission. Valentine had the distinction of being the great T. B. Maston's first Southwestern Seminary doctoral graduate in ethics in 1949. His dissertation was titled, "A Historical Study of Southern Baptists and Race Relations, 1917 to 1947."

In his first address to the convention in the CLC's report, Valentine said, "The Commission urges our Southern Baptist people to make use of every opportunity to help Negro citizens to secure [equal] rights through peaceful and legal means and to thoughtfully oppose any customs which may tend to humiliate them in any way."[13] In a sermon following the report, he also condemned communism.

Valentine came to the CLC just as what was to become the "turbulent 1960s" began. It was a marriage made in heaven. Valentine had a far more vigorous and confrontational leadership style than Miller and was more progressive on many of the issues that confronted American culture and Southern Baptists.

At the 1961 annual meeting, the convention further revised the CLC's program statement, instructing the CLC to "assist Southern Baptists in the propagation of the Gospel" by applying

Christian ethics "in family life, human relations, moral issues, economic life, and daily work, citizenship, and related fields."[14]

Two court cases of the early 1960s were important to understandings of public religion. The 1962 *Engle v. Vitale* case ruled state officials could not compose a prayer and encourage its use in public schools, citing Thomas Jefferson's "wall of separation" between church and state. The following year, the court ruled in *Abington School District v. Schempp* against any state-sanctioned prayer or Bible reading in the nation's public schools. It would be fair to say that a significant majority of Americans and Southern Baptists disagreed with the court's decisions.

Because of the 1947 restructuring, religious liberty issues were the primary concern of the Baptist Joint Committee, not the CLC. However, it was clear to most observers that Southern Baptists wanted the issue addressed and from a different perspective than the one offered by BJCPA, which had submitted testimony and resolutions supportive of the measure to ban school prayer.[15]

Back in 1960, in his first address to the SBC, Valentine had proclaimed that the entity "interprets its grave responsibility to this Convention to speak to the conscience of Southern Baptists on the application of Christian principles and everyday life."[16] This concept of the CLC as "the conscience" of the Convention, calling Southern Baptists and other Christians to be where the CLC thought they ought to be on the moral issues of the day became a vivid image in the mind of the CLC and Southern Baptists in the decades ahead.

In 1964, Valentine, in a massive understatement, claimed that America was undergoing a "crisis in morality." Valentine declared that Southern Baptists "have been part of a culture which has crippled the Negro and then blamed him for limping. Our failure to create a climate of Christian goodwill . . . has resulted in the racial protest movements which have been used for the redress of legitimate grievances."[17]

The CLC also began taking positions which were increasingly out of step with the majority of Southern Baptists. The 1964 Southern Baptist Convention rejected the CLC's recommendation that the SBC renounce capital punishment. As the 1960s progressed, the CLC became increasingly controversial as it held seminars that included liberal speakers such as Joseph Fletcher, the father of "situation ethics"; Anson Mount, manager of public affairs for *Playboy* magazine; Frank Stagg, a Southern Seminary professor who had become an anti-Vietnam War activist; and Julian Bond, speaking on "Black Power." Valentine's positions and activities led to attempts to defund the CLC, which failed, causing Valentine to respond to the SBC, "Thank you for my annual call."[18]

At the 1971 annual meeting, the CLC was significantly involved in drafting a resolution "On abortion," which was subtly pro-choice and used to erroneously convince the Supreme Court that Southern Baptists supported the legalization of abortions. In subsequent years, the CLC remained far more pro-choice on abortion while the SBC continued to grow ever more solidly pro-life.

Beginning in 1979, what became known as the "Conservative Resurgence" surfaced as an effort to elect inerrantist, conservative SBC presidents to ensure more conservative appointments to the SBC's boards, entities, and agencies. The CLC and the BJCPA continued, however, to feature speakers in national seminars and publications that signaled their sympathy for more moderate forces within SBC life. The appearance of former U.S. Attorney General Ramsey Clark (1980), Senator Ted Kennedy (1976), and Sarah Weddington, the attorney who argued for *Roe v. Wade* (1980), serve as excellent examples.

Frankly, the CLC was moving in one direction, and the SBC was moving in another, and the strains of that tension were increasingly clear. For example, in 1980 the SBC passed a much more strongly worded pro-life resolution on abortion. Additionally, in 1985 the SBC approved a Sanctity of Life Sunday on the denominational calendar. The CLC opposed its addition and then worked strenuously, albeit unsuccessfully, to get it moved away from January, so it would not be tied to the abortion issue.[19]

In 1986 Foy Valentine announced he was retiring due to a heart condition. It needs to be said that while Valentine's tenure became increasingly controversial, he was a seminal and important historical figure in SBC and American life in the mid–twentieth century. As Richard Land, president of the ERLC from 1988 to 2013, said at the time of Valentine's death in 2006: "Dr. Valentine gave 27 years of faithful service to Southern Baptists as head of the CLC. . . . While Dr. Valentine and I had significant differences of opinion on many issues, all Southern Baptists will be forever in his debt for his courageous and prophetic stance on racial reconciliation and racial equality in the turbulent middle of the 20th century."[20] Land added that it "had been important for him as a teenager in the 1960s to know that Dr. Valentine and the CLC were on the right side of the race issue, when there were too many institutions and individuals in American and Southern Baptist life who were on the wrong side."

Upon Valentine's retirement, the CLC trustees, with a small but growing number of theological conservatives, elected Nathan Larry Baker, academic dean of Midwestern Baptist Theological Seminary in Kansas City, Missouri, in January 1987 as the new executive director/treasurer. Baker was perceived as more conservative on the abortion issue than Valentine, but he was still seen as hostile to the overall goals of the Conservative Resurgence.

After serving for nineteen months, Baker resigned in May 1988 to accept the pastorate of First Baptist Church, Pineville, Louisiana.

In September 1998, the CLC trustees elected Richard Land as the fifth executive director of the CLC. At the time, Land was serving as vice president for academic affairs and professor of theology and church history at Criswell College in Dallas, Texas, having just finished an eighteen-month stint as executive assistant to Texas governor William Clements (while on a leave of absence from Criswell). Unlike his predecessors Brimm, Miller, Valentine, and Baker, Land's academic background was in theology rather than ethics. At the age of forty-one, Richard Land was the first baby boomer national entity head, thirteen years younger than the next youngest entity head, a child of the civil rights revolution, and a harbinger of generational change. Land had become a prominent spokesman for the pro-life cause and on other social issues, leading the church to take a stand for the dignity of the preborn.

After his election, Land explained to the trustees that he had been led by the Holy Spirit to accept the CLC's call because he had been given a vision of three overarching goals he felt led to pursue. First, he felt inspired to lead the CLC and Southern Baptists to take a strong, uncompromising pro-life stance for the unborn at the national and international level. Second, he felt convicted to make the racial reconciliation issue a "Gospel" issue that transcended any and all political or cultural labels for Southern Baptists and the nation.[21]

Accordingly, Land led the CLC, in the early months of his tenure, in January 1989, to convene a conference on racial reconciliation. He had told the search committee and the full CLC board, "The race issue is an issue of right and wrong, not an issue of right or left." To emphasize continuity on this topic between himself and Valentine, Land invited Valentine to speak at the racial reconciliation conference. Land's invitation and Valentine's acceptance provoked some intensely negative reactions. Land explained to Valentine, "Foy, *my* friends are going to be very upset that I have invited you to speak, and *your* friends are going to be very upset if you accept. But Foy, this issue is more important than our friends."[22] However, the point had been made. The torch had been passed on racial reconciliation. That conference led to the crucial 1995 SBC resolution in which Southern Baptists apologized for having supported slavery and segregation and asked for the forgiveness of our African American brothers and sisters.

Third, Land felt inspired to lead Southern Baptists to an understanding and acceptance of a doctrine of *accommodation* in terms of the people's expression of their religious belief in the public square according to the dictates of their own consciences. This would be a different model from the more liberal *avoidance* model favored by the BJCPA, which argued for "secularizing" the public square by avoiding religious displays, activities, or symbols therein. The accommodation model was also in contrast to the more conservative *acknowledgment* model, which favored the majority religion "on behalf of the people."[23]

Land believed that if Baptists were forced to choose between the avoidance and the acknowledgment models, the majority would reluctantly choose acknowledgment as the lesser of two evils. However, Land believed that if they were exposed to the accommodation model, they would find it more appealing, as it was far more in keeping with their Baptist convictions. The Convention agreed with Land's position, and in the early 1990s removed the issue of religious liberty from the BJCPA and gave it to the CLC.

Having acknowledged that the CLC had lost the confidence of a great many Southern Baptists, by the time of his election, Land made it a priority to restore that trust. He continually reminded the trustees and staff that as "the conscience of the Convention" the CLC had an obligation to seek to lead Southern Baptists and other Christians to be where the CLC believed they ought to be on the moral and ethical issues of the day. He often said, "If it is a controversial issue, it is probably our responsibility to address it. If we do our job right, we will make everybody mad sooner or later."

In this first role, the CLC was free to speak *to* Southern Baptists and seek to convince them of the biblical rightness of their position. However, the CLC also had the responsibility to let the courts, the legislators, presidents, and governors know where Southern Baptists *were* on various issues. In such cases, Land explained, the CLC had a moral obligation to tell the truth, to explain things as they are, even when they are not necessarily where we would like them to be. In that role, the CLC was speaking *for* Southern Baptists.

In 1997, the Southern Baptist Convention went through a major reorganization which resulted in all the "commissions" at the national level being integrated into other entities except for the CLC.[24] At this time, the religious liberty assignment was taken from the BJCPA and given to the CLC. Accordingly, the CLC was given additional funding, and it also requested to rename itself as the Ethics & Religious Liberty Commission (ERLC). In Land's tenure, the ERLC fulfilled their ministry assignment through his successful radio programs, printed publications, and web presence.

Land continued as president until 2013, dealing with numerous issues of public policy including immigration reform, marriage, judicial appointments, and the war on terror. He also served from 2001 to 2012 as a presidential and then senatorial appointee on the United States Commission on International Religious Freedom. Land was also an initial signatory of the Manhattan Declaration and oversaw the launch of the Psalm 139 Project, which places ultrasounds in pregnancy resource centers still today.[25] He retired in 2013, describing the opportunity to lead the Commission and "to serve the great people called Southern Baptists as the honor and privilege of a lifetime."

Later that year, the ERLC trustees elected Russell Moore, former dean of the School of Theology at The Southern Baptist Theological Seminary, as the next president. Moore's inaugural address emphasized the role of kingdom, culture, and mission for the work of the ERLC. Speaking blocks away from the U.S. Capitol, Moore pointed back to his own upbringings in southern Mississippi and reminded those in attendance "where the power of God is: in local congregations, in local churches, made up of people who have been redeemed by the gospel of Jesus Christ."[26] These local congregations—the seat of Baptist authority and identity—through their faithful giving were the foundation for the work that went forward during Moore's eight-year leadership of the organization.

The task given to the ERLC signifies the weight the SBC has placed on matters of public policy and the Christian life. Under Moore's leadership, the ERLC focused on how to "assist churches in applying the moral and ethical teachings of the Bible to the Christian life," continuing the long work of the Convention on matters of importance to Southern Baptists.[27] For example, the pro-life work of the ERLC continued and was expanded during the Moore administration. In January 2015, the ERLC—alongside Focus on the Family—hosted the Evangelicals for Life Conference (EFL). The conference coincided with the March for Life, the annual pro-life gathering in Washington, DC, to protest the heinous *Roe v. Wade* court decision creating a constitutional right to abortion. While the March for Life welcomed Christians and pro-life advocates of all stripes, EFL provided a distinctly evangelical space to advocate for the cause of life. The conference not only focused on the dignity of the unborn but also the dignity of every individual. Conference speakers spoke consistently about dignity as rooted in the *imago Dei* and how this informed advocacy on pro-life policies protecting the baby in the womb, but they also spoke on racial minorities, immigrants, and care for the elderly.

The Psalm 139 Project also saw significant expansion under Moore. Recognizing that seeing a child in the womb makes a woman much less likely to abort, the ERLC had long worked to provide ultrasound machines, and the training for their professional use, at no cost to qualifying pregnancy resource centers. The project is funded through donations of individuals (not the CP), while ERLC staff provides the logistical overhead, thanks to CP giving. In 2020, the ERLC set an ambitious goal of placing fifty machines before 2023, which would have marked the fiftieth anniversary of *Roe v. Wade*. Previously, the program placed roughly one to two machines a year. However, because of the faithful giving of Southern Baptists and other pro-life Christians, the ERLC met and exceeded that goal, providing more than fifty ultrasound machines to pregnancy resource centers.

The ERLC also faced new challenges as evidenced by the 2015 Supreme Court decision in *Obergefell v. Hodges* which legalized same-sex marriage. In their "Here We Stand: An Evangelical Declaration on Marriage" in response to the Court's decision, drawing support from the wider evangelical world, the ERLC declared forthrightly that "we dissent from the court's ruling that redefines marriage."[28] Further, it called for stronger protections of religious liberty because the statement authors (correctly) predicted that the new definition of marriage would conflict with the religious beliefs of thousands of faithful Christians. The statement was signed by evangelical leaders such as theologians J. I. Packer, editor of *WORLD* magazine Marvin Olasky, journalist and First Amendment attorney David French, and pastor David Jeremiah. Additionally, the ERLC worked with other partners to prepare churches for the new realities they faced. With Alliance Defending Freedom, a conservative Christian legal advocacy group, the ERLC released a guide to protecting churches and ministries, ensuring that they were taking adequate steps to protect their rights.[29]

Following *Obergefell*, cultural questions about gender and sexuality prompted evangelical leaders, including ERLC staff, to craft a statement clearly setting out the historic Christian position on marriage, gender, and sexuality. "The Nashville Statement," echoing the language and tone of earlier evangelical declarations such as the "Danvers Statement on Biblical Manhood and Womanhood" and the "Chicago Statement on Inerrancy," articulated a clear message of God's good design for marriage and sexuality.[30] The ERLC helped facilitate the statement at the annual gathering of its Research Institute in 2017 along with the Council for Biblical Manhood and Womanhood. Projects such as the "Nashville Statement" have served as helpful guideposts for local churches seeking to clarify their own position to a watching world.

Under Russell Moore, the ERLC continued its long history of advocating racial reconciliation and justice. In 2018, the ERLC, along with The Gospel Coalition, hosted the MLK50 conference, marking fifty years since Martin Luther King Jr.'s assassination in Memphis. The conference was a call to continue the work of King, particularly within evangelicalism, because if the church could not get this question right, there was no hope for the rest of the nation. The conference was one of the largest ever held by the ERLC and proved to be a catalyst for future work on the issue. Encouraging evangelicals, Moore called them to persevere in faithfulness to the challenging work of ending racial injustice. He called them to be a "gospel people," which means not to "seek a cheap reconciliation, but a cross reconciliation."[31] As Moore described the work of the ERLC and the long fight toward racial reconciliation in the SBC, he highlighted how the CP had often been wielded like a cudgel by some hoping to silence the CLC. However, its existence ensured that the Commission could continue to act as the conscience of the Convention, clearly teaching that each person was made in God's image.

Two unexpected areas of challenge arose during the tenure of Russell Moore. The first was the rise of technology and social media, which continues to profoundly shape our current cultural landscape. Recognizing that technology and the emergence of artificial intelligence posed new questions to the Christian faith, the ERLC convened a group of theologians, ethicists, ministers, and policy experts to create a framework for Christians navigating the new digital public square. In April 2019, the ERLC released "Artificial Intelligence: An Evangelical Statement of Principles," affirming the need to properly steward technology and innovation and proactively engaging the topic.[32] It was the first set of religious principles released by any denomination to address the subject. The statement formed the basis for the ERLC's ongoing Digital Public Square project, which has produced a number of books, resources, Bible studies, and podcasts helping Christians to think biblically about technology in a digital age. Because of God's provision through the CP, the ERLC staff is always thinking about how best to serve churches and equip them to address the cultural challenges of the day.

That same year, a more dark and wicked story would sweep the Southern Baptist Convention and nation as reports of sexual abuse in churches flooded the media. Following the *Houston Chronicle*'s Abuse of Faith series, which detailed the actions of some seven hundred ministers who had sexually abused those under their care,[33] the ERLC and the Southern Baptist Convention made the commitment to help churches strengthen themselves against this evil and become places of support for survivors of abuse. Alongside the Convention, the ERLC created the Caring Well Curriculum, which aimed to help churches prevent abuse from occurring and respond well if it should occur. Additionally, the Commission refocused its theme for a national conference that year to the topic of abuse prevention. The Caring Well Conference was an initial and crucial step toward making sure our churches are safe for survivors and safe from abuse. Further, the initiative serves as another representative of collaboration among churches, state conventions, and Convention entities.

Though the ERLC has always worked to help Christians thoughtfully engage the culture—a product of its earlier identity as the Christian Life Commission—much of its work centers on advocacy before federal and state governments on issues of primary concern to Southern Baptists, as well as before the courts. Many times, the ERLC has filed briefs before the Supreme Court on cases impacting religious liberty concerns such as *American Legion v. American Humanist Association* (defending the placement of religious statues on government property), *Obergefell v. Hodges* (opposing same-sex marriage legalization), *Masterpiece Cakeshop v. Colorado Civil Rights Commission* (defending Jack Phillips's right not to bake a cake for a same-sex marriage ceremony), and *Fulton v. Philadelphia* (defending the right of adoption agencies not to violate their religious beliefs).

One key case, *Our Lady of Guadalupe School v. Morrissey-Berru* (2020), involved the "ministerial exception," which had been established in the earlier Supreme Court decision *Hosanna-Tabor Evangelical Lutheran Church & School v. Equal Employment Opportunity Commission*. The *Hosanna-Tabor* case affirmed in a unanimous decision that the federal antidiscrimination laws do not apply to religious organizations, and therefore the federal government was barred from interfering with the right of religious groups to appoint and select their own leaders (i.e., a Christian church that believes homosexuality is wrong could not be sued because it refused to hire a gay individual). The *Our Lady of Guadalupe* case expanded the scope of the ministerial exception to say that it applied not only to those who held the title of clergy or ministers but also to those who help accomplish the mission of the organization (i.e., a teacher at a religious school). The U.S. Supreme Court cited the ERLC's brief in defense of the ministerial exception and affirmed that religious groups should be able to define who is or is not a minister, not the government—a significant victory for religious freedom.

In the late 2010s, Moore led the Commission through a challenging cultural epoch punctuated by the 2016 election, Donald Trump's tenure as president, and a global pandemic. During this season, his leadership sought to assist Southern Baptists in navigating cultural conflicts that often centered on collisions between church and state.

Moore departed to join *Christianity Today* as editor in chief in 2021. The following year, trustees elected Frederick Brent Leatherwood as the new president. Interestingly, Land, Moore, and Leatherwood all came to the helm of the organization at the same age of forty-one. Under Leatherwood's administration, the ERLC has focused even more on the policy concerns of Southern Baptists, drawing on Leatherwood's years of experience as a senior advisor on Capitol Hill and as the director of the Tennessee Republican Party. In particular, the ERLC has given new attention to the role of state legislatures for advancing policies in the face of Washington gridlock.

This focus on state-level advocacy is especially important following the 2022 Supreme Court decision in *Dobbs v. Jackson Women's Whole Health*. In a five to four decision, the court overturned *Roe v. Wade*. The decision did not outlaw abortion but rather returned more decision-making authority to the states. The ERLC, recognizing this new landscape for the pro-life movement, began working closely with state partners and conventions to advocate for laws which would outlaw the practice at the state level. Thankfully, a number of states, largely in the South and Midwest, had already established "trigger laws," which went into effect after the *Dobbs* decision effectively outlawing the procedure. However, other states, such as California and New York, took steps to enshrine abortion into law even up to the point of birth, further proclaiming themselves abortion destinations and sanctuaries. The work of state-level advocacy has never been more important in the life of the ERLC and the pro-life movement.

The ERLC and its Baptist state partners have engaged on other critical issues before they reach the Supreme Court. In light of recent debates surrounding gender identity and the rights of parents, the ERLC joined briefs with state partners in Iowa, Minnesota, and Wisconsin. The briefs argued that schools violated parental rights by allowing students to use different names and pronouns at school without notifying the parents absent a student's consent. Southern Baptists have consistently affirmed, as in their 2014 "Resolution on Transgender Identity," that individuals should live in accordance with their biological sex and oppose any attempts by government officials to "validate transgender identity as morally praiseworthy."[34] This work demonstrates the ERLC recognizes that not every battle is going to be fought on Capitol Hill and that Baptist cooperation is the key to advancing policies consistent with a biblical worldview at both the federal and state levels.

The early years of the Leatherwood administration also focused on fostering relationships with local churches and listening to the concerns of its members and pastors. These individuals, who live, serve, and minister in their local communities, are those best equipped to identify problems, bring solutions, and build bridges with others who can make a difference where they live. While presidential politics have always loomed large in the work of the ERLC, local leaders—both pastors and elected officials—are critical to the flourishing of communities. The local church is and should always be the starting point for all cultural engagement.

Of course, even as this work is advanced, the Commission's work at the federal level continues apace. While the majority of the ERLC's work typically focuses on the Legislative Branch, congressional gridlock has necessitated increased attention toward the administrative rule-making process. U.S. presidents from both parties have recently viewed this route as a legitimate way to push forward preferred policies.

As a result, the ERLC has placed new emphasis on formally registering its deep opposition to harmful proposals on a range of topics including abortion tourism, violations of religious liberty in adoption and foster care, and transgender ideology. This public comment capability is an important tool for engaging the administrative state and pointing to solutions that lead to the flourishing of all people.

Throughout its history, this entity has been tasked with bringing forth the views of the churches that initiated it. In doing so, it ensures the highest policymakers in the land are held accountable by Southern Baptists who are unashamedly motivated by their shared, deeply held convictions. That engagement, that ministry, is needed now as much as ever. New issues emerge where church and state meet, and unique challenges arise for our fundamental rights. Whether on life, religious liberty, marriage and family, or human dignity, the cooperative efforts of the churches of the Southern Baptist Convention ensure the ERLC will remain a vibrant voice of truth and grace in the public square for generations to come.

Personal Reflection

Richard Land

As a Christian who was led to the Lord, nurtured in the faith, called to preach, and prepared for ministry in a Southern Baptist context, I owe an incalculable debt of gratitude to the CP and the sacrificial giving of generations of Southern Baptists that financially undergirded it. The CP helped sponsor the founding of the mission church in a new postwar neighborhood in Houston where I was led to salvation through the ministry of the godly leaders of the church.

The CP helped finance the education of the pastors and church staff who nurtured my faith through faithful tutelage in God's Word. The CP helped make possible the Baptist retreat centers that played a pivotal role in my spiritual growth as a youngster and in my call to ministry as a teenager. The CP financially undergirded the ministries of the faithful, devoted missionaries who periodically came to speak at our church about how God was using them to proclaim the gospel around the world. The CP helped engender a passion for missions in my heart, even at an early age, as well as the hearts of fellow church members.

When God called me to seminary preparation, approximately 80 percent of my educational costs at New Orleans Baptist Theological Seminary were underwritten by the CP. For this I was, and am, grateful. It would have been much more difficult for me to attend seminary on a full-time basis without the CP's substantial assistance. In the decades since seminary graduation, I have experienced the many ways in which the CP has enabled and undergirded Southern Baptist ministries at the associational, state convention, and national Convention levels.

The Southern Baptist entity which I was privileged to lead for twenty-five years, the ERLC, was made possible only by the generous and ongoing support of the CP. Many were the occasions when I was so grateful for CP support as I watched many of my public policy advocate colleagues having to spend so much of their valuable time raising money instead of pursuing their ministries. And lastly, my wife (whom I met in seminary) and I were privileged to have two of our three children graduate from one of our Southern Baptist seminaries, and their education was greatly assisted financially by the CP.

Brent Leatherwood

As a colleague and I were discussing matters of the Southern Baptist Convention one afternoon, he shared his view that the CP is the finest initiative ever devised by man to spread the gospel across the globe. Similar sentiments have been communicated by others. I could not agree more. Of course, Baptists are right to rejoice about our successes. From combating lostness on the mission field, to planting new churches in challenging contexts, to funding excellent training for future pastors and ministry leaders, to ensuring the gospel is proclaimed in the public square, with all of this and more fueled by the CP. Think of how novel the idea was at its founding. Churches from across the country would join together to cooperatively pool the resources to ensure that the Great Commission was carried out. Our own age of doubt and distrust further enhances just how revolutionary and selfless an initiative this was and still is.

Reflecting on my own experience in SBC life, and now as head of the entity most reliant on CP funding, I cannot help but rejoice for all the ways the CP has been a cornerstone for ministries that have enriched the lives of so many. Personally, I would not be able to focus all my vocational attention to public policy without the CP. I would not see as many preborn lives saved without the CP. I would not feel as optimistic as I do about our nation's safeguards for religious liberty without the CP. I would not see significant advancements in protecting the family and respecting human dignity without the backing of the CP. In short, the work of this agency would not happen without the CP. On so many issues, I am convinced Baptist cooperation is the key to finding a solution. The CP makes that cooperation a reality, and for that I am grateful.

10

What Has God Done in North America?

Kevin Ezell and Mike Ebert

> *"The kingdom of heaven is like a mustard seed that a man took and sowed in his field. It's the smallest of all the seeds, but when grown, it's taller than the garden plants and becomes a tree, so that the birds of the sky come and nest in its branches."*
> Matt. 13:31–32

Some of the biggest things in life start small. It's a reality that pervades just about every realm. The most valuable company in the world, Apple, worth an estimated $2.97 trillion at the time of this writing,[1] started in the garage belonging to Steve Jobs's parents. Sam Walton, founder of Walmart, the world's largest private employer, began as Walton's Five-and-Dime in a small building in Bentonville, Arkansas.[2] Not all small things grow into something big. But when the right combination falls into place, boom! What started off small can grow into something we never imagined.

In God's kingdom, small things, done faithfully and with a humble spirit, can be used by him to accomplish great things. But it takes a willingness to depend on something beyond ourselves. It also means setting some things aside and letting some of our own opinions and preferences go. When we do that, God can work in big ways.

Hilltop

Hilltop Baptist Church in Fort Worth was the first church I (Kevin) pastored. It was located in a one-room building in a part of town that a lot of people avoided. Its only claim to fame was that the church building showed up twice on the television show *Cops* because there was so much crime in the neighborhood. The church building was broken into so many times we finally put a sign on our front door that said "Unlocked. Please come in," so people would stop breaking down the door.

When I came to the church as a student at Southwestern Baptist Theological Seminary, they were looking for a pastor, but, almost more than that, they were looking for a pastor who was willing to live in their parsonage. A few of the men who had considered the job ultimately turned it down because their wives didn't want to live in such a crime-ridden part of town. It was one thing to pastor a church there but another thing altogether to live there! Fortunately, my wife Lynette was up for the adventure. We said yes to the parsonage, and the church voted me in 7–0. To this day, it was the only unanimous vote I have received!

As I look back on those years, I can see that God was teaching me much more than any wisdom I had to share with those dear folks at Hilltop. One sweet woman, Lennie Fenton, taught me so much about what a privilege it is to give to the Lord's work. She lived in a modest home (some would call it a shack) and got by on a meager income each month, but she loved to give to the church. She literally would weep when she talked about the honor it was to give and be a part of the larger work God was doing through what the people at Hilltop were able to give. Ms. Finny (we affectionately called her Ms. Finny, a combination of her first and last names) was exactly right. With every dollar she sacrificially gave, our church forwarded a portion through the Cooperative Program (CP). It was then combined with hundreds, then thousands, then millions of other dollars given in offering plates each Sunday morning by Southern Baptists all over the United States.

Do you think God took Ms. Finny's faithfulness and turned it into something much larger? I absolutely believe he did! Yes, Hilltop Baptist Church was small. But because of those generous hearts and their sacrificial giving, the impact was big once their offerings were combined with all the other giving God orchestrated through Southern Baptists. That Hilltop congregation impacted the world through their little church located in that tough part of town.

That's what we celebrate. The CP alone is not the reason we give or what we applaud. But when we look back at what God has done through Southern Baptists since the CP was established in 1925, we celebrate what it has fueled.

The Power of Together

"I am the vine; you are the branches. The one who remains in me and I in him produces much fruit, because you can do nothing without me."
(John 15:5)

When we look at the enormity of lostness—an estimated 281 million people in North America alone who do not have a relationship with Christ[3]—it's enough to overwhelm even the most optimistic overachiever among us. But maybe that is the point. We were created to be dependent, not independent. And if we are going to succeed in taking the gospel to North America—and the greater world beyond—we must be fully dependent on Jesus (the vine) and his church (our fellow branches).

Southern Baptists, from our earliest days, insisted on the autonomy of the local church but realized the importance of joining together to reach the unchurched in the United States and beyond. At the first gathering in 1845, Southern Baptists formed the Foreign Mission Board and the Board of Domestic Missions.[4] The effort started off small (remember the mustard seed?). In 1847, the Domestic Board had just thirty missionaries covering a fourteen-state territory. That amounted to 955,644 square miles with a population of eight million people.[5]

Even though our forebearers agreed in those early days that they needed a domestic missions entity, there was no plan to fund it. That meant Board representatives had to travel throughout the South from church to church, requesting financial support for the fledgling entity. Still, somehow by 1860, the Board had 159 missionaries with works that included outreach to Chinese immigrants in California and Native Americans in the West.[6]

The Domestic Board struggled greatly in the years after the Civil War. In 1874, the entity was renamed the Home Mission Board (HMB), and the financial ups and downs continued.[7] In 1888, the Woman's Missionary Union (WMU) was officially organized and became a steadfast advocate for both mission boards. Annie Armstrong, the group's first corresponding secretary, personally visited churches and rallied support for missions.[8] By the early 1900s, Southern Baptists began to expand domestic mission efforts once again. The HMB formed an evangelism department and began ministry in Panama (the Panama Canal Zone was then a U.S. territory). Ministries to deaf and Jewish people were started, and the Board operated thirty-seven mountain mission schools.[9]

The CP began in 1925, but soon afterward the HMB endured a double calamity. Financial scandal struck when it was discovered that the Board's treasurer had embezzled nearly a million dollars over a ten-year period. Then, the 1929 stock market crash ushered in the Great Depression. The Home Mission Board was left debt-ridden. Its missionary force was cut from 1,600 to 106. The evangelism department and mountain schools were eliminated.[10] Needless to say, the condition of the Board was dire, and its future viability seemed perilous.

But Southern Baptists' faithfulness through the CP, the Annie Armstrong Easter Offering, and other special financial initiatives that arose even during the Great Depression allowed the HMB to work toward financial improvement, and by 1943, all its debts had been repaid.[11] The new stability allowed for a refocus on expanding the mission, following the population growth in the South and Western United States. World War II scattered Southern Baptists to different regions of the U.S., and wherever they went, new churches followed. As the U.S. became more urbanized, Southern Baptists increased their focus on reaching cities.[12]

With debts paid and Southern Baptist CP giving thriving, the HMB began student missions efforts in 1944, with seventy-one summer missionaries. The evangelism department was reestablished, and missions to migrants began. In the late 1950s, the HMB formed agreements with state Baptist conventions, which led to greater coordination of ministry efforts and budgets. The 1960s saw great expansion into ethnic and language work with nearly half of the missionary force focused on ministry to the varied people groups who had arrived in the States.[13]

During that same period, HMB work expanded into Canada and Puerto Rico, while the rise of communism in Cuba curtailed its work there, with some missionaries imprisoned before eventually being allowed to return to the United States. The HMB helped thousands of Cubans resettle to the U.S.[14] The HMB worked with the Brotherhood Commission to fund many disaster relief responses as Southern Baptists became more involved in this rapidly expanding area of ministry.[15] In the mid-1970s, Southern Baptists adopted Bold Mission Thrust with the goal of giving every person in the United States an opportunity to hear the gospel and accept Christ and be part of a New Testament church. The HMB helped more than three thousand refugees from Vietnam, Cambodia, and Laos resettle after the Vietnam War.[16]

In 1977, the Board continued to expand as the entity rolled out a plan to engage volunteers in short-term missions. It was called Mission Service Corps (MSC). The HMB partnered with state and local ministries to address hunger needs.[17] The SBC reasserted its commitment to the inerrancy of Scripture in the 1980s and shifted back to more conservative leadership. Concurrently, the Home Mission Board recommitted to advancing the cause of Bold Mission Thrust by setting a goal of reaching fifty thousand Southern Baptist congregations by the year 2000.[18]

As the 1990s drew to a close, Southern Baptists adopted the Covenant for a New Century, which implemented a significant restructuring of the SBC and culminated in consolidating three separate entities—the Home Mission Board, the Brotherhood Commission, and FamilyNet (formerly the Radio and Television Commission)—into one, naming the resulting entity the North

American Mission Board (NAMB).[19] Later, Southern Baptist messengers overwhelmingly approved recommendations from the Great Commission Resurgence Task Force in 2010, which focused NAMB's efforts more exclusively on church planting and directed it to invest more of its resources outside the South.[20]

A Means, Not the End

We must remember that, for all its brilliance and all it has allowed Southern Baptists to achieve, the CP is a vehicle, not the destination. The driving force that has kept Southern Baptists united and propelling forward is the overarching goal of seeing the Great Commission fulfilled at home and around the world. This is why we sacrificially give and send resources to the mission field as we do.

For this reason, we must exercise wisdom in the language we employ to celebrate CP giving. We celebrate churches that send a high percentage of their annual giving, but we must also applaud a church's giving to our other, historic Great Commission-focused efforts. We want churches in our faith family to be actively committed to leading people into a relationship with Christ. As autonomous partners in the gospel, we believe a church must seek and follow the Holy Spirit's guidance when making decisions about where best to invest its resources and how best to engage in the ministry of gospel reconciliation.

That said, we wholeheartedly believe that no modern-day giving model comes close to achieving so much for the sake of the Great Commission as does the CP. Any church—regardless of size—can give a dollar and know it is playing an active role in sharing the gospel throughout its state, across our home continent, and all over the world. More than that, the CP is making it possible for our next generation of church pastors and leaders to receive the best seminary training in the world.

Even our largest megachurches, when held up against the backdrop of the entire world, are small in comparison. Yet, when their giving is combined with thousands of other churches of all sizes and unleashed into the Great Commission network Southern Baptists have built faithfully for generations, the resulting power and effectiveness are unmatched by anything else happening in ministry and missions today.

The Obligation of Abundance

Here is where the people and entities that receive CP funding must do their part to maintain the trust and accountability that are critical to keeping the CP healthy and viable long into the future. Talk to any missionary who serves with just about any other denomination or Christian ministry, and you will learn that missionaries all over the world from other faith traditions look longingly at our CP. So many must scrape together funding by going from church to church and person to person. Some are even forced to leave their field of ministry so they can come back home and raise funds. The CP allows our missionaries to concentrate on the main reason they are on the mission field—making new disciples for Christ, planting churches, and responding to those in need.

But our missionaries and the entities that undergird their efforts should never take CP dollars for granted. I (Kevin) have regularly reminded our staff that we can never minimize the funding that comes from Southern Baptists each month. It is a gift and a huge responsibility. Just like Lennie Fenton back at my first church, millions of Southern Baptists, some who have meager incomes, give sacrificially to make those dollars available, and they are trusting that each dollar is being wisely spent and invested in ministry that will help share the gospel with those who need to hear.

At NAMB, one of our four core values is: "Do more with less." I regularly remind our team that we will be the best stewards of everything Southern Baptists send us. Whether offerings go up or offerings go down, we will prudently deploy the funds entrusted to us and stretch them as far as possible. Part of that wise spending means always being willing to look at what we are doing and weigh its effectiveness. We will never settle for maintaining a ministry that is no longer impacting lostness. We won't shirk from making hard decisions when we need to set aside the good to achieve what is best.

Keeping the Best Ahead

For as long as anyone can remember, evangelical church plants in Montreal were doomed to fail. But in 2013, David Pothier launched La Chapelle church in the heart of the city with an optimistic spirit and a heart for connecting with residents who had become jaded toward Christianity. At the time, the historic city had few evangelical churches and virtually no church of any denomination numbered fifty or more in weekly attendance.

But in its first year, La Chapelle baptized more than seventy new believers and added a second Sunday morning worship service to accommodate more than 750 weekly attendees. Today, in partnership with Send Network, NAMB's church planting arm, the church has started five new churches, and they saw more than thirty-seven hundred attend Christmas services in 2023.

As we look back on the history of Southern Baptists, there is much to celebrate. God has allowed us to be part of the incredible story he is weaving through the lives of millions of people who have come to faith in him as a result of our mission endeavors through the generations. He has also allowed us, as Southern Baptists, to benefit greatly in our missions-sending efforts from a century of CP giving.

Stories like La Chapelle in Montreal remind us that, if we keep the Great Commission at the center of everything we do, our best years as a network of churches are still ahead of us. At NAMB, everything we do is about the gospel. The entire reason we help Southern Baptists start new churches is so new people will be introduced to Christ. Compassion ministry through Send Relief lets us serve people and meet needs with the goal of pointing them to Christ, the only One who can give them eternal hope. We endorse chaplains who serve in the military, law enforcement, firefighters, and in prisons and hospitals for the same reason—to introduce people to Christ.

But as we do this, we are careful to keep pastors and the churches they lead front and center in this effort to advance the gospel. If you visit NAMB and ask any member of our staff who our number one "customer" is, they will tell you, "pastors." NAMB does not start new churches—churches do. NAMB does not send missionaries—churches do. NAMB does not baptize anyone—churches do.

It is an incredible blessing to serve at a missions entity that is solidly funded largely through a strategic budgeting mechanism, but it also comes with a risk. Missionaries can start to feel independent from the churches who have sent them. A missions entity can start to see itself as headquarters instead of acting as a servant to the churches that created it. Before long, this independent mentality can take hold, and missionaries operate as islands, not connected to or dependent on the churches that sent them. This is why we keep all our efforts at NAMB tied closely to the local church. Our Send Relief Ministry Centers rely on partnerships with local churches. And we require every church we help plant to have a sending church that takes the primary responsibility of overseeing key aspects of the plant. We believe in the New Testament model: churches plant churches, so we have developed our church-planting strategy around that belief.

When Matt Lahey started Killbride Community Church in St. John's, Newfoundland, in 2021, it was the first time in nearly 130 years that Killbride had an evangelical church. Ministry in the Canadian province is challenging, with many residents suspicious of churches. But Lahey is blessed with a strong sending church, Calvary Baptist in nearby Mount Pearl. NAMB has come alongside Calvary Baptist to help fund its vision for church planting in the region, and thanks to the partnership, planters like Lahey are ministering in communities that have long been without a gospel presence. At NAMB, our number one "customer" is pastors and the churches they lead. We do not, and will not, operate independently from churches.

Conclusion

Joining together in cooperative missions means setting aside some personal preferences. Some things may not be done exactly the way you would do them yourself. But what can be achieved by working together is so much more compelling. It makes our personal preferences pale in comparison. The larger mission, the larger goal, is fulfilling the Great Commission. It is sending missionaries. It is starting new churches where new believers can worship. And it is introducing people to Christ who have never heard of him before.

When I (Kevin) met Dan Coleman, he was working on his own, trying to convince churches to support church-planting efforts in Maine. He had great enthusiasm and passion, but New

England is one of the least churched parts of the United States. Fundraising was slow going, and it took him away from pastoring. He had relaunched his church, Central Church in Augusta, Maine, and they were holding two services at the time in what can best be described as a large garage.

Not long after we connected, Dan became a NAMB-endorsed church planter, eligible for all the resources we are able to share because of the faithful generosity of Southern Baptists through CP and Annie Armstrong giving. Dan called one day and told me the local Catholic church was closing its doors and the building was available but at a price far above what he and his church could afford. On top of that, no bank will give a loan to a new church.

But Southern Baptist giving allows NAMB to provide loans to church plants—loans that most banks would not fund. Now that former Catholic Church building is home to Dan's church. They baptized more than one hundred in 2023 and hosted more than three thousand people at their most recent Christmas services. That's what God can do when Southern Baptists choose to come together. Dan was faithful, and God used Southern Baptist cooperation to grow that mustard seed of faith into something much larger than Dan ever imagined in an area where healthy, successful churches are few and far between.

We have seen it repeatedly during the 179 years of Southern Baptist mission efforts, and especially over the past 100 years of CP giving. God takes Southern Baptist faithfulness and multiplies it into a force strong enough to move mountains. He is moving the mountain of lostness. He is moving the mountain of unbelief. He is moving the mountains of unchurched communities because thousands of Southern Baptists are joining together in a way that is much bigger and more powerful than any single church could ever be on its own.

Yes, we are all independent. We are all autonomous. But our interdependence and our decision to voluntarily come together bring the greatest synergy and power. If we stay united for the sake of the Great Commission, and if we continue to sacrificially pool our resources and relationships together on mission, we will continue to see God move mountains and push back lostness in North America and throughout the world.

Personal Reflection

Kevin Ezell

When I was young, my parents were led to Christ by some faithful believers who were out one evening doing door-to-door evangelism in our neighborhood. I am forever grateful that those men were obedient to the command Jesus gave to "make disciples of all nations," starting with the people right in their own neighborhood.

My first years of churchgoing were in independent Baptist churches. My parents wanted to be members of a church that was actively involved in evangelism, and the local independent Baptist church stood out. Those years gave me a heart for sharing Christ and a love for Scripture. Then, God made a path for me to attend college through a tennis scholarship to Union University in Jackson, Tennessee. There, at that Southern Baptist university supported by the CP giving of Tennessee Baptist churches, I began to better understand the bigger picture of how Southern Baptists work together to advance the gospel around the world. It was also there that I sensed God's call to ministry.

God gave me an opportunity to serve as a student intern with First Baptist Church of Paducah, Kentucky. The wonderful people there encouraged me to attend seminary, even offering to help pay part of the cost. The CP also covered a generous portion of my seminary tuition. I'm not sure how or if I ever would have afforded seminary without the incredible financial blessings from FBC Paducah and the CP.

As a pastor, I saw firsthand how churches of all sizes have the incredible opportunity to impact the world, supporting evangelistic efforts through the CP. By directly funding the training and deployment of missionaries, Southern Baptists have had an incalculable impact on lostness for generations. Beyond that, we have created an infrastructure that educates pastors and missions personnel and sustains the development and support of missionaries, allowing them to focus on the task of reaching people for Christ.

Since 2010, I have had the remarkable privilege of leading the North American Mission Board. This new perspective has given me an even greater appreciation for just what a blessing the CP has been. There is nothing else like it in Christendom, and it is one of the most precious gifts God has entrusted Southern Baptists to steward.

Mike Ebert

My spiritual legacy is tied directly to Southern Baptist mission efforts and the funding the CP provides. In the late 1960s during the Vietnam War, my dad served in the United States Navy and was stationed at a naval base in Japan. A fellow service member invited my parents to church. That church was pastored by a missionary serving with the Southern Baptist Foreign Mission Board (now the International Mission Board, or IMB). Not long after my parents began attending that church, my dad placed his faith in Jesus Christ. My mom did the same a short time later. It is incredible that God brought two Americans who had grown up attending church to a church in Japan pastored by a Foreign Mission Board missionary, and that's where they both came to know the Lord. But that is how God works, and that is the gospel reach Southern Baptists have, thanks to the CP.

The spiritual foundation established in Japan meant that I was raised in a Christian home, attending a Southern Baptist church, and at a young age I placed my faith in Christ. At a Royal Ambassador (RA) camp one summer (supported through CP funding), I sensed God's call on my life to serve in ministry. That calling eventually led me to the North American Mission Board (also supported through the CP) where I have now served for twenty-six years.

Because so many Southern Baptists faithfully funded the CP fifty-five years ago, my parents walked into a church where they heard the plan of salvation in a way that connected with them for the first time. Later, my siblings and I all placed our faith in Christ. My wife, Linda, and I raised our four children in the church, and they have placed their faith in Christ. Now they are starting their own families and telling their children about Jesus, too.

This is the legacy of just one family. When I think of how God has used Southern Baptists, and their missions and ministry efforts funded through the CP, to change the lives of millions of families like ours around the world in these last one hundred years, the impact is beyond comprehension. It is a Great Commission legacy. It is a legacy worth protecting and preserving.

11

What Has God Done around the World?

Paul Chitwood, Melanie Clinton, and Julie Nall McGowan

Since 1845, almost twenty-five thousand Southern Baptist international missionaries have shared the gospel, made disciples, planted churches, and planted their lives in 185 countries around the world, a sacred effort made possible through Southern Baptists' financial support of nearly $4 billion in Cooperative Program (CP) giving to the International Mission Board (IMB).[1]

This centennial anniversary of the CP affords Southern Baptists an opportunity to reflect on the impact of our efforts to create a sustainable model to financially undergird our brothers and sisters on mission through the IMB. A look around the world and across the decades finds missionaries whose stories remind us of the power of God and the courage of his people. So many significant moments in Southern Baptist history invite us to celebrate God's faithfulness through these one hundred years of remarkable CP giving. Ultimately, we pray and trust that our missional efforts of the past, present, and future will contribute to the future biblical vision that burns in our hearts and fuels our cooperation: "A vast multitude from every nation, tribe, people, and language, which no one could number, standing before the throne and before the Lamb. They were clothed in white robes with palm branches in their hands. And they cried out in a loud voice: Salvation belongs to our God, who is seated on the throne, and to the Lamb!" (Rev. 7:9–10). I invite you to walk with me through these historical moments in grateful celebration. To God be the glory.

1845–1925: A Challenging Launch into Missions

In 1845, the Foreign Mission Board (FMB, today's IMB) was formed so Southern Baptists could take the gospel to foreign lands. Within months, several missionaries were appointed to China and Liberia.[2] In 1846, the FMB appointed pastor James B. Taylor as its first leader (officially titled "corresponding secretary"). He served until mere days before his death in 1871, guiding the organization through its early growth and the tumultuous Civil War years.

No other period in FMB history endured such turmoil and tragedy as the Civil War years.[3] Baptist churches were so distraught over conflicts on the home front that the missions cause was largely forgotten. Although executive leader James B. Taylor worked valiantly to keep up support levels, missionaries often were left to fend for themselves. Sometimes money for salaries simply did not exist. In other cases, reliable methods of transporting funds overseas, particularly to Africa, were no longer operational. Some missionaries managed to find local jobs, but others virtually starved.

In the early part of this decade, four missionaries were lost at sea, including a couple going to begin Baptist work in Japan. In China, Taiping rebels killed Landrum Holmes, making him the first Southern Baptist missionary to be murdered on the field. Another missionary to China died in a typhoon.

Amid war between the states, news of these tragedies devastated Southern Baptist leaders. After the war, they received more discouraging news that several missionaries had died in Africa, the Liberia mission was in disarray, and the work in Nigeria was at a standstill due to civil war there. Besides the loss of life and stability at home, the toll of the American Civil War left the Foreign Mission Board with only $1.78 in its bank account. Southern Baptists feared the organization might not survive.

Taylor valiantly traveled from state to state, raising funds to pay off debts and replenish reservoirs. Eventually, hopeful reports from the field reached the U.S. and bolstered the spirits of Baptist leaders and churches, such as news that missionaries Matthew Yates, T. P. Crawford, and Rosewell Graves were being used of God to lead the Chinese to Christ. By 1871, all debts were paid, and the FMB was poised to send out more missionaries to new and existing mission fields.

After the devastating chaos of the U.S. Civil War, the 1870s were a period of new beginnings.[4] The FMB opened work in Italy, and new ministry efforts were being launched in Africa. This decade also ushered in the explosion of the women's missionary movement. By the 1870s, more Baptist women were desiring to go overseas. New FMB leader Henry Allen Tupper was eager to appoint them, both married and single, for ministry in lands where women were not permitted to associate with men outside their families. In 1872, Edmonia Moon (sister to Southern Baptists' beloved missionary, Lottie Moon) went to China, and Lottie followed a year later.

Because the FMB, still recovering from the financial devastation of the Civil War, could not afford to support the Moon sisters, Tupper encouraged churches and women's societies to raise funds for their salaries. Thus began the long-standing tradition of women's missionary groups supporting missionaries through prayer, fundraising, and advocating for overseas needs. In 1888, the Woman's Missionary Union formed and instituted a Christmas offering for missions.[5] To this day, the support of the WMU in the thriving of Southern Baptists' international missions efforts cannot be overstated.

As a new century dawned, the Foreign Mission Board faced enormous pressures to unite with other mission-minded denominations to start churches overseas.[6] Southern Baptists held fast to the essentials of their faith, insisting that if we ignored biblical truths about ecclesiology, we could also choose to ignore what it says about salvation or other essential doctrines.

Although the Woman's Missionary Union continued to collect money, the FMB's constant financial challenges forced Southern Baptist leaders to acknowledge that churches were failing to give according to their ability and must be challenged to do more. After World War I ended, ambitious plans were made to expand Southern Baptist work around the world, funded by the $75 Million Campaign, which would launch the following decade.

1925–1929: A Stable Solution and Revival in China

During the 1920s, the Southern Baptist Convention made grand efforts to support and expand missions work, first through the $75 Million Campaign and then through the Cooperative Program (CP).[7]

The Southern Baptist Convention's $75 Million Campaign was the first Convention-wide attempt to raise funds in a unified manner. Over the next five years, $92 million was pledged, and four thousand young people committed to full-time Christian service (some overseas, some in the U.S.). But only $58.6 million of the $92 million pledged was received, and the FMB fell deeply into debt to support the many new missionaries who had been guaranteed funding. Yet in many ways, the $75 Million Campaign was a success because it rallied Southern Baptists around the common cause of global missions and unified a denomination that had come dangerously close to falling apart.

The 1925 creation of the CP began to provide a more reliable, ongoing source of funding for Baptist entities. The giving formula encouraged every Southern Baptist church to give half of all the church's receipts to mission work through the CP. State conventions were recommended to keep half of the receipts for state mission work and send half on to the national and international work.[8]

Despite financial challenges, during this decade FMB missionaries experienced what some consider the greatest revival in Baptist church history. In China's Shantung province, missionaries had been disheartened by the apathy of the Chinese people. No one was coming to faith in Christ, and churches were stagnant and dying. Missionary Mary Crawford said groups began earnestly praying for revival, some as early as 1925, the same year the CP began. John Abernathy and others faithfully taught the Bible and preached about sin. In 1927, an outpouring of the Holy Spirit brought about earnest repentance from sin and renewed spiritual fervor among missionaries and Christians across many denominations. This decade-long revival spread from Shantung province in the north throughout the entire country.

1930s: First Native American Missionary Goes to Mexico

The 1930s found the Foreign Mission Board's work still severely hampered by debt and impacted by a looming world war.[9] Conflict in Europe resulted in rising persecution against Baptists, and in Asia many missionaries were evacuated after Japan attacked China.

The Dust Bowl, caused by severe drought in the Great Plains, wreaked havoc and added to the financial crisis of the Great Depression, which marked its beginning with the stock market crash of October 1929. In a devastating financial climate, the FMB found itself significantly overextended. More than thirty furloughing missionaries had to get jobs in the U.S. until sufficient funds were found, while others were told they likely could never go back overseas. The FMB was widely considered a "basket case" that no one wanted to touch. But well-known Baptist Charles Maddry was up for the challenge. After he was elected FMB executive leader, he reminded bankers that they had never lost a cent from the Board and guaranteed Southern Baptists would pay back every penny. The FMB continued to function. By the time Maddry retired in 1944, the debt had been paid, and the organization retained almost $700,000 in the bank.

Among other significant accomplishments in this decade, Maddry began republishing *The Commission* magazine, which brought the stories of foreign missions into thousands of Southern Baptist households. He also started a missionary pension plan and appointed field leaders to help administrate work overseas. In October 1938, the FMB appointed the first Native American Southern Baptist missionary, Jewell Starr Reid of Cherokee ancestry.[10] She and her husband, Orvil, served in Mexico, where she died in 1940.

Southern Baptists' gifts through the CP helped undergird the FMB's ability to begin sending missionaries again, specifically by underwriting the salary of FMB leader Charles Maddry, by paying for the publishing of *The Commission*, and by covering the practical costs for sending missionaries such as Orville and Jewell Starr Reid.

1940s: A Century in International Missions

By the 1940s the United States was fully engaged in World War II, a global conflict resulting in the death of between seventy and eighty-five million people. Just over twenty years after "the War to End All Wars," this new war involved more than thirty countries. Most Foreign Mission Board missionaries in China and Japan had evacuated during the previous decade.[11]

Once the U.S. officially entered the war, ninety missionaries remaining in China, Japan, and Manila were interned or imprisoned, including M. Theron Rankin, the field leader for the Orient. In 1942, Rankin and thirty-nine other Baptist missionaries were exchanged for Japanese prisoners of war. Of the remaining prisoners, thirty-nine were repatriated in 1943, one died in captivity, and ten were liberated in 1945. Two years after Rankin's return, he was elected to serve as the seventh executive leader of the FMB and the first missionary to lead the organization.

After the war ended, Rankin and other leaders surveyed the lands that had experienced the most damage. Africa was barely impacted, but in Europe buildings had been bombed, seminary programs were shut down, and some missionaries had relocated. By far, the worst damage was in China and Japan, where nuclear fallout and widespread devastation led to urgent appeals for aid. By 1946, relief and development projects were taking place in Asia and Europe thanks to almost $4 million collected by Southern Baptists.

With the financial support Southern Baptists were providing through the twenty-year-old CP, the FMB reached its one hundredth anniversary in 1945. The next year, in 1946, the FMB appointed its first Hispanic missionary, Alfredo Celso Muller, a native of Mexico. He served until his death in 1962. His wife, Damaris, who was Swiss, retired in 1968.

Following the war, many servicemen and women who had witnessed global needs during wartime deployment signed up for mission service. This postwar period of energy and growth, which lasted through the 1970s, is unparalleled in FMB history.

1950s: Work Launches in New Asian, Pacific, and African Fields

During the 1950s, Southern Baptists experienced a massive growth spurt.[12] Congregations were growing, resources were flowing, and Southern Baptist churches were missions-saturated environments. Missions education programs, including Sunbeams, Girls In Action (GAs), Royal Ambassadors (RAs), Woman's Missionary Union, and Brotherhood, ensured most Southern Baptists were aware of, and concerned about, global missions. Financial support for the Foreign Mission Board was strong, and many new missionaries were sent out to new lands. In 1950, the FMB appointed 111 missionaries. This was the first time more than 100 missionaries were appointed in a single year. By 1955, more than 1,000 FMB missionaries were on the field.

In 1951, the FMB was grieved when the last missionary in China was forced to leave due to the communist government's opposition to missionary presence. But much as the persecution in the book of Acts helped spread the gospel to new areas, the hostility in China led to an expansion of ministry into many new parts of Asia. God graciously used these circumstances to open countries like Taiwan, the Philippines, and Indonesia to missionary presence. On Christmas Day 1951, three missionaries who previously served in China moved to Indonesia, which soon became one of Southern Baptists' biggest mission fields.

Baker James Cauthen, former missionary to China and field strategy leader for the Orient, was elected executive leader of the FMB in October 1953. He led Southern Baptists for the next quarter-century in historic mission advance around the globe, including growth from 908 missionaries in thirty-three countries in 1953 to 2,981 missionaries in ninety-four countries in 1979.

In 1955, the Foreign Mission Board appointed its first ethnically East Asian missionaries, Reiji and Alice Hoshizaki, of Japanese descent. They served in Japan until their retirement in 1984.

In Africa, where missionaries were working only in Nigeria, Ghana, and Southern Rhodesia (modern-day Zimbabwe), a field leader called for additional workers to help minister to a massive continent where large populations of Muslims and Roman Catholics were resistant to the gospel. In 1956, missionaries moved out of Nigeria to start work in Tanzania. Soon, new missionaries arrived in other parts of eastern and southern Africa, where many nations were starting to declare independence from European colonial rule.

After two hundred years of British rule, India and Pakistan (which included modern-day Bangladesh) were granted their independence in 1947.[13] These countries were partitioned to create two states, one primarily Hindu and the other primarily Muslim, leading to the displacement of around fourteen million people, subsequent violence, and much death. The FMB opened work in East Pakistan, now known as Bangladesh, in 1957, following the partition.

1960s: Journeyman Program Commences

In the 1960s, Foreign Mission Board work continued to expand rapidly as missionaries entered or reentered almost thirty countries.[14] During this decade, the FMB started new programs to enable larger numbers of Southern Baptists to serve overseas, particularly those who did not meet the age or educational requirements for career missionary service. The most popular of these initiatives was the Journeyman program, a Peace Corps-inspired initiative that sent young people overseas for two years of missionary service; it launched in June 1965. Since the inception of the Journeyman program, more than sixty-four hundred young adults have served among the nations.

When Mary Sue Thompson was appointed as a missionary in 1967, decades had passed since the FMB appointed any African Americans for career missionary service.[15] Thompson, a highly educated schoolteacher, wanted to teach in Nigeria and build a ministry that would support the FMB's missionary work in Africa. She served for more than a decade.

As increasing numbers of missionaries were mobilized, the FMB recognized the need to provide extensive training for overseas service. New missionaries were already required to attend a weeklong orientation session, but in 1967, orientation expanded to a full sixteen weeks. Sessions included studying the linguistics and customs of the countries to which the missionaries were headed, along with practical topics like health and mechanics. To this day, missionary training remains a vital service dependent on CP gifts.

In 1968, mission strategy studies via on-the-field research began with a commission to examine church development factors in Latin America. Over the years, church development studies and church-planting assessments continued, and in the 1990s missionaries were assigned to full-time research positions around the world. Their research helps field leaders make decisions about where to send missionaries and resources.

1970s: Access in Vietnam and the Middle East

During an unparalleled season of growth from 1945 to 1979, the number of Foreign Mission Board missionaries increased from 504 to 3,010, the annual income grew from $2.8 million to $70.1 million, and missionary presence expanded from fifteen to eighty countries.[16]

One of these missionaries, Sam James, experienced unexpected response to the gospel as he taught theological education classes in the Vietnamese villages of Southeast Asia. Non-Christians attended in record numbers and, after hearing the gospel, proclaimed faith in Christ. Some stayed up all night to study the Word. At that time, communist forces started taking over the countryside, and James realized the Holy Spirit was preparing the Vietnamese for "the deepest crisis of their lives."

George Braswell Jr. served in Central Asia as a missionary in Tehran, Iran, during the 1970s.[17] He was particularly curious about the mullahs, the Muslim clergymen. Upon meeting and conversing with a local mullah, George was surprised how freely and openly the mullah spoke with him regarding spiritual matters. As they shared cups of tea, the mullah spoke with George as he would a close confidant. George soon learned the more tea you drink, the more you are immersed in another's life.

Missionaries such as George make the most of their opportunities to be present among others, never knowing when that opportunity may end. An anti-Western and anti-American group of Iranian students seized the U.S. embassy in Tehran in November 1979, directly impacting access to present day.

The 1970s witnessed unprecedented humanitarian aid efforts as Southern Baptists ministered in times of disaster. Missionaries had met human needs since the FMB's earliest days, but now Southern Baptist laymen joined in the efforts. A hurricane in Honduras and an earthquake in Guatemala led to the deployment of short-term teams to help with medical relief and construction efforts. Within a year, both nations experienced record numbers of baptisms. These experiences cemented in Baptists' minds the conviction that gospel proclamation and gospel demonstration work hand in hand.

In 1971, the Kenbak I became the first "commercially available personal computer." The Apple II, which came out in 1977, was the first personal computer to become publicly successful. The Foreign Mission Board had installed its first computer system in 1967, a 9200 Univac Card system. Today, CP funding makes it possible for missionaries to use the latest technology to expand the efficiency and effectiveness of getting the gospel into otherwise nearly inaccessible places.

1980s: Securing Access to Forbidden Lands

The 1980s were characterized by world events with far-reaching consequences for sharing the gospel increasingly through creative and nontraditional means.[18] China began slowly opening to the outside world after years of isolation. Although Foreign Mission Board missionaries were not allowed to reenter China, in the mid-1980s Cooperative Services International formed to meet needs expressed by Chinese Christian and secular institutions, particularly their desire for teachers.

As the FMB wrestled with how to reach the quarter of the world's population living in countries where missionary presence is forbidden, the concept of the nonresidential missionary was developed in 1986. Nonresidential missionaries would reside outside a country's borders but develop strategies for sharing the gospel with particular people groups in that country. Within five years, nonresidential missionaries were at work in thirty countries.

In 1981, under the leadership of R. Keith Parks, FMB leaders began seriously considering the concept of "hidden peoples"—people who do not have churches or active evangelism happening among them. Up to that point, missionaries had focused mostly on geopolitical countries and official languages, yet thousands of ethnic groups, each with a distinct language and culture, needed access to the gospel.

In 1984, news of the famine in Ethiopia raised Baptists' awareness of hunger needs around the world, and they responded by giving a record $7.2 million in relief funds, part of which went to Ethiopia. A year later, Baptists partnered with local Christians to minister to Colombians affected by a volcanic eruption. CP gifts support missionary presence. Because missionaries live and work alongside national partners around the world, Southern Baptists have on-site resources and established relationships to maximize response when unexpected crises occur.

As 1989 drew to a close, the FMB's first deaf missionary, Yvette Aarons, was commissioned for a four-year special assignment to Trinidad.[19] She was appointed as a career missionary to Trinidad in 1993 and served in St. Lucia and Thailand before retiring in 2016.

1990s: Focus Shifts to Unreached People

The 1990s became a decade of significant paradigm shifts within the Foreign Mission Board. The organization's name changed to the International Mission Board in 1997.[20] Many missionaries served in nations with significant numbers of churches and Christians, often holding roles like pastors, doctors, and educators in Board-funded institutions. Although good work was happening, thousands of unreached people groups still did not have access to the gospel.

Southern Baptists began realizing that although the world is made up of almost two hundred countries, a more appropriate way to understand the world missiologically is by recognizing its more than twelve thousand people groups—ethnolinguistic groups with a common self-identity shared by their members.[21] The gospel often does not easily transmit from one people group to another, so even if one or two groups within a nation are evangelized, others still might be "unreached." This understanding deeply impacts IMB strategy to this day.

During the 1990s, George and Veda Rae Lozuks served in Moscow, Russia, as some of the first missionaries to enter the country after the Iron Curtain fell.[22] George's father had moved to America from Russia when he was just a boy and became the pastor of the Russian Baptist Church in Fort Worth, Texas. Both George and Veda Rae had a heart for Eastern European missions. The Lozuks served in Moscow from 1991 to 1993, building and strengthening ties between the Southern Baptist Convention and the existing Russian Baptist Convention.

In 1997, IMB president Jerry Rankin announced New Directions, a strategy for getting the gospel to every people, tribe, and language. Within four years, the number of people groups engaged by IMB personnel increased from 584 to 1,015. Today, just over 3,000 people groups remain that have no known evangelical work among them, so they are considered both unreached and unengaged.[23] They continue to be the focus of the IMB's most aggressive efforts.

In the 1990s, the IMB also emphasized the direct involvement of all Southern Baptists in fulfilling the Great Commission. Rankin did not consider the IMB responsible for "doing missions" on behalf of Southern Baptists; he knew every church and Christian must play their part. There was an increase in IMB-sponsored short-term mission trips, and programs started to enable churches to pray for a people group and work alongside missionaries to take the gospel to them.

2000s: Love Triumphs over Terror

At the turn of the new millennium, the number of International Mission Board missionaries exceeded five thousand for the first time.[24] Even the global age of terror, which hit the United States in full force on September 11, 2001, did not dampen missionary enthusiasm. Two months after the September 11 attacks, the largest group of new missionaries to date, 124, was appointed to serve around the world. Tragically, throughout the decade, Southern Baptist missionaries and volunteers died in terrorist attacks, including relief workers in Iraq, medical professionals in Yemen, and a missionary in the Philippines.

One of these martyrs was Dr. Martha Myers.[25] She served in Yemen for twenty-five years as an IMB missionary doctor of obstetrics and gynecology. As such, she delivered hundreds of babies, but she was even better known for her love for the Yemeni people. This endeared her to many but also made her a target of Al-Qaeda extremists. On December 30, 2002, a man burst into the Jibla hospital and gunned down Martha and two colleagues in hopes of keeping Christianity out of his country. Instead, because of her love and respect, forty thousand Yemenis filed past her casket on the day of her funeral.

In 2002, the IMB began emphasizing the use of chronological Bible storying to share God's Word with oral learners (those who learn through nonliterate means). Orality became a major emphasis as missionary teams started to engage millions who either couldn't read or who preferred to digest Scripture through oral methods like storytelling and song. CP funds help purchase tools such as "storying cloths" to aid in Bible storying around the world.

As missionaries continued to engage greater numbers of unreached people groups throughout the decade, often in areas with open hostility to the gospel, they had to find creative ways to share God's Word and make disciples. Some were able to live in countries by taking on jobs as teachers and business owners; others had to make disciples in secret.

2010s: Urbanization, SD Cards, and Budget Shortfalls

During the 2010s, the International Mission Board grappled with the realities of worldwide urbanization.[26] By 2008, more than half the world's population was living in cities, and missionaries developed networks across the world to think through ensuring that every population segment in every city has access to the gospel. Increasingly, they started relying on partners to help tackle this overwhelming task, including local Christians, U.S. Southern Baptists, and like-minded missions organizations.

Pastor and former IMB missionary Tom Elliff was elected IMB president in 2011. During his three-year tenure, he challenged Southern Baptist churches to do "whatever it takes" to get the gospel to the world's thirty-eight thousand unengaged, unreached people groups.

In 2012, missionaries Brennan and Veronica Masterson (names changed for security) began regularly visiting a remote South Asian village—home to an illiterate man who prayed for three years for help to share his newfound faith.[27] In the village, they found a group of thirty "believers" whose biblical knowledge was, according to the Mastersons, "incomplete at best." The missionaries taught the small group thirty-five chronological Bible storying lessons. Because the people group is illiterate, the Mastersons created picture books to match the thirty-five Bible lessons and a micro-SD card containing the full audio Bible and teaching tools. The Mastersons intentionally designed the SD card to work on any mobile phone.

The thirty believers embraced the training and began sharing the gospel story house-to-house with their families and neighbors. In just one month, the thirty believers started six Bible studies each—a total of 180 Bible studies in this remote area. As those disciples made disciples, the gospel began to spread beyond the boundaries of the village. Over the years, a church planting effort has continued to grow into many new churches and tens of thousands who have heard the gospel.

In 2015, budget shortfalls once again forced the IMB to address funding challenges. Then-president David Platt acknowledged that current income could not continue to support missionary work around the world.[28] The painful decision was made to draw down personnel numbers. More than eleven hundred missionaries and staff left of their own volition. The IMB also announced new pathways for serving on mission overseas, including pathways that did not involve financial support from the IMB. Southern Baptists were given opportunities to serve on missionary teams while living in countries as professionals, students, and retirees.

In early December 2019, residents of Wuhan, including vendors at a seafood market, began exhibiting pneumonia-like symptoms. On December 31, China notified the World Health Organization of this "pneumonia of unknown cause," which came to be called COVID-19. The ensuing pandemic would challenge international missions access and resolve into the first years of the new decade. It would also prove, without a doubt, that Southern Baptists are tenacious about the Great Commission. Around the world, missionaries would find ways to share the gospel, whether through digital gatherings in Asia, by singing hymns from their open windows in Europe, or by leaving notes of love on their neighbors' doorsteps in South America.[29] As the world reopened, Southern Baptists once again began appointing missionaries to the nations, tackling the world's greatest problem: lostness.

Personal Reflection

Paul Chitwood

At 203 South 4th Street in Murray, Kentucky, a marker stands alongside the sidewalk. In the background is Murray's First Baptist Church. Historical Marker No. 1770, placed by the Kentucky Historical Society, commemorates Pastor Harvey Boyce Taylor and his contribution to the formation of the Southern Baptist Convention's CP.[30]

As the story goes, in the early years of the twentieth century, Pastor Taylor's desire to see First Baptist Church support more missionaries conflicted with his frustration over a growing number of financial appeals coming from missionaries, ministries, and denominational workers. So Taylor tried something new.[31] He placed a box in the sanctuary and told the congregation they could put extra offerings in the box to contribute to a missions fund that would be divided up by percentage for specific, stipulated causes. The members were soon giving more to mission work through Taylor's Box Plan than they had been giving for the individual appeals during Sunday gatherings. The effort was so successful that Taylor was soon sharing about it across his state.

In 1905, Taylor began serving on the executive board of the General Association of Baptists in Kentucky, today's Kentucky Baptist Convention, a position he would hold for the next twenty years. In 1913, Taylor was named chairman of a committee to consider the question of unifying Baptist work across the state. He used the leadership role as an opportunity to shape the future of missions giving in his state and, ultimately, across the SBC.

On November 16, 1915, the General Association of Baptists in Kentucky held its annual meeting at the First Baptist Church of Jellico, Tennessee, just a few hundred feet from the Kentucky state line. During that meeting, the convention messengers adopted a unified budget plan for the support of all denominational projects throughout the state and Convention. As an aside, First Jellico is the church where I came to faith and where I was baptized, ordained, and married. Ten years later, in 1925, the Kentucky plan served as a model for the unified missions budgeting plan set forth for the entire Southern Baptist Convention, the plan being called the Cooperative Program.

The blessings I have experienced of that giving plan, the model for which was first adopted at my home church, are innumerable. I hold three degrees from Baptist institutions paid for, in part, by the CP. As an employee of the Kentucky Baptist Convention and now the International Mission Board, my livelihood has been provided exclusively by the generosity of Southern Baptists through their faithful CP giving. Most importantly, as a Southern Baptist church member, I have, throughout my life, enjoyed the assurance that I was a part of advancing God's kingdom across North America and among the nations through CP-funded ministry and mission work.

When I was elected IMB president in November 2018, my first official action in office was to urge Southern Baptist state conventions and churches to consider anew the part they each could play in training and sending out their members to serve overseas. By recounting the stories of God at work through IMB missionaries, I have the honor and duty to encourage Southern Baptists to consider anew how to work together toward "a vast multitude from every nation, tribe, people, and language" (Rev. 7:9) who know and worship our Lord Jesus Christ. This includes a consistent reminder of the unique opportunity afforded us as Southern Baptists to partner through CP giving to do more together than we could ever do alone. I know of no better way to address lostness, the world's greatest problem, with the solution of the gospel other than through a cooperative missions effort, and I know no greater efforts than those funded by the CP.

PART 3

12

Current Challenges and Opportunities in the Southern Baptist Convention

Bart Barber

The Southern Baptist Convention (SBC or Convention) is not doomed, is not dying, is not unraveling, is not drifting, is not sliding off into irrelevance, and is not facing any challenges of a different nature or a greater severity than those it has faced before. Be of good cheer.

The SBC is not perfect, is not indispensable, is not the sum total of the kingdom of God, is not immune to the challenges that affect other groups of churches, and is not altogether healthy right now. Be vigilant.

The nature of the SBC is predominantly that of a family of local, autonomous churches. That is to say, whatever challenges and opportunities lie before the SBC, they primarily consist of the aggregation of the challenges and opportunities that lie before the individual churches who are in friendly cooperation with one another through the Convention. The situation in the churches bubbles up into the gatherings and operations of the Convention.

To a far lesser degree, the nature of the SBC is that of a family of separate and independent entities who serve those churches and are mostly supported by those churches.[1] The needs and accomplishments of these entities can often shape the environment in which the various churches practice voluntary cooperation.

Opportunities Facing the Southern Baptist Convention

Organizations like the SBC owe their existence to the widely held view among Baptist churches that the world ought to have a lot more Baptist churches populated by a lot more Christians who hold Baptist views. Southern support for the American system of racial slavery split the old Triennial Convention through which Baptists had been supporting missionaries like Adoniram Judson, but after the slavery question had been resolved by warfare, Southern Baptists maintained their separation from the North primarily because of a different set of priorities related to the planting of Baptist churches in the South, in the West, and around the world.

The appetite to plant healthy Baptist churches persists.

- Thousands of localized ethnolinguistic groups around the world lack any healthy Baptist churches. Indeed, thousands lack any evangelical[2] churches at all. The need

- to plant Baptist churches around the world is great.
- Some overwhelmingly unreached, unconverted, unbaptized places in the world now lie within the United States of America. The need to plant Baptist churches in "pioneer areas" within the United States is great.
- In some locales with a healthy number of existing Baptist churches, the population is growing at a rate that far outstrips the growth rate of those churches. The need to plant Baptist churches within the strongest quadrants of our own Southern Baptist "territory" is great.
- Among some families with long, multigenerational histories of faithful membership in Baptist churches, the generations currently emerging are either not embracing the gospel at all or are migrating out of Baptist life into other streams of Christianity. The need to preach the gospel and to teach sound doctrine within our own existing churches and families is great.

We face the same needs we faced in 1814, the founding of the Triennial Convention; 1845, the founding of the SBC; and 1925, the founding of the Cooperative Program. Even greater opportunities lie before us than lay before us in any of those years.

The opportunities are greater because the resources at hand to face those needs is greater than before. Southern Baptists have two strong mission boards with healthy financial reserves.

We have tens of thousands of existing churches with millions of members and billions of dollars. God has given us those resources in a moment in time when jet travel can take a person from the United States of America to any place in the world within forty-eight hours and when Christian resources on the Internet are far more difficult for hostile world leaders to keep out of their nations than were our books, pamphlets, and personnel just thirty years ago. We have robust institutions dedicated to training those who will take up this task—some of the largest and highest quality seminaries in the world. One need not be triumphalist to acknowledge these widely known facts.

The more lugubrious members of our Southern Baptist family will doubtless point us to the hardness of the soil into which we are planting. The culture has changed. The milieu is, we read, a "negative world," as though that were something novel.[3]

Years ago, I preached the Sunday morning service at one of the oldest Baptist churches in the state of Arkansas. Framed in the foyer was a brief historical narrative describing the church's founding. It has been a few decades since I stood there and read the story, but the gist of the story was hard to forget.

Only a few years had passed since Thomas Jefferson extended religious liberty to the area by way of the Louisiana Purchase. A traveling evangelist sympathetic to the work of John Mason Peck came upon this little glade in the Ozarks and erected a brush arbor. He went throughout the countryside and invited all the population to attend a revival meeting at the site.

When the evening came for the campaign to start, the evangelist had just stepped up to the pulpit to commence the service when a group of armed men on horseback rode up to the brush arbor and called him out. They were decidedly of the opinion that the area did not need organized religion, and they threatened armed violence unless he would disband the service and leave the region.

The evangelist reached down into his pulpit and withdrew from it two loaded revolvers, inviting the ruffians to try their luck. They slipped away quietly. Rather than returning the revolvers to the interior of the pulpit, the evangelist placed them atop the pulpit in full view of the congregation and then continued the service. The church was born out of his efforts.

Without endorsing pistols on our pulpits, one can commend his bravery and determination.

The more important lesson taught by this anecdote is that "hard soil" is best met by hard heads unwaveringly committed to preach the gospel or die trying. The First Great Awakening came at a moment when the soil was hard. "All we like sheep have gone astray" (Isa. 53:6 KJV). All soil is hard. Conversion is always miraculous. The opportunity is as apparent as your faith in the work of the Holy Spirit is strong.

Challenges Facing the Southern Baptist Convention

Seizing opportunity always means overcoming challenges. Some of the challenges Southern Baptist churches face are percolating up into the SBC.

The degree of confidence and enthusiasm in Baptist belief held by churches in the SBC is visibly waning. Above lies a sentence that discussed "the widely held view among Baptist churches that the world ought to have a lot more Baptist churches populated by a lot more Christians who hold Baptist views." Did that sentence strike you as gauche or excessively parochial? I offer that feeling as Exhibit A.

For more than a century, the primary institutions by which Southern Baptists taught their distinctive beliefs were our mission auxiliaries and what we once called "Training Union." Local churches attenuated their support of these teaching vehicles starting in the 1980s, and the attenuation was substantial enough that by 2024 an entire generation has been raised in Southern Baptist churches without any substantial or consistent exposure to the deliberate teaching of Baptist doctrine.

This rejection of doctrinal discipleship may arise less out of a disdain for doctrine and more out of declining willingness to produce and attend church events beyond the Sunday morning time slot. Training Union, RAs, and GAs generally took place at other times of the week. The societal trend toward less time spent with a group of believers studying the Bible and more time spent alone at home in front of a screen has produced a measurable impact not only on Baptists also but on all evangelical Christians. In the 2022 survey titled "The State of Theology," Ligonier Ministries and Lifeway Research found that among evangelical Christians who reported attending church at least once weekly:

- Thirty-six percent were open to the possibility that God learns and adapts to different circumstances.
- Fifty-eight percent described an Arian belief about Jesus: "Jesus is the first and greatest being created by God."
- Forty-one percent said that the Holy Spirit is a force and not a personal being.
- Thirty-five percent said that small sins do not deserve eternal damnation.

- Thirty-three percent said that worshipping alone or with one's family is a valid replacement for regularly attending church.
- And yet, remarkably, 100 percent said that the Bible was the highest authority for what they believed.[4]

With such erosion in confidence about basic doctrines of Christian orthodoxy, a decline in commitment to distinctive Baptist beliefs is not surprising. Several of the distinctive beliefs that define the Baptist movement are showing evidence of this trend.

Congregational church governance is less widely practiced among Baptist churches than the near universal adherence it enjoyed not long ago. Congregationalism is entirely compatible with elder leadership in churches and always has been. One church meets relatively rarely to choose her leaders, offer transparent reporting, and set broad priorities, entrusting the day-to-day implementation of those priorities to the congregation's designees. Another church meets monthly and makes detailed decisions about expenditures, volunteer assignments, calendar events, and facilities maintenance. The former church is no less congregationally governed than the latter. But some churches have moved to self-perpetuating leadership structures, rare or incomplete reporting, or even an utter lack of congregational voting. These things are not congregational church governance.

A departure from congregational governance in the local churches impacts the operations of the SBC. Even the pastor who is the least congregationally minded in his local church tends to desire the broadly held decision-making and transparent reporting of congregationalism when he sits as a messenger at the annual meeting. If the elected and employed leaders of Southern

Baptist institutions are drawn from congregations that are less and less congregational in their polity, they will tend to bring to their roles the governance styles they have learned in their local churches.

Support for universal religious liberty is a distinctively Baptist belief. Since the 1500s, Anabaptists and Baptists have consistently championed a free church in a free state. Two recent factors have challenged the Baptist commitment to the biblical doctrine of religious liberty. First, increasing (and increasingly ferocious) Islamic terrorism led some Southern Baptists in the aftermath of the attacks on September 11, 2001, to toy with excluding all forms of Islam from the Baptist doctrine of universal religious liberty. Second, some non-Baptist political movements have set their sights on wooing Southern Baptists away from Baptist belief about religious liberty.

Because establishmentarian Christian political theory directly contradicts the SBC's statement of faith, if this rejection of universal religious liberty were to spread (and if those converted to these sentiments lacked the integrity to admit that they were no longer Baptists and to leave the SBC), the SBC could face sharp disagreement over this point of doctrine in coming years.

The autonomy of the local church is a distinctive belief of Baptists, but Southern Baptist exploration of multisite church campuses tests the boundaries of this important doctrine. The trend toward multisite ministry, like most trends eventually do, seems to be ebbing at least a little. Also, few Southern Baptist practitioners have intentionally and expressly rejected the idea of local church autonomy. This seems to be more a debate about what local church autonomy means rather than a debate about whether the autonomy of the local church is sound biblical ecclesiology. Nevertheless, most of those who have preceded us in the

Baptist movement would likely be alarmed to see the widespread practice of having the congregation meeting in one location be subservient to the decisions of a congregation meeting in another location.

The list could go on. Commitment to believer's baptism is, in some cases, yielding to experimentation with open church membership. The idea of regenerate church membership seems impossible to reconcile with the existence of Baptist churches that do not track church membership at all! The dismissal and reception of church members from one Baptist church to another is a dying practice. The active use of a church membership covenant, reviving now somewhat after a noticeable retreat, is one hopeful development. In a dozen different ways, what Southern Baptists once assumed of one another is now tenuous. What is true about our faltering grasp of our doctrines of the local church is even more true about our doctrinal convictions that shape the nature and organization of our cooperative work—what we mean, for example, when we say that the Southern Baptist Convention is "a convention, not a denomination."

I mention these things not to position myself as the putative chief of the Baptist doctrine police. I am merely pointing out that the group who cannot clearly and consistently subscribe to (or even identify!) "Baptist views" can hardly mobilize itself for work around the assumedly common view that "the world ought to have a lot more Baptist churches populated by a lot more Christians who hold Baptist views."

The solution is to recommit ourselves to teaching our beliefs. This objective is within easy reach! Our statement of faith is sound, and it includes all the Baptist beliefs I have mentioned above, plus many more. Our seminaries are populated with faculty members who believe the truths taught in our statement of faith. The SBC contains a surfeit of highly creative teachers who can make sure the next generation to emerge from our churches is well acquainted with the doctrines we have cherished for four centuries.

I pen these words in early 2024, while a Cooperation Group commissioned by Southern Baptists is actively considering (among other things) the effect that a failure to indoctrinate Southern Baptists is having on Southern Baptist cooperation. Whether by that vehicle or another, I am hopeful that Southern Baptists can reinvigorate our commitment to the "definite doctrines that Baptists believe, cherish, and with which they have been and are now closely identified."[5]

Alongside these doctrinal challenges, we face significant behavioral challenges. Not since the 1920s have so many prominent Southern Baptists behaved so badly. In one recent week during my term as SBC president, four different churches reached out to me for advice about how to handle breaking news about sexual abuse that had occurred at the hand of a church staff member or volunteer within the context of their churches. Recently the interim head of the Executive Committee of the SBC, as a part of the process by which he nearly came to hold that position indefinitely, admitted that he had falsified large portions of his resume. Southern Baptists are filing lawsuits against one another at what feels like an unprecedented pace. More than one Southern Baptist has gotten in trouble for his demeanor displayed in online social media outlets. Abuse of alcohol and other intoxicants by leaders in local Southern Baptist churches is a consistent discovery. Forced termination of institutional heads within the Southern Baptist panoply of related institutions is far from rare.

With regard to sexual abuse, Southern Baptists have taken significant steps since 2021. Most Southern Baptists do not commit sexual abuse. Most Southern Baptists are opposed to sexual abuse and wish to prevent it. We face three obstacles in achieving that goal.

- Many of our churches, especially some of our smaller ones, either do not know how to prevent sexual abuse in the best possible ways or do not know how to fund those preventative measures.
- Many of our churches, sometimes including some of our larger ones, do not know where to seek good advice when they discover that abuse has occurred within their church. Sometimes they choose whom to trust when they seek that advice without considering whether those who give them advice have any positive experience or expertise in responding to abuse in a way that best cares for survivors and sides with truth and righteousness.
- When our churches discover someone who has tried to abuse vulnerable people within their church, sometimes those churches do not know how, as one autonomous church, they can warn other autonomous churches about dangerous people. Sometimes the churches who are the most vigilant are the ones who face this problem in the most pressing manner because in their vigilance, they have uncovered a predator before he was able to commit a crime.

By the time that this essay is published, I hope we will have completed our work to launch the Abuse Response Commission

(ARC), an independent nonprofit designed to serve the churches of the SBC. The mission of ARC is to assist churches in solving all three of those problems. I am optimistic about the direction of this new organization. This much is certain: none of those three problems is something we can safely ignore.

Indeed, the overall question of Southern Baptist behavior demands our attention. It is caused, at least to some degree, by the behavioral degradation of our society as a whole. Sexual abuse is not a uniquely Southern Baptist phenomenon. Our society marinates in pornography, and every American institution is struggling to prevent abuse, including our public schools, branches of military service, the entertainment industry, sports, journalism, and government. Our society counts boorishness as strength, confusion about the fundamental attributes of our personal identities as courage, vulgarity as passion, and imperviousness to reasonable critique as wisdom.

The cultural source of these problems notwithstanding, blaming the culture for our behavioral problems is no way to save people from the culture as brands plucked from the fire. We have a biblical message about human sexuality and gender identity that our society needs so desperately to hear—a message that reconnects sex with love and our bodies with God's good design—and yet, who will hear it if we are acting in denial of a growing sex abuse problem in our churches? We have a biblical message about strong family institutions our society needs to hear, but who will hear it if we are having to remove pastors and denominational leaders for their adultery?

One final challenge deserves to be the final note ringing in your ears. Both because of a retreating commitment to our Baptist work together and because of a sense of scandal and fatigue in response to the sin uncovered in our midst, our commitment to the Cooperative Program (CP) is measurably diminishing. This is unfortunate.

The CP is not terribly mysterious. It is simply our commitment (1) to develop a budget together and then (2) to fund that budget together. The development of the budget starts with recipient entities and the trustees appointed by the messenger body to oversee them. It involves voluntary cooperation between state conventions and the national SBC. The capstone moment of the development of the budget is that moment when the messengers hear the budget, discuss the budget, and then adopt the budget.

The funding of the budget together occurs when each autonomous church voluntarily chooses to send money to fund the CP. The heart of the CP is a willingness to send *my* money to fund *our* plan. After all, the same thing happens in our local churches. Our church adopts a budget together. It is likely that no individual gets exactly what he or she would want in the adopted church budget. We give a little and take a little. We negotiate a budget for our local church that works best for all of us. Then, as evidence of our love for one another and our spirit of cooperation, each individual gives away his own money to fund a plan that everyone developed together.

In the same way, First Baptist Church of Farmersville (my church) sends 10 percent of our undesignated receipts to a CP allocation budget that is never exactly what we would do if we alone were in charge of the SBC. We would have different priorities. Some things the SBC does, we might cut altogether. Some things the SBC has chosen not to do, we might add (like that potluck Sunday the convention declined to add a few years back).[6] Do we get our way all of the time, in every vote? We do not.

We support the CP anyway. We do it because we had our fair say in the process, and we aren't inclined to take our ball and go home. We do it because every bit of the work is guided by *The Baptist Faith and Message 2000* and is biblically sound. We do it because we are passionate about planting more Baptist churches in every part of the world.

The SBC did, it is true, survive for eighty years without the CP, but those eight decades represented a time when, for the most part, our local churches did not adopt budgets, either. There is no going back to the 1870s. If Southern Baptist churches are so far removed from cooperation with one another that we cannot successfully adopt a budget that we can all fund in good conscience, then societal giving will not save us. How will we, who cannot agree on a budget, possibly agree on which missionaries to appoint, which textbooks to use, or which locations to plant churches? When the fights on the budget end, those fights will take their place.

The CP is more than a program; it is a mindset and a worldview. Without it, it is difficult to imagine that the Southern Baptist Convention can survive.

A Hopeful Conclusion

It would be hopeful enough to say that there are solutions within reach for us to meet these challenges and seize our opportunities, but I can go beyond that. The messenger body of the SBC has already expressed our willingness to address every one of these problems. We have ended people's employment where we needed to do so. We have articulated solid Baptist doctrine in our statement of faith and in our many adopted resolutions. We have overwhelmingly adopted resolutions decrying every one of the behavioral problems I have identified above. What's more, in response to widespread concerns about the CP allocation budgets adopted by the various state conventions several years ago, state conventions successfully made changes that restored confidence in the CP at the state level. The same outcome is within reach for the SBC. We know the right thing to do. We have even moved forward in trying to do the right thing in circumstance after circumstance.

All that remains is for us to prove to be steadfast in the implementation of it all.

We must be steadfast not only in meeting the challenges, but we must also be steadfast in our commitment to the mission that undergirds it all and makes it all worthwhile. I believe we will do so, and I look forward to taking that journey arm in arm with you.

Personal Reflection

On November 4, 2023, I stood looking down the hill across the charred rubble of what had once been Lahaina, Hawaii, on the Island of Maui. To see such an ugly scar marring such a beautiful vista was disturbing. But the gospel exists to thwart the curse that despoils God's good creation with bad scars. The damage done by the fire lay before me, but Southern Baptists stood all around me, helping those in need and sharing the gospel, and the CP underwrote it all. State convention disaster relief units from several states were on duty the week I was there. The heroic work of pastor Erik Naylor and Lahaina Baptist Church was a CP story of its own. CP funds sent Naylor there before the fire as a Southern Baptist church planter. Now Send Relief and disaster relief efforts were helping him to serve his community and point them to Christ.

Four weeks later, on December 1, I stood with my friend Mahoss (his African name), a CP-funded missionary who was guiding me and others through a small village in the Casamance region of Senegal. FBC Farmersville has been sharing the gospel and planting churches there in partnership with the IMB since 2012. The money we have invested through the CP to provide seminary education to Mahoss, to help him learn the Wolof language, and to fund his efforts in the area have been well spent. We stop to share lunch with a young woman. Her family opposes her for her decision to follow Christ, but she remains faithful to the fledgling church she attends, clinging to the hope of the gospel. In this area torn by war and by a brutal traditional religion that impoverishes the population and incites them to practice dangerous and sometimes violent rituals, work funded by the CP offers hope in a hopeless region.

My two years serving our Convention as president have convinced me all the more that the CP is ethically good, practically wise, and spiritually beautiful. I wish I could take every Southern Baptist with me to stand where I have stood and see what I have seen. At the very least, I can testify that it all brings glory to God, and I can encourage my fellow Southern Baptists to support sacrificially the work we do together.

The Ethics of Kingdom Cooperation

RaShan Frost

As we reflect on one hundred years of the Cooperative Program (CP), it benefits us to remember that God has always prioritized cooperation and collaboration among his people. God created humanity for community, and for us as Christians to thrive, we have to work together. Scripture outlines how God first embodies and demonstrates cooperation within himself as the triune God. In creation, recorded in Genesis 1–2, we see that God created man and woman, in his image, to come together, make families, build communities and nations, and shape the world around them. We see it throughout the Old Testament as God established his law for his people to demonstrate what a society should look like under his rule. We see collaboration in the Gospels as Jesus selects twelve men as his disciples and models to them what God's mission looks like and charges and empowers them to accomplish it. Finally, we see it in Acts and the rest of the New Testament, as the gospel spreads from Jerusalem, in all Judea, and to the end of the earth (Acts 1:8) through the church. The legacy of Southern Baptist cooperation is grounded in God's redemptive work in humanity as outlined in Scripture. Cooperation is a principle of the kingdom of God. It is answering the prayer that Jesus prayed in John 17:21, "May they all be one, as you, Father, are in me and I am in you. May they also be in us, so that the world may believe you sent me."

My journey in kingdom collaboration, leading to Southern Baptist life and ministry and the CP, began with my work on staff with a national sports ministry, serving as a collegiate football chaplain. It would end up with me going to Southeastern Baptist Theological Seminary, becoming a church planter and pastor within the Convention, and serving as a college professor at a South Carolina Baptist Convention-affiliated university. What I discovered as I partnered with local churches in the Charleston, South Carolina, area was that the most kingdom-minded churches were SBC churches. The churches within the Charleston Baptist Association had a shared vision and collaborated to see every man, woman, and child impacted by the gospel where they lived, learned, worked, and played. They shared my passion for reaching the next generation and collaborating with others who shared that same vision. Even more important for me was that I saw and experienced how the state and local levels of the Convention, the Charleston Baptist Association, and the South Carolina Baptist Convention, collaborated through finances and other resources in a manner that demonstrated a desire to be obedient to the Great Commission and reflect the desire to embody the love of Christ in practice. They were serious about reaching every man, woman, and child with the gospel, and where they put their money reflected that.

The call to reach every man, woman, and child has not changed, nor will it. However, as Southern Baptists move forward to the next one hundred years and beyond, we will need to understand that if we want to impact future generations effectively, then we must be willing to consider and evaluate our methods while staying true to the gospel. Gen Z (those born between 1999 and 2015) is the largest American generation to date with approximately seventy million teens and young adults, and their characteristics will shape how we do ministry. The Barna Group's research provides some key insights about how the characteristics of Gen Z help shape the larger discussion on how we need to view an ethic of cooperation:

- Gen Zers are twice as likely as adults to say they are atheist.
- About half of Gen Z is nonwhite.
- Half say happiness (success) is their ultimate goal in life.
- Three out of five Gen Z Christians who don't think church is important say, "I find God elsewhere."
- One out of five Gen Zers chooses a negative judgmental image to represent a Christian church.[1]

Reaching the next generation requires us to cast a vision to them that speaks to God's redemptive mission, demonstrates authentic biblical unity across ethnic and generational lines, and invites them to participate in this work where they live, learn, work, and play. This vision is anchored in the kingdom of God.

The Kingdom in the Ethics of Kingdom Cooperation

The kingdom of God implies a political connotation to Christian life that informs our ethics of cooperation. I am not referring to the political nature of the Christian faith as an attachment or allegiance to particular political parties or partisanship. I am saying the Christian's political existence and thus our cooperative efforts are based on the reality that we represent a kingdom and therefore a King. The Christian faith is inherently political because the statement "Jesus is Lord" is a political statement. The lordship of Christ encompasses and informs every aspect of our lives, and his dominion expands over all creation. As Abraham Kuyper famously stated, "There is not a square inch in the whole domain of our human existence over which Christ, who is Sovereign over all, does not cry: 'Mine!'"[2] The political nature of the Christian faith establishes a foundation by which we order our lives, individually and collectively as the church, under the lordship of Christ.

Why does this matter if we are talking about the CP? The CP is one way Southern Baptists collaborate and participate in the kingdom of God regardless of geographical location. It supports missions, church planting, and theological education, as well as other endeavors for the purposes of fulfilling the Great Commission (Matt. 28:18–20). The end goal of the CP is demonstrating a unity of purpose that says, "Your kingdom come. Your will be done on earth as it is in heaven" (Matt. 6:10). When we talk about kingdom cooperation, we are acknowledging our role as representatives of God's heavenly kingdom in our context. It is affirming the fact that because we have been given a ministry of reconciliation as his ambassadors (2 Cor. 5:18–20), our collective work is a demonstration of our obedience to King Jesus. Not only that, but it is also continuing the work of the first-century churches in which they provided financial assistance to other churches (1 Cor. 16:1–4; 2 Cor. 8:1–9, 15; Rom. 15:25–27; Acts 21; Phil. 4:10). Churches supporting churches for the purposes of support and cooperation in ministry is a biblical model.

The kingdom of God governs how we live and accomplish God's mission where we live, learn, work, and play. When we ask the question, "What does God want?," we are not asking what he wants for our lives, although that is important. We are addressing the ultimate purpose for our cooperative mission in relationship to the kingdom of God: his glory reflected in all endeavors (Ps. 115:1; 1 Cor. 10:31; 2 Cor. 4:6; Eph. 1:12–14; Col. 3:17, 23). In other words, all of life is worship, and we are to pursue the glory of God in everything we do and everywhere we go. When we consider the glory of God as the ultimate goal, then the ethics of the kingdom of God constitute the operating system that informs our ethic of kingdom collaboration. Without a proper vision of the kingdom in our collective endeavors, our work, while well intentioned, will not make the deeper, eternal impact we hope it might make. Keeping our eyes focused on the kingdom of God ensures that our earthly, missional activity maintains its eternal emphasis.

God's kingdom is greater than any one church, and the CP is a reminder of what can be accomplished when local churches come together under a unified vision and mission. As we pursue the glory of God by participating in his redemptive mission, we are demonstrating the transformational power of God's kingdom through his multiethnic and multigenerational community. We are kingdom citizens who, through King Jesus, have been given a ministry of proclaiming the good news of Jesus Christ in word and deed. The kingdom of God is to be proclaimed and demonstrated anywhere the brokenness of sin is evident. God has given us the local church as the context for us to do ministry, and he has also given us a local and broad community to do ministry with. In this community we pool our resources together so we can maximize our ministry impact wherever God calls us to go—locally, nationally, and internationally.

I wanted to start with the idea of the kingdom in the ethics of cooperation because we need to have a proper view of what God wants, what he is doing, and how he invites us to participate in his redemptive work as his kingdom representatives. As we look at a vision of how the CP will last for future generations, we need to see how God's kingdom encompasses the beauty of God's cause and community. These two factors transcend time and location and, I believe, are the key to bridging Southern Baptists today with future generations with the same mission, even if methods change. God's cause is the gospel. God's community is his people (the church). Through our collective efforts within our spheres of influence, we are calling the next generation to live with a kingdom DNA that conveys the transcendent cause of the gospel, the transcendent joy of his people, and the transcendent urgency of his mission.

The Transcendence of the Gospel

One thing the years between 2020 and 2024 have shown us is that Gen Z is driven by purpose and is cause oriented. Christians have the greatest cause to advocate for, and to be involved in, because the gospel of Jesus Christ has literally changed the course of human history. The gospel is God's good news that articulates God's redemptive work throughout human history. Genesis 1–2 chronicles how God created a good world in perfect harmony with him and the rest of creation. Humanity, created in his image, was in perfect relationship with him and one another. However, that relational harmony was disrupted by sin (Gen. 3), and the rest of Scripture shows how all aspects of the human experience have been negatively impacted ever since. The good news is that Scripture also communicates—through the incarnation, life, atonement, and resurrection of Christ—that humanity has the opportunity to be reconciled to God and to one another. Ultimately, God will bring a complete restoration to the created world under the lordship of Jesus, but in the meantime, God has instituted his churches to serve as carriers of this great cause to spread from the neighborhood block to the world.

As we communicate the message of the gospel within our ethics of kingdom cooperation, we must remember that the overarching message of the gospel is God's love for humanity and his heart and mission for reconciliation. The ultimate cause and purpose of the gospel are to reconcile people to God and one another.[3] The beauty of the gospel is that God cared about his creation so much that he would step into it in order to save humanity. The gospel demonstrates how God is transcendent, being above and outside creation, and yet simultaneously immanent, being personal and working within it. God's love, and thus the heart of the gospel, is a reconciliatory love that bears the weight of human pain, suffering, and estrangement from God. Through Christ, who bore that sin and suffering on the cross, and whose victory was solidified in the resurrection, we see the redemptive power of his love. As we engage the next generation, we are communicating this larger vision of God's love, redemption, and reconciliation because sin pervades every aspect of the human experience. Therefore, our cooperative efforts in evangelism and mission must address the brokenness that sin has caused individually and corporately, and our resources must prioritize a mission that addresses the entirety of human brokenness with the gospel of Jesus Christ.

The gospel is wholistic, meaning it affects every aspect of the human experience. Because God understands humanity as both Creator and Savior, there is no issue we as human beings experience that his gospel is not equipped to address. The gospel, therefore, is a verbal proclamation of God's good news through Christ that is necessarily demonstrated in how we live. We share the gospel with our words and reflect it in our actions, recognizing that words without action lack the opportunity to demonstrate the love of God and the power of the gospel through meeting someone's needs and seeing how such acts of love can transform lives. Gospel-centered Christian action displays the love of God through service in times of hardship and disaster. Acts of service and love—especially in times of need, hardship, and disaster—are a practical way we can demonstrate the gospel. As Christians, we know the gospel is transformative, and we must ensure that all our evangelistic efforts reflect that. Thus, a key component of the CP is that our collective efforts serve to advance the gospel in a way that meets the human need holistically. So the gospel informs not only our words but also our ministry priorities and practices.

The gospel is the foundation of everything we do and the motivation for our outreach and evangelism. As we look forward to the future, Southern Baptists have the responsibility to articulate the large vision of the church's mission and how all of us are called to actively participate in it. As a church planter, pastor, and professor, I had to learn how to adapt to whatever context I am in because ministry by nature is contextual. Some methods are effective in some areas and not in others. Their effectiveness is based on the people we are serving and the opportunities and potential obstacles within the ministry context. Methods and strategies change based on context, but the gospel does not. The gospel is our vision, our motivation, and our cause. What makes the CP so effective is that it stays committed to the gospel while being flexible to the ministry demands of the moment. In other words, the CP is not bound by methodology as much as it is bound to cooperative evangelistic effectiveness. As a result, we can affirm the nonnegotiable nature of the gospel while we evaluate our strategies and methods within our context. When we communicate the transcendence of the gospel as the center of everything we do, we can show Gen Z and future generations they have a crucial role in this great cause as do (and did) Millennials, Gen Xers (my generation), baby boomers, and the multitude of generations that have engaged in cooperative ministry before us.

The Transcendence of God's Community

The gospel is more than a message of salvation and personal transformation. When we place our faith in Jesus, we are transformed from sinners to saints, but God does not stop there. He also brings us into his family as siblings, and that family is the church (John 1:12–13; Rom. 8:14–17; Gal. 3:26–29; Eph. 2:11–22; 3:6–10; 1 John 3:1–2). God's family is multiethnic and multigenerational, spanning across time, generations, geography, and cultures as we are a part of the "vast multitude from every nation, tribe, people, and language" (Rev. 7:9). The beauty of God's redemptive work is that the mystery of the gospel communicates how God can bring Jew and Gentile into his family, together (Eph. 3:6–11). The gospel is a unifier, and we are unified into the body of Christ, but we are also responsible for protecting the bonds of familial unity (Eph. 4:3–6). This sibling theology is important to our ethics of kingdom cooperation because it points to the fact that Christians were never intended to live out the Christian life alone. Rather, the kingdom ethic is to be lived out within the context of Christ's unified multiethnic, multigenerational family.

If we want to embody an ethic of kingdom cooperation, as Southern Baptists we have to be a trustworthy community. That is to say, we need to embody a love, unity, and purpose in all our interactions in a way that affords us relational and missional credibility with people. Research on Gen Z and millennials reveals a suspicion of religion, and their first critique is the hypocrisy of religious people and institutions.[4] This suspicion attacks the heart of evangelism because one of the biggest barriers to the gospel today is our public witness—how we interact with one another and how we live. A proper understanding of the transcendence of God's community means our lives are eternally linked with our brothers and sisters, on display through our interactions with them and with the larger society. The world needs to see the beautiful community of believers working together as God's incarnational presence. The church is God's only plan to carry the gospel to the ends of the earth, and all believers are part of that plan. As God's incarnational community, our credibility matters as do our ethics and moral dispositions. Simply put, our public witness matters.

If we want to see the CP flourish in the next one hundred years, we need to show the beauty and harmony of the love and unity within God's family, the church (and the churches). When we collaborate by sharing resources under a shared vision, and when we are unified in public witness, future generations will see the beauty of the larger church in action. This means the CP has to be more than the sharing of resources; it is the applied disposition of Christian unity and love for the purpose of loving and reaching the lost. Our affection for the CP must come out of our love for those who are within our missional proximity but are far from God. We are called to love in action and truth, and the life of God's family must be an embodied demonstration of the trustworthiness of the gospel.

Additionally, the CP, by virtue of its existence, communicates the benefits of local churches collaborating and serving in cooperation with other churches both locally and abroad. This is vital to next-generation involvement because the CP speaks to the larger relational need for belonging, discipleship, and personal connection. In other words, people need to feel like they belong to something bigger than themselves, while being connected to that community and cause. The church was created by God to make disciples of all peoples, everywhere, wherever they live, learn, work, and play (Matt 28:19–20; Acts 1:8; 2:42–47). While the benefits of biblical community are not limited to Southern Baptists, the CP affirms the allocation of its resources to that end. Simply put, the CP is an opportunity to "put your money where your mouth is." Because Southern Baptists care about the gospel, and the gospel cares about reconciling people to God, our resources—both tangible and intangible—are allocated throughout the church community.

The Transcendence of God's Mission

While Gen Z is often stereotyped as selfish and self-centered, Barna's research has found that they are one of the most likely generations to be cause-oriented and involved in organizational volunteer work.[5] This is encouraging because their volunteerism reminds us that when they see the value of a cause and community, they will get involved in the work of its mission. The church, as God's community, has the greatest cause in human history, the gospel, and therefore participates in the greatest mission of all time. Christ sends his people to be salt and light, making its mission "everything the church is sent into the world to do."[6] Regarding the heart of Christian mission, Carl F. H. Henry notes, "The Christian is not simply to abstain from evil and to deal justly with other men, but he is also to seek his neighbor's regeneration. Wherever his life touches human need, the believer is to respond. His involvement in social responsibility grows not so much out of a comprehensive social theory as out of direct obedience to God and genuine personal interest in his neighbors."[7] Christian mission is a comprehensive endeavor embracing evangelism through verbal proclamation that works itself out in acts of justice, mercy, and compassion for the purpose of drawing people to a reconciliatory and regenerative faith in Christ.

The comprehensiveness of Christian mission is an important concept we must clearly articulate if we want to connect with future generations and engage them in the mission. Barna's research shows that American teens and young adults are concerned about issues of public importance and are looking for and expecting the church to find ways to engage their neighbors and/or issues of justice that impact their community.[8] This is a great opportunity for the church as it contextualizes gospel mission within one's social location. If upcoming generations are cause-oriented and concerned about social issues, then the church ought to demonstrate their involvement in dealing with the needs of the community in clear and tangible ways. Outreach is more than going door to door and sharing the gospel, although it is certainly not less; it is also looking at the needs of the community and addressing the various barriers to people receiving the gospel. Sometimes those barriers exist because we have not communicated a robust view of how the gospel addresses every issue of life. Thus, Christian mission facilitates God's intentions for the church by becoming the living, incarnational expression of God's love for humanity in word and deed.

The CP is a structure already in place that can help address the concerns younger generations have by providing resources toward missions already being practiced. Send Relief is one example of CP resources in action, dealing with justice and mercy causes and compassion care. As a collaborative initiative between the North American Mission Board and the International Mission Board, Send Relief addresses issues like refugee care, strengthening communities through local ministry centers, protecting children and families, fighting human trafficking, and responding to crises like natural disasters. The whole purpose of Send Relief is to be a ministry of compassion and care that meets physical and spiritual needs. The means by which these points of emphasis are addressed depend on the issues at hand. Send Relief is just one example of how Southern Baptists can share with the next generation the various ways we are practically involved in important issues, inviting them to contribute to and participate in what God is already doing through his church.

When we present a clear vision of the transcendence of God's mission, we can cultivate a multiethnic and multigenerational synergy that empowers a giving that aligns with the collective passions of the people. People support causes, but our responsibility as the church is to articulate how we can fully participate within it where we live, learn, work, and play. What the CP does in this greater cause of God's mission is galvanize our collective, unified efforts to create a missional ecosystem that facilitates this larger vision of Christian mission, impacting all aspects of life with practical and tangible ways to both share and apply the gospel. The CP exists as a way for Christians to participate in Christian mission in multiple ways and in multiple locations. Through the generosity of churches in cooperation, churches in Charleston, South Carolina, can help impact gospel mission not only in their own backyards and neighborhoods, but in Boston, Los Angeles, China, Ukraine, Nigeria, Brazil, or anywhere CP funds are being deployed for the glory of God and the good of our neighbors.

Be the Bridge: Putting It All Together

My ministry as a church planter, pastor, and college professor is dedicated to this idea of "being the bridge," connecting people to God and one another by making disciples of Jesus Christ. This means that as people know God, grow in their maturity as Christians through God's family, and live out God's mission, we can make an eternal impact in people's lives in practical and tangible ways. This mission is informed by a larger ministry vision to see every man, woman, and child exposed to, impacted by, and responding to the gospel where they live, learn, work, and play. That is a phrase we say a lot because it is the heart of our missional DNA. We are an intentionally multiethnic and multigenerational church where every member is a missionary disciple who lives with "Mondays in mind," meaning that we are called to be disciples—the church mobilized—tasked with making disciples in whatever our social context throughout the week. Our systems and structures are dedicated to cultivating what happens when we look at the gospel, God's family, and God's mission as a whole life endeavor. So, how can we galvanize the next generation with this vision to "be the bridge," calling people to participate in God's mission within his community? What follows are some ideas I believe can be helpful.

First, establish relationships with those in younger generations and develop personal connections with them. In a generation that has low trust in institutions, one of the most effective things the church can do is be trustworthy through developing deep relational bonds within it. We want to create an environment where trust and relational equity are cultivated. A key part of relational equity is faithfully demonstrating that you are doing life with them by investing in them and pouring into them. Authentic relationships allow older believers to help younger believers discover their passions and, through discipleship, channel their passions through a biblical missional alignment. We want to help them identify their kingdom gifts (1 Cor. 12:4–11, 28–31; Eph. 4:11–12; Rom. 12:1–8) and give them opportunities to use and grow in that giftedness. Show them how their gifts and passions align with God's mission and serve alongside them. This reminds them that we are in this together. When we cultivate relationships, we can help the next generation of believers find belonging within God's family and develop the bonds of multiethnic and multigenerational relationships when we are unified in our shared identity in Christ.

Second, expand the vision of kingdom effectiveness by connecting generosity and vocation as gifts to the church that are key parts of living out God's mission. In other words, connect giving—financial and talent resources—to vocational calling. This vision should communicate how the local church emboldens its people for ministry outside the four walls of the church, since that is where the majority of ministry takes place. Cultivate a mindset within the church that every believer is a missionary. What one does for a living matters, and one of the crucial roles of the local church is to equip believers for ministry in the broad marketplace. While every member is not going to be a pastor or serve on a church staff, every member is still called to ministry. It does not matter what one's station in life is. Whether a student, stay-at-home parent, or marketplace worker, everyone has a ministry and a sphere of influence where that ministry is to take place. Taking this vision a step further, local churches need to communicate how the CP helps each person fulfill vocational callings for the work of ministry.

When we put our resources together as the church, we are reminding people that what God has called them to do vocationally can have an eternal impact, and we want to help finance those missional efforts. What I am suggesting is connecting how our various vocational callings and our generosity in funding and fueling ministry can be used collectively for local ministry and abroad. This vision reminds people that God has given them passions, talents, and resources to be the church in their context and that the local church is tasked with cultivating a conception of how we are to be the church outside of the Sunday gathering or small group. Ultimately, this vision is about presenting a concept of radical generosity—leveraging our time, talents, and treasure individually and collectively to accomplish the larger mission to make disciples for the glory of God and the good of the city.

Third and finally, we need to share stories of gospel movement by everyday missional disciples within every sphere of life by way of living parables. People are willing to give of themselves and their resources when they can see themselves as part of a movement. The gospel is that movement, the church is God's people mobilized for it, and God's mission is how we participate in it. Stories take the transcendence of God's cause, community, and mission and make it personal and relational, inviting people around them and within the church to share in the beauty of participating, within their context, in the greatest story of all, the gospel. Stories testify to what happens when the church is mobilized for ministry where they live, learn, work, and play. From the "block to the boardroom," every believer has a mission field where stories of gospel transformation can take place, and those stories must be told. When we tell those stories of life change around us, it invites others to see themselves as participants and affirms their place as colaborers in God's harvest. Finally, telling these stories also facilitates missional synergy by creating excitement about what God is doing and how he is using his people to accomplish his purposes. Storytelling produces a certain galvanization within missional community that invites others to become participants of ministry rather than spectators. Because younger generations are cause-oriented, storytelling—testifying about God's redemptive activity around them—will produce an excitement for others to get involved.

Personal Reflection

I am a beneficiary of the CP from being a Southeastern Baptist Theological Seminary graduate to being a church planter and participating in South Carolina Baptist Convention initiatives like the Start Network. The CP has provided me with the resources to effectively live out God's mission in accordance with his calling on my life. My story is not unique, nor should it be. If we are communicating the larger vision of the transcendent cause of the gospel, God's community and God's mission, then we can experience the stories of the transformative work God is doing in and through our obedience to the Great Commission. In the end, it is about God's multiethnic and multigenerational family collaborating in a work that is of eternal significance, pursuing the glory of God and the good of the world around us. I am grateful the Lord in his grace has allowed me to participate in his redemptive work.

Today's and Tomorrow's Mission Field

Scott McConnell

Much of what I will share about today's and tomorrow's mission field stems from my current work in statistics and research. But my motivation to share this information goes back to numerous experiences God has placed in my life.

The most profound influence on my life has been God's Word. Reading it regularly continues to remind me of God's grace extended to me and his love for all people. "For he stands at the right hand of the needy" (Ps. 109:31). "For the Son of Man has come to seek and to save the lost" (Luke 19:10).

Another significant influence has been the diverse people I have met in high school, college, and international travel. As I sought to understand these different people, I saw that each was an image bearer of God. They were valuable, deserved my respect, and had much to offer that made my life better. God gave me a love for them and a deep desire for them to know Jesus Christ.

Another influence stems from my interest in world affairs, politics, cultures, and social trends. In college, I used my electives outside of my major to take courses in urban studies and political science. Through the years, the more I have studied, traveled, or followed world events with interest, the more I have seen the same needs in every culture that can only be met by Jesus Christ.

The final influence that motivates my interest in today's mission field is the countless missions and ministries I have seen up close throughout my life. Living at a missionary-sending headquarters during middle school and high school, I heard many foreign missionaries tell stories of their work. I helped mail newsletters of believers' testimonies to Africa and Asia for missionaries who had served in those places. My first mission trip was to the 500,000-watt Trans World Radio station in Bonaire. I attended church with people who worked closely with Billy Graham. I benefited from numerous evangelical ministries. And God called me to work at Lifeway to serve the local church.

As I have worked with Southern Baptist churches and Southern Baptist entities, I have had the joy to experience our collective heart for sharing the gospel with those who are not yet followers of Christ, as is evidenced in one hundred years of their faithful, sacrificial Cooperative Program (CP) giving. As we consider the trends and the trajectory of missions today, our task is not getting easier. Southern Baptists must continue the cooperative work of pursuing the lost around the world with the gospel, and we must be willing to adjust our methods and our role in this work as we have in generations past.

The U.S. Mission Field Represents a Growing Need

The mission field in the United States has changed in three noteworthy ways in the past one hundred years. The population has grown dramatically. The population has become more diverse ethnically. And recently, population growth has slowed noticeably.

According to the Census Bureau, the U.S. population was 106 million in 1920. It grew to 203 million in 1970 and to 331 million in 2020.[1] Population growth has slowed to just 7.4 percent in the last decade due to lower birth rates and lower immigration. Growth is expected to continue at a low rate until 2080 when the U.S. population is projected to begin declining.[2] Many individual communities have a stagnant population size, and four states ended the last decade with fewer residents than in 2010.[3]

Census data on ethnicity of Americans is harder to compare over time because the questions have changed dramatically through the decades. For example, it was not until 1980 that all Americans were asked if they were Hispanic. While immigrants to the U.S. had come from many different countries, most voluntary immigration had been from European countries. This changed with the passage of the 1965 Immigration and Nationality Act which changed U.S. policy to allow more visas for people from Asia, Latin America, and other non-European regions.

In 1930, the U.S. Census reported that 89 percent of Americans were white and 10 percent Negro.[4] By 1980, the white population declined to 79.7 percent while the black population grew to 11.5 percent. Growth was also seen among the new

Spanish origin category (6.4%) and Asian and Pacific Islanders (1.6%).[5]

Changes in the ethnic makeup of the U.S. accelerated in the next forty years. In 2020, 57.8 percent of American residents were white, 18.7 percent Hispanic or Latino, 12.1 percent black or African American, 5.9 percent Asian, 0.6 percent American Indian or Alaska Native, 0.2 percent Native Hawaiian or other Pacific Islander, 0.5 percent other race, and 4.1 percent two or more races.[6]

The Census Bureau's main series of projections estimate that in 2060, 44.9 percent of the population will be white, 26.9 percent Hispanic, and 13 percent black.[7]

While the number and ethnicity of Americans has been changing, our shared mission involves the hearts of these people. The World Christian Database estimates that in 1900 there were 79,254,000 Christians in North America. This grew to 202,363,000 in 1970 and 254,184,000 in 2000. While growth continued for several years, the database indicates the number of Christians has peaked, with the expectation to plateau at 271 million in 2025. They predict it will decline to less than 257 million in 2050.[8]

The Pew Research Center has also made some future projections about the number of Christians in the United States. Their analysis begins with the current trend line. From 1972 to 2020, the percentage of Americans self-identifying as Christian declined from 90 percent to 64 percent. They then set out four projections for 2070 based on different assumptions if recent trends continue.

Using the Pew data, the best-case scenario is that no additional people switch religions. Even with this unrealistic assumption, the impact of migration, births, and deaths would put Christians at 54 percent of the population. If the rate of switching continues as we have seen recently, it would be 46 percent. Since each generation has seen acceleration in switching away from Christianity and deceleration in those who switch to Christianity, the final projections include these trends estimating the percentage of Americans in 2070 who are Christians to be 39 percent or 35 percent, depending on whether they limit those rates of switching.[9]

The Holy Spirit moved in many Americans to draw them to Christ during much of the first century of the CP. We praise God for this! Statistically speaking, population growth and higher levels of residential moves made church growth easier during that time period. However, the recent rapid decline in population growth is making it increasingly difficult to see new faces visiting our churches. Additionally, new people in our communities include ethnicities that require focused intentionality to welcome them and sometimes proficiency in language skills to reach them.

Changes to Southern Baptist Ministry within the U.S. Mission Field

The mission field of the United States has changed dramatically since 1925. How Southern Baptists have engaged the missional task has also changed significantly. These trends provide context for potentially necessary changes as we look toward the future.

After the depression of 1920–1921, the U.S. economy largely fit the moniker of the Roaring Twenties. However, stability hardly described the finances among Southern Baptist entities. Neither was there a clear doctrinal unity among us going into 1925. But things were changing. The Cooperative Program began in 1925, and the annual SBC meeting also marked the first time Baptists embraced a formal confession of faith, with the approval of the 1925 *Baptist Faith and Message*.

Whether it was the confessional firestorm, the consolidation of financial appeals, delayed impacts from the Spanish flu, or other factors of the time, the SBC had 3,176 fewer churches in 1925 than they had the year before. This is the largest ever annual net loss in SBC-cooperating churches. It happened in the middle of an eight-year stretch that saw a net cooperating church decline six out of eight years. In fact, it took until 1951 for the church total to get back to what it had been in 1922. While the church count was slowly rebuilding, membership doubled in this same time period. In 1925, Southern Baptist churches claimed 3,649,330 members; by 1951 the total membership had grown to 7,373,498.[10]

Another noteworthy report and appeal were made at the 1925 annual meeting by the Sunday School Board (now Lifeway), describing an emerging ministry:

> **Daily Vacation Bible School:** We heartily commend the Board for launching a great program of Bible teaching of the children in the vacation months of the summer through the Daily Vacation Bible School Department. With its sixty hours of training in four weeks, five days a week, three hours a day in our church educational plants that stand idle six days a week, a Daily Vacation Bible School can accomplish wonders for the child and the church. We heartily recommend the department's program as it is being outlined and hope that its goal of ten thousand vacation schools in ten years will be realized. We hope every pastor will seriously

study its claims with a view to have a school in his church at the earliest possible date.[11]

In 1925, the year the CP was born, the first year VBS enrollment was asked on the Annual Church Profile (called the Uniform Associational Letter at the time), with 28,167 reported participants. This next-generation ministry grew rapidly, exceeding a quarter of a million participants in 1937, half a million in 1940, and a million in 1946.[12]

While the typical church VBS would not remain a full summer program as it was first envisioned, the evangelistic effectiveness of this annual event has far exceeded early hopes. Lifeway Research found that the concept has incredible staying power. Six in ten American adults attended Vacation Bible School while growing up. Among those who attended, nine in ten agree they have positive memories about participating, and 89 percent say it positively influenced their spiritual growth. Possibly the best endorsement of VBS comes from American parents; 69 percent agree they will encourage their child to participate in a Vacation Bible School event at a church they do not regularly attend if invited by one of their friends.[13]

Annual Church Profile data for 1925 also reveals high levels of involvement in Sunday school. In that year, 74 percent of all members were enrolled in Sunday school as well. While this percentage dipped a bit in the 1940s, it stayed above 70 percent from 1950 to 1965, during which period some of the fastest growth occurred in the SBC with congregations adding a million members every four to five years.[14]

Over time, Southern Baptists began tracking weekly worship attendance and weekly Sunday school/small group attendance. In the early 1990s between 82 and 86 percent of worship attendees were in a Sunday school class or small group. However, this dropped to 70 percent in 2002 and has been below 66 percent since 2015.[15] Analysis by Lifeway Research has found that this ratio is predictive of future worship attendance within a church. A higher ratio of Sunday school/small group attendance to worship attendance predicts higher worship attendance numbers in five years.[16]

Another trend stands out among Southern Baptist annual statistics: the impact of church planting. The net number of SBC churches took off after World War II. From 1948 to 1959, the number of active SBC churches grew by 5,084, reaching 31,906 total congregations. Church planting continued at a slower but steady pace, adding another 5,879 churches by 1989, bringing the total number of congregations to 37,785. The next twenty years saw a jump of 7,225 churches to 45,010 in 2009. While church planting continued, the total number of members peaked in 2006 at 16,306,246, and weekly worship attendance peaked in 2009 at 6.2 million, revealing weaknesses in many existing SBC churches.[17]

Despite these declines within churches, strong church planting allowed the number of SBC congregations to grow until a peak in 2017. While church planting continues at a rapid pace, a larger number of congregations are currently closing each year. By 2022 there were 3.1 million fewer members of U.S. Southern Baptist congregations than the 2006 peak.[18]

The most recent trends reveal other changes within the SBC that go beyond the volume of churches and people. Between 2000 and 2020 the number of SBC congregations grew by 8 percent from 46,831 to 50,696.[19] Research done by the Ethnic Research Network, using ACP data, shows the way these congregation count trends varied depending on the congregations' largest ethnic group. In that twenty-year span, the number of congregations in which the largest ethnic group was white almost plateaued, only notching upward from 39.3 thousand to 39.4 thousand.[20]

Meanwhile, congregations whose largest ethnic group was not white saw rapid growth. African American congregation counts grew from 2,300 to 3,900; Hispanic congregations grew from 2,200 to 3,400; and Asian congregations grew from 1,300 to 2,100. While smaller in size, growth was also seen in the number of Native American congregations from 354 to 422 and in all other ethnicities from 755 to 1,500 congregations.[21] The Report on Ethnic Diversity and Participation in the SBC stated in 2021, "Since 1990, ethnic and racially diverse congregations have increased . . . from 3.9 percent to 22.3 percent."[22]

In 2022, two language questions were added to the Annual Church Profile. In the first year of asking this information, data was collected from just 9,654 congregations. Yet these Southern Baptist congregations reported having regular worship services in forty-five specific languages. Additionally, several indicated they held worship services in other African and Asian languages. These numbers will continue to grow as churches expand current ministries to include worship services and as more congregations report the languages they use.[23]

The progress we see of disciples being made and congregations forming among different ethnic groups also represents the disciples who, going forward, will be making disciples. Minh Ha Nguyen, director of gift care and data stewardship at the International Mission Board, said, "Ethnic minority leaders want to be considered as part of the mission force and not the mission field. The Great Commission belongs to them, too."[24]

Southern Baptists saw incredible numbers of Americans come to faith in Christ and assimilate into local churches in the twentieth century. This immense blessing challenged us to be good stewards of numerical growth. But as the American culture has changed and fewer people acknowledge Jesus as their Lord, Southern Baptists must shift with these changes. Our challenge today is to focus our energies on being a witness in our communities rather than preparing for crowds in our buildings.

The gospel message has not changed, but our methods of evangelism may have to evolve to fit the people with whom we are sharing that gospel. As more people have no experience with church or the Bible, more and more evangelism will need to take place in personal conversations. Appeals will need to meet people where they are by addressing common needs for hope, purpose, and peace in their lives. Invitations to church are still appropriate and important, but we need to be intentional about explaining the value of church in the message of hope in Christ, now as much as (if not more than) ever.

Outreach can no longer simply be inviting people back to church. Instead, the focus will need to be on introducing people to Jesus Christ. As fewer people in the U.S. have an affinity to Christianity, believers must be willing to demonstrate courage to share the message and value of their faith in everyday conversations. Increasingly, there is also the need for believers to form long-term relationships with these people to ensure they hear and see the gospel repeatedly.

Sunday school and small-group Bible studies, vacation Bible school, gospel-focused preaching, and church planting served Southern Baptists well over the last one hundred years, and they all have an important place in our future as well. Continued faithfulness and innovations in these methods, as well as developing new innovations and methods, will be needed to reach those in the U.S. who are not yet followers of Jesus Christ in the coming century.

The Global Mission Field Today and Tomorrow

The Great Commission calls and compels believers to make disciples of every nation. In 1900, 34.5 percent of the world's population was Christian. It is estimated by the World Christian Database that in 2050, 34.4 percent of the world's population will be Christian. The bad news is this percentage did not grow. The good news is that the spread of Christianity kept pace with rapid global population growth from 1.6 billion in 1900 to an estimated 8.2 billion today. Growth is expected to continue at a slower pace, to 9.7 billion in 2050.[25]

I am confident that in the age to come we will find that the number of names in the Lamb's Book of Life are not restricted by our statistics and estimates. John's Revelation tells us of a "vast multitude . . . which no one could number, standing before the throne and before the Lamb" (Rev. 7:9). Nevertheless, in estimating the size of the church today and the missionary task that awaits our generation, these statistics are helpful.

Important details and shifts in these global religion statistics also inform the task. Between 1900 and 2050, Roman Catholics and Protestants will have shifted in different directions as a share of the world population. Catholics made up 16.4 percent of the global population in 1900 and are expected to be 15.6 percent in 2050. Protestants were 8.3 percent of the population in 1900 and are expected to grow modestly to 9.1 percent in 2050.

Two religious populations that can exist across some of these Christian groups are evangelicals and Pentecostals/charismatics. In 1900, 5.0 percent of the world's population was evangelical Christian. It is estimated that in 2050, 6.4 percent of people in the world will be evangelical Christian. In 1900, less than a tenth of 1 percent of the world's population was Pentecostal; in 2050 it is estimated that 10.6 percent will be Pentecostal.[26]

Among Protestants, much has changed as well. In 1910, the top ten countries by Protestant population were located in North American or Europe. By 2015, only three of the largest were in North America or Europe (United States, United Kingdom, and Germany). Nigeria, Brazil, China, India, Kenya, Indonesia, and Ethiopia have now joined the top ten countries with the largest population of Protestants.[27]

This dewesternization of the location of Protestants is also seen in the list of the largest Protestant denominations in a country. The SBC in the United States is the seventh largest. The largest are the Han house churches in China, Three-Self Patriotic Movement in China, Assembleias de Deus in Brazil, Evangelische Kirche in Deutschland (Germany), the Church of England in the United Kingdom, and the Anglican Church of Nigeria.

The distribution of Christians has also shifted from North to South. In 1970, 57 percent of Christians were in the Global North, and 43 percent were in the Global South. In a stark trend reversal, by 2018, 34 percent were in the Global North, and 66 percent were in the Global South. Since 2018, Africa has been the continent with the highest Christian population.[28]

Many changes over the past one hundred years impact global evangelization today. These changes include increased speed of transportation, multiplication of communication methods, changes in language use, literacy growth, and access to lost people. Missionaries don't have to spend weeks on a ship to reach their mission field. You can get almost anywhere in the world within forty-eight hours. Instead of living from letter to letter in hopes of staying in touch with a few family members or friends, missionaries can talk, text, post pictures, and video chat with folks at home when they are on the field and can talk with friends on the field when they are Stateside.

First, radio broadcasts allowed millions of people to be reached with the gospel without missionaries being physically present among them. Now, a host of new technologies such as email, text, social media platforms, and videoconferencing allows individual believers who know a language and culture to cross continents and borders virtually and instantaneously to connect with people in most parts of the world.

According to Ethnologue, there are 7,168 languages in use in the world today. Roughly 40 percent of languages are now endangered. In other words, the users of 3,045 languages have begun to teach and speak a more dominant language to their children within the community. Many of these endangered languages know fewer than a thousand users remaining. Today, more than half the world's population can speak one of the twenty-three largest languages. These dominant languages are like linguistic interstate highways for communicating the gospel with many in the world today.[29]

While the number of languages is declining, most of the global missionary task requires learning a language other than English in order to effectively communicate the gospel. Even in places where English is spoken as a trade language, relationships and meaningful conversations are often still reserved for the indigenous, or "heart," language.

Most of those in the world who need to hear the gospel do not speak English, although the use of English has grown substantially in the last century. Most Americans speak only English and do not aspire to reach fluency when they take language classes in school. For American believers, learning a second language should be encouraged and celebrated. This opens opportunities to share the gospel with more people in your community and with those in other countries through technology or travel.

Access to Scripture in one's own language is an important part of making disciples of all people. The entire Bible has been translated into 73 languages that are used by six billion people. In addition, the New Testament is available in 1,658 languages, and portions of the Bible have been translated into 1,264 more languages. In total, at least some Scripture is available in 3,658 languages. These languages are spoken by 7.23 billion people (up to 97% of all people).[30]

The World Christian Database estimates that in 1900 a mere 27.6 percent of the global population was literate. A century later that leaped to 76.7 percent, and by 2025 it stands at 84.3 percent. This is expected to continue to grow so that by 2050, 88 percent of the world's population will be literate.[31]

For those who are literate, technology allows churches around the world to easily share Scripture, articles, commentaries, Bible study plans, encouragement, and other teaching materials along with traditional book distribution. Technology also enables many forms of gospel witness to reach people who are less literate. Cell phones or other portable devices can play videos sharing the gospel and audio recordings of Scripture being read in other languages to people from anywhere in the world. Technology has also standardized information on the missionary task, improved the sharing of diverse missionary efforts, and enabled the combination of these reports with other research efforts to generate and update statistics like those in this chapter.

Unreached People Groups

Despite these advances in infrastructure, processes, and communication, there are still people and places in the world today without a gospel witness—people who do not have resources that they understand through which to learn of God's gift of salvation or existing local Christian churches in their area to share the hope of the gospel.

For hundreds of years, the missionary task was defined and directed toward reaching people in countries. This is a valid way of thinking of a destination, a government to issue you a visa, and a portion of a person's identity. But in the 1960s Ralf and Roberta Winters, founders of the U.S. Center for World Mission (now Frontier Ventures), advocated for a focus on unreached people groups in missions.[32] A people group is an ethnolinguistic group with a shared self-identity. They speak the same language and share ethnic factors such as history, customs, and clan identity.[33] Shifting our thinking from country to people group has been helpful because someone's people group matters in evangelism. The Lausanne Movement is a group who works to connect influencers and ideas for global mission. At a 1982 meeting in Chicago, they wrote, "For evangelization purposes, a people group is the largest group within which the Gospel can spread as a church planting movement without encountering barriers of understanding or acceptance."[34]

According to the International Mission Board, there are 7,250 Unreached People Groups (a people group in which less than 2 percent of the population are evangelical Christians). The population of these groups totals almost five billion (4,793,964,310); 336 of these people groups have no known evangelical Christians or churches and no access to major evangelical resources.[35] Let that sink in. There are 3,072 people groups who have no missionary presence today.

According to the International Mission Board, 59 percent of the world's population (4.6 billion people) is considered unreached. This means there are less than 2 percent evangelical Christians within their people group or nearby.[36] The International Mission Board works with The Joshua Project, a research initiative seeking to highlight the ethnic people groups of the world with the fewest followers of Christ. The Joshua Project breaks the world's people groups and their populations into five groups:

- 42.4% Unreached
- 3.1%   Minimally reached
- 6.8%   Superficially reached
- 24.8% Partially reached
- 22.8% Significantly reached[37]

Barriers

While obstacles to sharing the gospel have changed in the past century, many real barriers persist that relate to access and hostility to the gospel. Traditionally, the largest access barrier was getting to people in remote places. Some people who need the gospel are still in remote, difficult to reach places. But urbanization has improved access to many unreached people groups as they migrated from remote locations to urban centers.

In 1900, 14.4 percent of the world's population lived in urban settings. This more than doubled to 36.5 percent in 1970. The urban percentage of the global population has grown to 58.2 percent in 2025 and is expected to reach 68 percent in 2050. This has brought many lost people into the proximity of Christian churches. But within urban centers, significant barriers exist.

Many of those who move to an urban area are relegated to low-paying jobs and are forced to live in substandard housing and even shelters they make out of whatever material they can find. The World Christian Database estimates that in 2050, 1.5 billion people will live in urban slums.[38]

Jesus Christ's death on the cross in our place is good news both for those at the socioeconomic bottom and for those at the socioeconomic top. But physical access can be limited to both groups. In urban slums, some homes can only be accessed through another person's home. You typically have to know someone living there to safely navigate the community. Similarly, upper-class residents in urban apartments or gated communities may only be accessed when accompanied by a resident.

Access to people can also be interrupted, either temporarily or for extended periods of time, due to war, natural disaster, and migration. These factors will change over time, but their frequency, and the size of migrations in particular, have grown substantially. Interruptions to people's lives can create an openness to considering the gospel if they hear it. But these events can also create barriers to accessing these people during these critical times. CP-supported Send Relief, an arm of the North American Mission Board, has established international responses to such events to show the love of Christ by partnering with local churches and believers in sustainable ways.

Many countries will not give a person a visa or permission to enter the country for the purpose of being a missionary. So individuals wanting to take the gospel to one of these countries need another stated reason to be in the country. This can be necessary to have legitimacy with the government, but it also may be needed to have credibility among the people group among whom the believer intends to live. People groups that do not welcome Christianity often reject someone coming to proselytize them without ever affording them a chance to share their message or show the love of Christ. Followers of Christ usually need to have another occupational platform, or government-approved reason, to be present in these communities.

Both governments and local people can also be overtly hostile to those who share the gospel. Open Doors International annually ranks countries based on the level of persecution or hostility toward Christians. In 2023, they identified eleven countries with extremely high, forty-four countries with very high, and twenty-one countries with high levels of persecution of Christians.[39]

Today, more than 360 million Christians suffer high levels of persecution and discrimination for their faith. Worldwide, one in seven Christians now experiences at least "high" levels of persecution or discrimination; one in five in Africa, two in five in Asia, and one in fifteen in Latin America.[40]

Persecution itself cannot stop the spread of the gospel, but it does create barriers to when, where, and how the gospel is shared. While the stories are more difficult to document numerically, historically there have been occasions in which the gospel has spread rapidly in hostile places. The risk a believer takes in sharing his or her faith with someone in these hostile places is not lost on the hearer. They may listen more intently, knowing this message is valuable enough for you to risk your well-being to share it.

Conclusion

Tomorrow's mission field includes both those who are among an unreached people group and those who are lost and living where churches have already been established. We must continue focused efforts to establish gospel witnesses among unreached people groups. The United States and other traditionally sending countries will also need to work hard at partnering with local churches around the world.

As people come to follow Christ among a people group and churches are formed, the responsibility to evangelize this people group shifts from vocational missionaries to local churches. These local churches and pastors still may need training, resources, fellowship, encouragement, and joint missions ventures with believers in other places to effectively evangelize lost people in their communities. Increasingly, ours may not be the only missionary presence in a community. We will be called upon to be one member of the body of Christ, allowing the local church to take the lead and to determine what service(s) we may need to provide.

The apostle Paul's analogy of the church being a body can apply not only to a local congregation but also to our future missions efforts. There will be seasons in which we need to offer a local church in another country the gift of mercy or knowledge or wisdom or service or teaching or encouragement or giving. We are used to providing leadership, but increasingly the global church will need us to offer other gifts. One of the greatest tests for our generation will be whether we are willing to have a more modest role in the body of Christ while still giving our all for the sake of the gospel.

We often want to meet needs with financial gifts. There will be times when we need to continue to do this. But this often comes with unintended consequences that tend to change the relationship with that individual believer or local church. Financial gifts often mean we are no longer a partner; we are a patron. As equals in the missionary task, Western believers must increasingly put relationship first and seek to partner with spiritual gifts. It is not that we should never finance global missions efforts, but how we fellowship with and learn from global believers will be an important measure of our missions involvement going forward.

It can be easy for us as Southern Baptists to take pride in how many missionary efforts we support when we give through the CP. There was a season beginning in the 1950s when the United States was supplying two-thirds of the forty-three thousand Protestant missionaries around the world.[41]

As we look at the global missions task and the changes in the church today, it is humbling. The average Christian today is not in the North and not in the West. We are not the center of the church. We are not the originating point of missions. The growth of churches in Africa, Asia, and South America has allowed them to send increasing numbers of missionaries. The church of Jesus Christ has always had multiple centers, and disciples in all locations have been called to go. Let us focus on being grateful for the missions efforts we can support through the CP and being good stewards of these opportunities.

We celebrate the thousands of Southern Baptist and other evangelical missionaries who have devoted their lives to the Great Commission in the last century. We celebrate progress in the availability of resources to support churches. We celebrate progress in Scripture translation and access to evangelical witness around the world. Yet we are humbled that lostness remains, at least statistically, at essentially the same place it was 125 years ago.

Not unlike 1925, we live in a world in which a staggering number of people need to hear the gospel while some question whether they want to remain Southern Baptist. May we seek the Lord of the harvest together, to continue sending workers from among us. And may we remain faithful in cooperating to share the gospel in innovative ways in our generation.

Global researcher Jason Mandryk shares the following encouragement in the face of our immense task: "Urgency and patience must go hand in hand in world evangelization. For reasons we cannot fathom, God's agenda awaits our obedience."[42]

Mandryk surfaced a helpful quote from John P. Jones's book, *The Missionary Challenge*. Jones was a Welsh-born Congregationalist missionary who served in India for many years around the turn of the twentieth century. Jones's insights are as applicable to our outlook on the missionary task today as when he wrote this in 1910.

> This enterprise is not only the greatest that the world has ever known; it is also the most difficult of achievement. Let us not fall into the error of thinking that Christianizing the nations and bringing the world to the feet of our Lord is the task of a day or of a generation. Its magnitude should be fully realized by the people of God in order that they may prosecute it with all seriousness and brace themselves up with a faith that is invincible, with a courage that will never yield, and with a purpose to lean hard upon God, that He may lead in the conflict and give patience in the work to the very end.[43]

Personal Reflection

I have been a member of Hermitage Hills Baptist Church for more than twenty-seven years since moving to Tennessee from Philadelphia, Pennsylvania. As my family has given to our church, we have been aware they give a percentage of receipts to the CP. That work sometimes sounds distant because it is so massive and diverse. But as I reflect, numerous experiences have made CP-funded ministries personally meaningful.

From our own church, we have seen one friend become a Journeyman and other friends follow God's call to work full-time overseas with the International Mission Board. Hearing their experiences, we are grateful for their training, development, and financial support.

Our studies at Lifeway Research have included numerous research projects in concert with state conventions, the North American Mission Board, the International Mission Board, the Ethics & Religious Liberty Commission, and the Executive Committee. At each entity there are kingdom-minded people serving faithfully in specialized ways. As we partnered to learn more about an aspect of ministry, I would see their heart, notice their expertise, and see God's work through them.

In our first Latin American study, I stayed with Joe and Kim Busching in Caracas. They gathered local church leaders seeking to reach this city whose millions of residents knew some things about God, but few had a relationship with him. There and later in Peru they modeled supporting existing churches in megacities in Latin America.

In a research visit to Buenos Aires, I stayed in a seminary building with plaques on the walls recognizing the long-standing partnership of Southern Baptists helping establish Christian education among Baptists in Argentina. As religious liberty, human dignity, and respect have come under attack in the United States, I have seen the ERLC stand up for biblical values. As I have regularly sat down with student cohorts, I have seen the impact of our seminaries on the next generation of pastors, missionaries, educators, and church staff. One of those is my son-in-law, who is finishing studies at one of our seminaries and serving as a youth pastor in a local church. My wife, Debbie, has trained VBS trainers through our state convention.

Of the hundreds of firsthand encounters with the work of the CP, none has impacted me more than when my daughter went to college at Austin Peay University here in Tennessee. She was outside of our daily influence and in the Lord's hands. When Debbie and I learned she was enjoying the ministry of the Baptist Collegiate Ministry on campus, we were beyond grateful.

CP funds paid for a building on campus where the students meet regularly. Local churches come alongside this ministry through their association to provide weekly meals and ministry opportunities. A faithful staff member, Stacy Murphree, invests in students and student leaders to share the gospel and disciple college students. CP ministry through our state convention impacted our daughter's life in ways we could not have planned if we tried.

15

A Charge for Our Future

Daniel Dickard

One hundred years of Cooperative Program (CP) participation is behind us, but what lies before us? Southern Baptists stand at an intersection moment. The denomination which we love finds herself at a point of convergence. Navigating the uncharted waters of our one sacred effort moving forward will not be easy, but Southern Baptists have all we need to sail any choppy waters that may lie before us on our cooperative voyage.[1] We have the Word of God as our compass, the Spirit of God as our guiding Captain, the mission of God as our directional aim, and a cooperative spirit as our unmitigated resolve. Mark Twain famously quipped, "What are the two most important days in your life? The day you are born and the day you find out why."[2] With each passing year, Southern Baptists must remember not only the day our cooperative sacred effort began, but we must likewise remember *why* our cooperative sacred effort began.

For Southern Baptists, an important day came in May 1845 when William Bullein Johnson was elected as our first president and our cooperative mission began. As the first convention convened, the following resolution was adopted: "Resolved, that for peace and harmony, and in order to accomplish the greatest amount of good, and for the maintenance of those scriptural principles on which the General Missionary Convention of the Baptist denomination of the United States was originally formed, it is proper that this Convention at once proceed to organize a Society for the propagation of the Gospel."[3]

Since that historic day, Southern Baptists have been a Great Commission people. The SBC is a family of churches that believe we can make a greater influence for the kingdom of God together than we can separately and independently. As the old African proverb states, "If you want to go fast, go alone; if you want to go far, go together." Southern Baptists believe that together we can go further with the mission of God. We believe that together we can plant more churches. We believe that together we can engage more unreached people groups. We believe that together we can pursue the lost, with Christ. We believe that together our evangelistic arm is stronger and our gospel reach is wider. As we look to fulfill the Great Commission in this next chapter of our journey as a convention of churches, it will be imperative that we remember *why* we partner together.

Southern Baptists join our hands, hearts, and heads together for the propagation of the gospel, the joy of the nations, and the redemption of the lost. Inevitably, there will be difficulties, challenges, and even choppy waters ahead. The real issue is not that we will experience challenges and difficulties among our Southern Baptist family but how we handle such challenges and difficulties as they come. George Mueller once said, "Ninety percent of the difficulties of life are overcome when hearts are ready to do the Lord's will, whatever it may be."[4] As we seek the will of God together, may it be with a laser-focused zeal in evangelism, missions, and the propagation of the gospel to the nations.

It has been said that the real measure of a person is not *how much* is said about that person but *what* is said about that person. Could it be that the real measure of the SBC, moving forward, is not how much is said about our collective efforts but what is said about our collective efforts? When the new history books are written generations from now, may we have the same tenacity toward togetherness that a previous generation did, and may we have the same boldness to impact lostness, one life at a time, as did our founding Southern Baptist ancestors.[5] So what will it take for Southern Baptists to navigate the future and build upon our legacy of cooperative togetherness? Southern Baptists, moving forward, must avoid unnecessary distractions and lay aside unneeded barriers that would prevent us from the fulfillment of our cooperative efforts. In order to fulfill the assignment of intercongregational financial cooperation, it will require seven foundational pillars: a call to persistent prayer, an unwavering commitment to biblical truth, convictional agreement in doctrinal essentials, benevolent charity in theological differences, a posture of congregational yieldedness, a presence-centered people, refocus in mission and ministry, and sacrificial generosity.

A Call to Persistent Prayer

The history of the SBC is a record that cannot be written apart from understanding the value and emphasis of persistent prayer.[6] From its inception, Southern Baptists have been a praying people. The clarion commitment to prayer must not be a value of the past that is discarded in the present or future. Prayer must remain an indispensable foundation of Southern Baptists moving forward. The reason Southern Baptists must remain committed to the discipline of prayer is because prayer is our spiritual lifeline. Too often, Christians and churches treat prayer as an emergency 911 call. Prayer, however, is much more than sending spiritual distress signals to God. Prayer is continual and constant dependency, whether trouble is near or far. In other words, prayer is our expression of full-scale reliance on God. Prayer is when our need for God gets a voice. There are many things we can do, but there is one thing we must do as Southern Baptists: pray. When our family of churches is committed to unwavering prayer, it is an acknowledgment of our divine reliance. Needy people pray, and prayer is when our need for God gets a voice.

Prayer cannot be *a* ministry of Southern Baptists. If we are to be an effective convention of churches in our collective efforts, prayer is to be the *first* ministry of Southern Baptists. It must be the first ministry above all others. Why? The future success of the SBC is not contingent on our past successes, well-equipped agencies, thoughtful strategies, or beloved institutions. Our future success will rise and fall on our dependence on God and on his blessings poured out to us as we seek him. Southern Baptists would do well to remember that Jesus launched the early church not as powerful preachers shared eloquent words of human wisdom but as dependent believers gave themselves to the ministry of prayer (Acts 1:14–2:4). A convention of churches will not rise because of the giftedness of its leaders, the excellences of its programs, or the strength of its agencies; a convention of churches will rise when dependent believers lower themselves in prayer. This must not be casual prayer or convenient prayer. The type of prayer that will be required for our future success is tenacious prayer. The prayers that God hears are those persistently tenacious prayers (Matt. 7:7; Luke 18:1–9). The power of God at work in our lives often comes down to the right attitude at work within us: deference or indifference. The attitude of deference yields to God's will but doesn't stop praying; the attitude of indifference stops prayer because some assume God isn't listening or doesn't care. The truth of the matter is that Satan is not alarmed by Southern Baptist institutions or our feeble efforts. But he is severely weakened when believers unite their hearts to God in prayer.

The fulfillment of our cooperative efforts begins here. Prayer must be to Southern Baptists what wet is to water. Christians do not pray because we need more of us; we pray because we need more of God. We do not pray because we have it all figured out; we pray because God does. We do not pray because we have it all under control; we pray because we do not have control, but there is a sovereign One who does. We do not pray to demonstrate our self-righteousness; we pray because he is righteous, and we need more of his righteousness in our lives. We do not pray because we know all there is to know about God; we pray because this is what God wills for our lives. We do not pray to arm wrestle God into submission and bring him around to our way of thinking; we pray so that God can wrestle our wayward spirits into submission and bring us around to his way of thinking. In other words, prayer is for us, but it is not about us. Prayer is about God. That is, prayer is more dialogue than monologue. If prayer is a monologue, it is likely that we, as a convention of churches, are trying to get our will done in heaven; if prayer is a dialogue, the implication is that God accomplishes his perfect will on earth as it is in heaven.

The greatest strength of the SBC moving forward will begin with our most determined weakness. We must admit our weakness. God is attracted to weakness. God does not resist those who possess humility and admit how desperately they need him. Our weakness makes room for his power, and God's power comes when we are dependent in prayer. D. Martyn Lloyd Jones once said, "Man is at his greatest and highest when upon his knees and he comes face to face with God."[7] Prayer cannot be an addendum to the mission of Southern Baptists; it is the baseline of our collective ministry efforts. We can accomplish more in one minute of dependent prayer with God than we can in a thousand hours of cooperative effort in our own strength and power. Charles Spurgeon said, "If God be near a church, it must pray. And if he be not there, one of the first tokens of his absence will be a slothfulness in prayer."[8] The same is true for a convention of churches. If God be near a convention of churches, there will be prayer; if he is not, there will be slothfulness in prayer.

An Unwavering Commitment to Biblical Truth

Faithful ministry in difficult days requires complete confidence in the Word of God. There is little to no objection that Southern Baptists are ministering in difficult days. The real question is not, Are we ministering in a difficult day? but rather, Will we be faithful to the Word of God in these difficult days? Every Christian is tempted to drift spiritually. So, too, is every church and every denomination. People do not drift toward truth; they drift away from truth. The future success of the SBC then, and our intercongregational financial cooperation, is contingent upon our willingness to hold fast to the clear teachings of Scripture.[9] The importance of truth cannot be overvalued. But we must also be reminded that there is a difference between valuing truth and valuing our version of the truth.

Theological tribalism that lacks grace, is rooted in theological preference, and is bent toward doctrinal superiority will destroy churches, organizations, and conventions. Our use of Scripture, as a convention of churches, should be like a precise scalpel in a skilled surgeon's careful fingertips rather than a heavy club in a reckless bully's clinched fist. When the Bible is used as a heavy club in a bully's grip, it turns friends into foes. When the Bible is used as a precise scalpel in a skilled surgeon's hand, with a warm and tender heart, it creates the kind of grace-and-truth Christians our Lord desires.

But how will we know if Southern Baptists possess an unwavering commitment to biblical truth? First, our churches must be convinced that all Scripture is given to us by God. Second Timothy 3:16 reminds us that "all Scripture is inspired by God and is profitable for teaching, for rebuking, for correcting, for training in righteousness." This passage is arguably the strongest statement the Bible makes about itself. It asserts the divine nature and dynamic work of the Scriptures. The Bible claims to be the Word of God, not the words of mere men (1 Thess. 2:13). The Bible is not a word about God; it is the Word of God. When it comes to the Bible, God is both the divine Source and the ultimate Author of all Scripture. The Bible is the product of the Holy Spirit's supernatural breath (2 Pet. 1:21). Scripture has been recorded by supernatural operation. The Bible is the Word of God. It has God as its source; it has Jesus as its supreme object; it has salvation as its purposed end. The Bible is not a human book about God; it is God's self-revelation. When God speaks, the Bible speaks. When the Bible speaks, God speaks. Thus, an unequivocal declaration that Scripture is the voice of God is a sure litmus test for our unwavering commitment to biblical truth.

Second, to possess an unwavering commitment to biblical truth, our churches must be convinced that the Bible is without error, fully trustworthy, and sufficient to accomplish its purpose of leading believers to God.[10] The inerrancy of the Scriptures and our affirmation of its epistemological truthfulness must be a nonnegotiable in our doctrinal position moving forward. A truthful God could not provide us an untruthful word. An attack on the nature of Scripture is an attack on the character of God. A genuine belief in the inerrancy of the Scriptures should create an attitude of trust in the God of the Scriptures. In other words, for Southern Baptists, the volume of Scripture's voice in our ears is in direct proportion to the response of our obedience in our hearts. And when God speaks, how we respond to the will of God through the Word of God determines the intensity of his voice.

When the Bible is seen as fully trustworthy, it becomes an authority that guides our life rather than the mere suggestion of good advice. So, scriptural inerrancy and authority are critical, but so too is scriptural sufficiency. That is, Southern Baptists must affirm the conviction that Scripture is sufficient to accomplish its purposes. Second Timothy 3:14–15 reminds us of the need to affirm scriptural sufficiency: "You know those who taught you, and you know that from infancy you have known the sacred Scriptures, which are able to give you wisdom for salvation through faith in Christ Jesus." A common follow-up question to the aforementioned verse is, "Does the Bible save us?" The answer is no. The Bible doesn't save; Jesus does. But a connection does exist because only through the Bible's special revelation do we know about Jesus. That is to say, if salvation is a house at the end of a long road, the Bible is the road that takes us to that house.

Finally, if our churches are to have an unwavering commitment to biblical truth, we must be a people who not only believe the Bible and preach it, but we must likewise be a people who live out its truths. My fear is not that Southern Baptists will swiftly depart from saying we believe the Word of God. My greatest fear as a fellow pastor in the SBC is that we would be a people who affirm the right things about the Scripture, but our practical actions do not align with our biblical affirmations. We must not just be a people who merely say we believe the Bible. We must be a people whose words and witness align. We must be a people whose doctrine and duty coalesce. Our commitment to biblical truth begins in the mind, but it leads us to a mission. Nothing can flow to the sanctuary of the heart and hands unless it first passes through the lobby of the mind. Thus, an unwavering commitment to biblical truth always starts in the mind, but it doesn't stay there.

Convictional Agreement in Doctrinal Essentials—Benevolent Charity in Secondary Differences

The third foundational pillar to intercongregational financial cooperation among Southern Baptists will require convictional agreement in doctrinal essentials with benevolent charity in secondary theological differences. An important distinction is needed here. This is not to say that Southern Baptists should loosen our doctrinal positions or minimize truth.[11] The minimization of biblical truth is the irrelevance of churches and conventions. If anything, our theological convictions and doctrinal affirmations must be stronger than ever. A confused world will require courageous and convictional churches. The world is noisy; our convictions, therefore, must be clear. The point is not that truth is minimized but rather that truth is to be held in humility. There is a difference between holding to biblical truth and holding to your version and/or interpretation of biblical truth. The success of the SBC will require benevolent charity in theological differences while maintaining convictional agreement in doctrinal essentials as stated in *The Baptist Faith in Message 2000*. In order to accomplish this end, two realities are necessary.

First, it is necessary that we affirm the importance of biblical convictions. Everyone has convictions. The real question is, Are they biblical convictions? At this point a bifurcation between beliefs and convictions must be made. Someone has said that a belief is something you hold onto while a conviction is something that holds onto you. Biblical convictions, rooted in the timelessness of Scripture, do not change. Nor should they. Why? A conviction is not something you discover; it is something you purpose in your heart based on the revelation of Scripture (cf. Dan. 1–3). In other words, convictions on the inside will always show up on the outside, in a person's lifestyle. And what are the external evidences of such convictions? Biblical conviction is the product of three things that characterize the Christ follower:

1. The commitment to Scripture as one's authority
2. The construction of specific beliefs and convictions based on that authority
3. The courage to act on those convictions

The implications are far-reaching. It means there is a recognition of Scripture as inspired and thus inerrant and the final word. The Bible is a compass to guide believers in the foggy malaise of life. It is a well-constructed map that brings about a well-ordered life. Whereas the commitment to Scripture as one's authority is the starting point of a conviction, it doesn't end there. It also requires the construction of specific beliefs based on that authority. The authority of the Scriptures leads us to construct specific beliefs. But there is one more step: not only the construction of the belief but the application of the belief. We hold tightly to certain beliefs, not because they seem good or they are popular in the moment; we hold tightly to certain beliefs because we love the God who gave us perfect commands. Obedience flows not from fear but from love. And those who love God have the courage to act on convictions. Those who love God are willing to be clear, even in the face of fear.

Second, not only is it necessary that we affirm biblical convictions, but we do so with benevolent charity. Southern Baptists must not only see the best in one another, but we must also believe the best about one another. Giving another Christian leader the benefit of the doubt, especially in our Convention of partnering churches, should be our default instinct. Sure, good debates are needed. Intense dialogue may even be necessary at times. But assuming motives and committing character assassinations without understanding the position of another Christian is not the spirit of Jesus. Partnering churches should begin with the posture of listening first and doing so with the best of intentions. It has been said that those who lead well are those who can articulate the positions of their opponents to such a degree that the opponent says, "Yes, that is exactly what I believe." It is my observation that digital dialogue in the twenty-first century argues before it listens. Such tactics, if continually applied to the work of Southern Baptists in the years ahead, will cripple our cooperative mission. We must believe the best in one another and not misassign motives or malign character unfairly if we are to move forward in cooperative mission.

A Posture of Congregational Yieldedness

The study of language teaches us that when a new word comes into an existing dictionary, it is at the expense of an existing word that is subsequently pushed out. The terms *surrender* and *yieldedness* can be scarcely found in the vernacular of many Christians today. Instead, the term *commitment* is used. This is a subtle change with massive implications. The idea of commitment implies that you are in charge; the idea of surrender implies that God is at the helm. The Christian life, however, is the surrendered life.[12] Christianity is not about what we can do for God but rather what God in Christ does in us and through us. If Southern Baptists are to faithfully steward the one sacred effort before us, it will require a heroic spirit of surrender and yieldedness.

But what does congregational yieldedness look like in the age of hyperindividuality? Congregational yieldedness is when churches assume a posture of humility. It is when deference is valued above desire and when the ethos of the church is to meet the needs of others rather than meeting the needs of self. In short, congregational yieldedness is to assume the best in others, believe the best in others, and strive for togetherness in a gentle, humble, and lowly posture. There is much talk about church growth and denominational growth these days. But the reality is that congregational humility is the soil from which denominational growth occurs. A convention of churches will rise when its leaders lower themselves in humility. The future success or failure of the SBC will be measured by the amount of courage we possess with the Scriptures in our hands and the humility we possess in our hearts.

Humility is a missing virtue, however, among worldly leaders today. Humility cannot be a missing virtue in Christian leaders. A posture of lowliness was the posture of Jesus from Bethlehem's manger to Calvary's cross. That same posture of lowliness is what will be needed to partner together as a convention of churches, to get people to the Savior. "Adopt the same attitude of Christ Jesus," Paul wrote. "He humbled himself" (Phil. 2:5, 8). The SBC is a conglomeration of differing churches with one singular mission. It will require wholesale surrender among leaders and a spirit of deference among our members if we are to have success in our cooperative mission. We sacrifice and yield to one another on this side of the bridge because we understand what is on the other side of that bridge: reaching the nations with the gospel.

Presence-Centered People

There is an ever-present temptation in the heart of every church leader to be attracted to good things and not the right things. Attracting people to our Convention of churches is a good thing, but attracting the presence of God in our churches is even more important. If our driving goal as Southern Baptists is to attract as many people as possible, we will settle for gimmicks. If our goal is to attract the presence of God, we will seek the Lord, obey the Scriptures, pray diligently, evangelize the lost, and stay laser-focused on the mission.

The success of Southern Baptists moving forward is contingent on desiring the right things.[13] If we want to see greater intercongregational cooperation, another pillar will be desiring God more than anything else. The greatest shift in ministry that makes an eternal difference is when churches move from attempting to attract consumers and to making a deliberate effort to attract God's presence. The delight of a denomination is when we aim to attract God's presence over our preferences. We cannot do the work of God without the power of God, and the power of God flows out of the presence of God. Jesus told his disciples in Acts 1:8, "But you will receive power when the Holy Spirit has come on you, and you will be my witnesses in Jerusalem, in all Judea and Samaria, and to the ends of the earth."

A concern of mine, as a fellow Southern Baptist pastor, is not that our churches lose a desire for God's power. Most churches want God's power. My fear is that our churches will want the power of God but not want God himself. They might be tempted to want all the things God can do but, in the midst of that, not want God. There is a word for that: idolatry. Even if we want the best things—people to be saved, churches to be planted, revival to come to our denomination—if we want those things and not God himself, that is idolatry. As Southern Baptists, we must be presence-centered people and not program-centered or personality-centered people. We have to want something more than God's power or human personality; we must desire God's presence above all else.

Refocus in Mission and Ministry

There is a high cost, often hidden, in taking the gospel to difficult places. We are at a pivotal moment in the life of our Southern Baptist family where there must be a refocus of mission and ministry. There are many values to which we have held tightly that need to be celebrated—values such as denominational cooperation, sacrificial giving, international missions, church planting, and evangelism. What is needed is not new values but a recommitment to old ones. David Livingstone reportedly said, "God has one Son and made Him a missionary."[14] As Southern Baptists refocus on our combined mission and ministry, we must remember that it starts with the mission. Most churches do not quickly remove the pulpit and stop preaching the gospel to the pew. Instead, they are no longer missionaries to their neighbors. Many are the churches in our convention that preach the Bible. But it is becoming increasingly rare that churches maintain theological fidelity and missional engagement. The evidence is in our declining baptism numbers.[15]

The tension we face moving forward is that we must be both theologically sound and missionally active. The lack of missional engagement could be an indictment not on our stated theological beliefs but our practical ones. In other words, a convention of churches devoid of evangelism and missions is not simply ineffective; it is theologically anemic. Pride in confessional statements about our mission without the actualization of that mission is not only defective missiology; it is flawed Christology.[16] The church's mission is not a suggestion for a few eager churches; it is the marching orders for the entire church.

Now, what will keep us from focus in ministry? Busyness and drift. One of the greatest distractions to hearing from God is busyness. If Satan cannot corrupt us, he will distract us. An overloaded calendar is often one of Satan's greatest tools to keep us from hearing from God. Efficiency is a good thing. Hard work is also commendable. But it is possible to put good things on our calendars and miss God altogether. The biblical author of Hebrews encourages us not to drift spiritually (Heb. 2:1). A ship that drifts is a ship that will eventually shipwreck. In other words, the Scriptures teach us to be careful. If we do not want to be spiritually shipwrecked, we must be anchored to Christ. The reality is that spiritual drift can occur personally, congregationally, and denominationally. Most people do not try to destroy their life, character, and reputation. Most people do not say, "I am going to do this explosive, terrible thing." Drift happens subtly, insidiously, one step at a time. We begin with small concessions and choices that compromise our character.

Big moral earthquakes typically do not happen overnight. It is not like a blowout on a tire; it is like a small leak. It happens when we drift mentally and spiritually. It can even happen in church. We serve in ministries but spend no personal time with the Lord. We get caught up in doing for the Lord rather than being with the Lord. We love leading worship more than worshipping God himself. Each of us is susceptible to spiritual drift. Our walk with God is the most crucial thing in our lives. If we blow it there, it doesn't matter what kind of job we have, how much money we own, or what kind of preacher, missionary, teacher, or educator we are. Spiritual drift in a denomination which refuses to do a U-turn will eventually result in a tragic wreck, and the collateral effect is denominationally damaging.

So, what is the answer? Obedience. One act of obedience to Christ is more important than hours of unapplied knowledge. A wavering heart is a wandering heart, and wondering hearts want things other than God. No one drifts into a holy life. No one drifts into sanctification and godly living. No one drifts into obedience. As Christians, we will always flow against the current of the world and the riptides of culture where there are sin, disobedience, wickedness, and evil. Drifting is dangerous. You do not drift upstream; you drift downstream. You never drift toward God but always away from him. You do not drift toward strong beliefs but away from them. That subtle, slow, imperceptible drift can happen to nearly anyone. Here is a principle we must remember: disobedience is spiritual inattention. And spiritual inattention doesn't always happen on purpose; it happens by neglect.

Drifting is caused by neglect. It is a neglect and failure to walk with God. A failure to spend time in the Word and on your knees in prayer. A failure to take the Christian life seriously. This type of neglect is due to inattention. This kind of neglect is what causes drifting. We neglect the things of God, and neglect produces a casualness in the Christian life. It brings about a laissez-faire attitude that drifts along with the cultural current. The progression is real: casual spirituality leads to coolness, which eventually takes us to the cliff of carelessness. It is discomforting to realize that we are not where we ought to be with the Lord and not where we want to be. It is even more alarming when we do not know how we got there.

Sacrificial Generosity

The final pillar of intercongregational cooperation is a determination to be sacrificially generous. The CP's strength is in numbers but not in church size. Southern Baptists have learned that we can do more together than we can alone. We must not assume that the success of the CP is limited to a few large, flagship churches. What makes the CP appealing is that any church, of any size, in any location, can make a large dent in spiritual darkness. It has been said that there are not big churches and small pastors; there are just churches and pastors. Each church is part of this mission. It will require radical generosity from every partnering church for us to send more missionaries to the field. It will require big hearts to fulfill a big vision. The heroic spirit Southern Baptists need moving forward is one in which we collectively say, "Lord, I will go anywhere for you, provided it is forward."[17] Looking and leaning forward, for Southern Baptists, will require that we give a little more so the gospel can go a lot further. God is not dependent on us to fulfill his missionary task. But he invites us into his mission. That is why we call it the Great Commission. It is his mission, and we have a small part in the thousands of ways God is at work in the world. So together we can do more, but it will require sacrificial generosity.

Conclusion

Every Christian has a divine assignment. Every church has a divine mission. Every denomination has a divine duty. For each, it is the fulfillment of the Great Commission, for the glory of God and the good of the nations. The effectiveness of the SBC moving forward will be contingent upon remembering why we partner together. We exist not for ourselves, but we partner for the sake of the nations. The Great Commission is our one aim, and the heavenly picture of Revelation 7:9 is our end: "After this I looked, and there was a vast multitude from every nation, tribe, people, and language, which no one could number, standing before the throne and before the Lamb. They were clothed in white robes with palm branches in their hands."

Jim Elliott famously said, "Wherever you are, be all there."[18] Southern Baptists, we have the opportunity to join God where he is at work. But we must be all there. God is working. The question is, Are we joining him in that work, or are we simply watching? A new generation of Southern Baptist leaders must lean into our cooperative commitments with relentless determination if we are to steward our season successfully to the glory of God. The effectiveness of the SBC moving forward will depend on our remembering why we partner together. We exist not for ourselves, but we partner for the sake of the nations. The Great Commission is our one aim, and the heavenly picture of Revelation 7:9 is our end. In closing, the humble farmer knows that he eats the fruit of trees he did not grow and drinks the water of wells he did not dig. Similarly, a new generation of Southern Baptists needs to be reminded that we are benefactors of spiritual fruit that was sown by a previous generation, and we are recipients of spiritual wells dug by our denominational ancestors. If humility is the soil from which spiritual growth occurs, then a humble posture of togetherness will be the soil in which the next generation of Southern Baptists plants its new ministry trees.

Personal Reflection

It is difficult to share my story about how the CP blessed me without giving the broader story of God's faithfulness to my family in the generations that preceded me. My father, who is a Southern Baptist pastor in South Carolina, is one of eight children. His dad (my grandfather) could not read and write his own name when he passed away at the age of sixty-three. At that time, no one in my extended family had ever graduated from high school. We were poor country farmers, far from five-star prospects in the eyes of some churches. But Rev. Joe Trodder of Corinth Baptist Church in Easley, South Carolina, a bivocational pastor who ministered most of his life in ministerial obscurity, was faithful to visit my family regularly despite our financial and educational shortcomings.

Pastor Trodder did not see my extended family the way many in the world did; he saw my family as Christ did. Pastor Trodder's name rarely, if ever, appeared in a Baptist newspaper or a church growth magazine. But his ministry was marked by faithfulness. Each month, he prayed that God would save those in my family and asked God to call the youngest two boys into ministry. By God's grace, those prayers were answered. The faithfulness of one pastor, who was more concerned about the souls of an illiterate family separated from Christ than he was the applause of men or growing a congregation that would be filled with members and respectable in the eyes of the world, set the example for the pastor I desire to be today. Pastor Trodder was a faithful pastor who believed Southern Baptists could do more together. His church gave generously through the CP. God used Pastor Trodder's missionary zeal and evangelistic steadfastness to introduce my father and his seven brothers and sisters to the church he pastored, and members of that CP-supporting church would lead them to the Lord.

Two of the brothers would later be called to ministry in Southern Baptist churches. These brothers went to Southern Baptist seminaries, directly benefiting from the CP. They began pastoring Southern Baptist churches that gave faithfully through our CP. I was born into one of those churches. God called me to ministry at the age of fifteen. Soon thereafter, I went to a Southern Baptist school where the CP helped lower tuition to make theological education affordable for me. I went on to Southwestern Baptist Theological Seminary, where I was a CP recipient as an MDiv student and a PhD student. I now pastor a Southern Baptist church that gives to the CP. It would be an understatement to say that the CP has been a blessing to me personally. And what it has done for me, it has done for thousands of others who possessed the call of God on their lives. *Solia de Gloria.*

Afterword

Tony Wolfe and W. Madison Grace II

One hundred years have passed, but the mission of Christ's churches remains and the need for intercongregational financial cooperation on that mission is greater today than ever before. The Cooperative Program of Southern Baptists (CP) is a tool in the hands of a unified and consecrated people. Should our unity dissolve, no mechanistic program can recover the effectiveness or the sacredness of our efforts. Our unity is as it must be, a unity of purpose.

"May they also be one in us, so that the world may believe you sent me," prayed the Lord Jesus to the Father (John 17:21). It is there, in that purest of unity, that we experience the strange glory shared by the Father and the Son. It is there that the world is compelled to believe the gospel we unite to proclaim. The Spirit of God knits our hearts together in this bond of peculiar peace, if we will endeavor to "[make] every effort to keep" it (Eph. 4:3). This Spirit-led walk of unity of purpose is the only walk worthy of the calling we have received in Christ (Eph. 4:1). For one hundred years, the CP has been evidence of that singular focus, that oneness of heart and mind.

As we celebrate the milestone of one hundred years of the CP, it is important to reflect again on our own spirit of cooperation, our present and future unity of purpose. As the authors in this volume have demonstrated over and over again, the desire to engage the world with Great Commission effort drove Baptists, and especially Southern Baptists, onward in their efforts. They saw it as a divine and sacred effort to unite in order to equip and send out God-called men and women for kingdom advance. More than a mere funding mechanism, the CP was a catalyst to change hearts. Through participation in giving to missional purposes, Southern Baptists believed themselves missionary participants. As their money went out from their churches to the world, so too did the gospel go out. And, as we have seen, the program did not only increase faraway missional engagement, but local churches were ignited with evangelistic fervor to reach their own communities as they cooperatively gave to reach the nations.

The CP is a mechanism, but it is one that does more than provide funding to Southern Baptists entities. It is an opportunity to hold hands together as Southern Baptists to engage the world for Christ. Small churches and large churches are unified in the purpose of kingdom work. With our sent missionaries, we rejoice when souls are saved around the globe because of the unified purpose we share. In the same way, when local churches send out their members to our seminaries or to the mission field, we recognize that we are sending them out together. These are *our* pastors, *our* church planters, *our* missionaries. The CP is a means for all of us to maximize what we can do together for the sake of the gospel.

However, the unity we share is ever delicate. It is incumbent on us for the next one hundred years to determine if we are going to continue in this unity of purpose. It will require focus on kingdom priorities over individual desires. For the sake of our greater mission, on some matters we will have to agree to disagree, and on some paths we will have to meet in the middle. As our history has shown, when we work together with a unified purpose, we accomplish with the Lord more than we ever could imagine. When we take our eyes off that mission and aim at lesser purposes that foster disunity, our history records our failures. The CP has been and can be the way forward. It can help ensure the Great Commission's central place in our Southern Baptist cooperation as it continues to provide the means for every individual Southern Baptist to extend his or her gospel witness together with the rest as one missionally minded family unified for that sole purpose.

At the 1924 convention, twelve months before the CP was born, M. E. Dodd warned Southern Baptists of a lifeless, Spiritless, directionless financial apparatus.

> In making these recommendations, your Committee is keenly sensible to the fact that all of this proposed machinery shall be but sounding brass and clanging cymbal, unless it be infilled and vitalized by the Spirit of God. We, therefore, call all our people everywhere to constant and persistent intercession on behalf of all our great causes which Christ has committed to our trust. We believe that Southern Baptists should go forward, and forward together, year by year, in holy and high endeavor until His kingdom shall stretch from shore to shore and His name shall be known from the river to the ends of the earth.[1]

May it be said of us, in our time, that the Holy Spirit of God vitalized our Great Commission cooperation with a unity of purpose never known before. May it be said of us that we rose to our time to fulfill the great causes Christ has committed to our trust. May it be said of us that we rose to the occasion of going forward together, year by year, in holy and high endeavor until the name and the glory of Christ are known from shore to shore and to the ends of the earth. May God help our people to see it.

Contributors

Bart Barber has served First Baptist Church in Farmersville, Texas, as pastor, since 1999. He has earned degrees from Baylor and Southwestern Baptist Theological Seminary, culminating in a PhD in church history. He is married to Tracy Brady Barber. Together they have two children, Jim and Sarah. He has a cow named Lottie Moooon.

Paul Chitwood, PhD, has been president of the International Mission Board since 2018. He pastored churches for eighteen years and served as executive director-treasurer of the Kentucky Baptist Convention for seven years. He and his wife, Michelle, have four children and reside in Virginia.

Melanie Clinton (publicity name). Melanie is a writer for the International Mission Board. She lives in Sub-Saharan Africa with her husband and children. She is working on an MDiv from Southeastern Baptist Theological Seminary.

James K. Dew Jr. is the president of New Orleans Baptist Theological Seminary and Leavell College where he also serves as professor of Christian philosophy. He's married to, Tara, and together they have two sets of twins: Natalie, Nathan, Samantha, and Samuel.

Daniel Dickard, PhD (Southwestern Baptist Theological Seminary), is pastor of Shandon Baptist Church in Columbia, South Carolina, and author of *Church Together: The Church of*

We in the Age of Me. Daniel is married to Cassie, and they have four children: Conrad, Kesyd, Carolina, and Kali-Jane.

Jason G. Duesing, PhD (Southwestern Baptist Theological Seminary), serves as professor of historical theology, provost, and senior vice president for Academic Administration at Midwestern Baptist Theological Seminary.

Mike Ebert serves as executive director of public relations for the North American Mission Board. He is a graduate of Oklahoma State University in radio, television, and film. Mike and his wife, Linda, have four adult children and a granddaughter.

Leo Endel, DMin (MBTS, 2012), serves as the executive director of the Minnesota-Wisconsin Baptist Convention and senior pastor of Emmanuel Baptist Church in Rochester, Minnesota. He is married to Sarah and has two adult daughters, Rachel and Lydia.

Kevin Ezell, DMin (The Southern Baptist Theological Seminary, 1994), serves as president of the North American Mission Board of the Southern Baptist Convention. He and his wife, Lynette, have six adult children and eight grandchildren.

RaShan Frost, PhD (Southeastern Baptist Theological Seminary), is a church planter and lead pastor of The Bridge Church in North Charleston, South Carolina. He is also an adjunct professor of Christian studies at Charleston Southern University and is senior fellow for human dignity for the Ethics & Religious Liberty Commission. He is married to DeAnna, and they have two adult sons.

W. Madison Grace II, PhD (Southwestern Baptist Theological Seminary), serves as provost and vice president for Academic

Administration, dean of the School of Theology, and professor of theology at Southwestern Baptist Theological Seminary in Fort Worth, Texas.

Taffey Hall serves as director of the Southern Baptist Historical Library and Archives in Nashville, Tennessee, and executive secretary-treasurer of the Association of Librarians and Archivists at Baptist Institutions.

Adam Harwood, PhD (Southwestern Baptist Theological Seminary, 2007), serves as McFarland Professor of Theology and divisional associate dean at New Orleans Baptist Theological Seminary and a NAMB-endorsed chaplain in the Louisiana Army National Guard. He and his wife, Laura, have four children.

Richard Land, BA (magna cum laude), Princeton; DPhil Oxford; and ThM, New Orleans Baptist Theological Seminary, was president of the Southern Baptists' Ethics & Religious Liberty Commission (1988–2013) and is the executive editor of the *Christian Post*.

Brent Leatherwood serves as president of the Ethics & Religious Liberty Commission. A husband, father, and deacon, he brings an expertise in public policy to his work, having worked for the Tennessee Republican Party, the Tennessee General Assembly, and on Capitol Hill.

Scott McConnell is executive director of Lifeway Research. Scott is a graduate of the University of Pennsylvania. He has researched the church and culture with Lifeway Christian Resources for twenty-eight years. Scott is married to Debbie and has two adult kids.

Julie Nall McGowan serves as associate vice president of public relations and corporate communications at the International Mission Board in Richmond, Virginia. She is a 1995 graduate of Oklahoma Baptist University. She and her husband, Tory, have one adult daughter.

Pete Ramirez, DMin (Gateway Seminary of the Southern Baptist Convention, 2024), serves as executive director-treasurer of the California Southern Baptist Convention. He is a lifelong Southern Baptist. He is married to Anabella, and they have two adult daughters and one grandson.

Chris Shaffer, PhD, serves as chief of staff and associate vice president at New Orleans Baptist Theological Seminary. He is a graduate of New Orleans Baptist Theological Seminary where he also serves as an assistant professor in Leavell College. He and his wife, Vanessa, live in New Orleans with their two children.

Tony Wolfe, PhD (The Southern Baptist Theological Seminary, 2024), serves as executive director-treasurer of the South Carolina Baptist Convention. He has served Southern Baptist churches for twenty-five years. Tony and his wife, Vanessa, have two adult sons.

Notes

Introduction

1. "Proceedings," *Annual of the Southern Baptist Convention 1925* (Nashville: Marshall & Bruce, 1925), accessed October 27, 2024, http://media2.sbhla.org.s3.amazonaws.com/annuals/SBC_Annual_1925.pdf, 28.
2. "Proceedings," *Annual of the Southern Baptist Convention 1925*, 25.
3. "Proceedings," *Annual of the Southern Baptist Convention 1925*, 25.
4. "Recommendations," *Annual of the Southern Baptist Convention 1924* (Nashville: Marshall & Bruce, 1924), 68, accessed October 27, 2024, http://media2.sbhla.org.s3.amazonaws.com/annuals/SBC_Annual_1924.pdf; "Proceedings," *Annual of the Southern Baptist Convention 1925*, 26–27.
5. Jewel Mae Daniel, *The Chimes of Shreveport: The Life of M. E. Dodd, the Heart of the Cooperative Program* (Franklin, TN: Providence House Publishers, 2001), 68–69. See chapter 6 for more on Elmon Dodd's report.
6. "Proceedings," *Annual of the Southern Baptist Convention 1925*, 31.
7. Daniel, *The Chimes of Shreveport*, 69.

Chapter 1

1. "Article XIV. Cooperation," *The Baptist Faith and Message 2000*, accessed October 26, 2024, https://bfm.sbc.net.
2. Eckhard J. Schnabel, *New Testament Theology* (Grand Rapids: Baker Academic, 2023), 900.

Chapter 2

1. Baptist historians have long debated Baptist beginnings. For a survey of views, see James M. Stayer, Werner Packull, and Klaus Deppermann, "From Monogenesis to Polygenesis: The Historical Discussion of Anabaptist Origins," *Mennonite Quarterly Review* 49:2 (April 1975): 83–121; William H. Brackney, *A Genetic History of Baptist Thought* (Macon, GA: Mercer University Press, 2004); Timothy George, "Dogma beyond Anathema:

Historical Theology in Service of the Church," in *Review and Expositor* 84:4 (Fall 1987): 691–713.

2. Jason G. Duesing, "Pre-beginnings," in John D. Massey, Mike Morris, and W. Madison Grace II, *Make Disciples of All Nations: A History of Southern Baptist International Missions* (Grand Rapids: Kregel Academic, 2021), 37.

3. Jason G. Duesing, "Baptist Contributions to the Christian Tradition," in Christopher W. Morgan, Matthew Y. Emerson, R. Lucas Stamps, eds., *Baptists and the Christian Tradition* (Nashville: B&H Academic, 2020), 339.

4. See Jason G. Duesing, "Preaching against the State: The Persecution of the Anabaptists as an Example for 21st-Century Evangelicals," *Midwestern Journal of Theology* 14:2 (2015): 54–82.

5. See Jason G. Duesing, "The Church in the Reformation," in Duesing and Nathan A. Finn, eds., *Historical Theology for the Church* (Nashville: B&H Academic, 2021), 237–39; and Duesing, "The Role of the Anabaptists in the Reformation and Today," ERLC *Light* 3:1 (Summer 2017): 34–36.

6. See Jason G. Duesing, "A Wrinkle on Catholicism: The Anglican Understanding of Church Government," in Thomas R. Schreiner and Benjamin L. Merkle, eds., *Shepherding God's Flock: Church Leadership in the New Testament and Beyond* (Grand Rapids: Kregel, 2014).

7. Tim Cooper summarizes, "Of all Protestant groupings in late sixteenth-century England, only the [S]eparatists rejected all forms of authority but the Bible, and that remained true of the [S]eparatists well into the seventeenth century," in "English Separatists, Puritan Conformists and the Bible," *Journal of Ecclesiastical History* 71:4 (October 2020): 796.

8. A portion of this original congregation were those "pilgrims" that sailed to the New World aboard a ship called the *Mayflower* in 1620.

9. Recent scholarship by Matthew C. Bingham, *Orthodox Radicals: Baptist Identity in the English Revolution* (Oxford: Oxford University Press, 2019) argues that long-standing classifications of early English Baptists as "General" and "Particular" should be rejected as anachronistic. As that thesis has been challenged in several venues, for clarity and consistency this chapter will use the conventional terminology for each group. See David Lyle, "Seventeenth-Century General Baptist Identity: A Response to Matthew C. Bingham," in *Baptist Quarterly* (November 21, 2023), and William H. Brackney, "Perticular or Particular? In Search of When English Calvinistic Baptists Became Particular Baptists," in *Baptist Quarterly* (2021).

10. See Jason G. Duesing, "The Wedge That Binds the Work: The Pastoral Theology of Henry Jacob (1563–1624) as a Keystone for His Congregational Ecclesiology," in *Baptist Quarterly*, 43:5 (Jan. 2010): 284–301.

11. See Jason G. Duesing, "Henry Jessey (1601–1663)," in Michael A. G. Haykin and Terry Wolever, eds., *The British Particular Baptists*, vol. 1, rev. ed. (Springfield, MO: Particular Baptist Press, 2019).

12. Gregory A. Wills underscores that church membership in these associations was "[t]he chief institutional expression of their denominational unity" in this era before mission boards and Conventions. See "Southern Baptist Identity: A Historical Perspective," in David S. Dockery, ed., *Southern Baptist Identity* (Wheaton, IL: Crossway, 2009), 70.

13. William L. Lumpkin, *Baptist Foundations in the South: Tracing through the Separates the Influence of the Great Awakening, 1754–1787* (Nashville: Broadman, 1961).

14. Lumpkin, *Baptist Foundations in the South*, 139.

15. Baptist pastor and religious liberty advocate John Leland opposed the formation of the convention during a sermon given in Philadelphia the week before the Convention convened. See Eric C. Smith, *John Leland: A Jeffersonian Baptist in Early America* (New York: Oxford University Press, 2022): 228–29. See also John Taylor, *Thoughts on Missions* (1819), for an extended argument against missionary societies and Luther Rice.

16. See *Proceedings of the Baptist Convention for Missionary Purposes* (Philadelphia, May 1814), 3, accessed October 27, 2024, https://archive.org/details/proceedingsofbap00amer/page/n1/mode/2up.

17. Stratford Caldecott, *Beauty for Truth's Sake* (Grand Rapids: Brazos, 2009), 12.

Chapter 3

1. Fisher Humphreys, *The Way We Were: How Southern Baptist Theology Has Changed and What It Means to Us All* (Macon, GA: Smyth & Helwys, 2002), 57.

2. For more on Furman, see James A. Rogers, *Richard Furman: Life and Legacy* (Macon, GA: Mercer University Press, 2001).

3. For a defense of slavery, see the address to the convention by pastor, slave owner, and the SBC's first president, William B. Johnson, in *Proceedings of the Southern Baptist Convention, Held in Augusta, Georgia, 1845* (Richmond: H. K. Ellyson, 1845), 17–20, accessed October 27, 2024, https://sbhla.org/digital-resources/sbc-annuals.

4. W. W. Barnes, *The Southern Baptist Convention: 1845–1953* (Nashville: Broadman, 1954), 38.

5. Albert L. Vail, *The Morning Hour of American Baptist Missions* (Philadelphia: American Baptist Publication Society, 1907), 150, in Robert A. Baker, *The Southern Baptist Convention and Its People: 1607–1972* (Nashville: Broadman, 1974), 100.

6. This chart is based on the content in Baker, *The Southern Baptist Convention and Its People*, 98–100.

7. Chad Owen Brand and David E. Hankins, *One Sacred Effort: The Cooperative Program of Southern Baptists* (Nashville: Broadman and Holman, 2005), 87.

8. Today, those SBC boards are known as the International Mission Board (IMB) and the North American Mission Board (NAMB), respectively.

9. Barnes, *The Southern Baptist Convention*, 10.

10. William R. Estep, *Whole Gospel—Whole World: The Foreign Mission Board of the Southern Baptist Convention 1845–1995* (Nashville: Broadman & Holman, 1994), 63.

11. Baker, *The Southern Baptist Convention and Its People*, 247.

12. Brand and Hankins, *One Sacred Effort*, 91.

13. "Appendix B: Fourteenth Annual Report, Board of Domestic and Indian Missions," in *Proceedings of the Seventh Biennial Session of the Southern Baptist Convention*, Held in the First Baptist Church, Richmond, Virginia, 1859 (Richmond: H. K. Ellyson, 1859), 57, accessed October 27, 2024, https://sbhla.org/digital-resources/sbc-annuals. The DMB was renamed the Board of Domestic and Indian Missions.

14. For more on Taylor's contribution, see W. Madison Grace II, "Beginnings: Southern Baptists, the Foreign Mission Board, and James Barnett Taylor," *Making Disciples of All Nations: A History of Southern Baptists International Missions*, ed. John D. Massey, Mike Morris, and W. Madison Grace II (Grand Rapids: Kregel, 2021), 53–92.

15. For more on Tupper's contribution, see Anthony L. Chute, "Growth and Controversy: The Administration of Henry Allen Tupper, 1872–1893," *Make Disciples of All Nations* (Grand Rapids: Kregel Academic), 93–126.

16. For more on Willingham's contribution, see Mike Morris, "The R. J. Willingham Era, 1893–1914," *Make Disciples of All Nations*, 127–52.

17. For more on Love's contribution, see David S. Dockery, "Hopefulness, Expansion, Disappointment, and Retrenchment: Paving the Way for the Next Generation of Southern Baptist Foreign Missions, 1915–1933," *Make Disciples of All Nations*, 153–88.

18. For more on her life, see Catherine B. Allen, *The New Lottie Moon Story*, 2nd ed. (Birmingham, AL: Woman's Missionary Union, 1997).

19. Keith Harper, "Introduction," *Send the Light: Lottie Moon's Letters and Other Writings*, ed. Keith Harper (Macon, GA: Mercer University Press, 2002), xi–xii.

20. Lottie Moon, correspondence to H. A. Tupper, November 1, 1873, in Harper, *Send the Light*, 6. Italics original.

21. Moon, correspondence to H. A. Tupper, May 21, 1874, in Harper, *Send the Light*, 9. Ten years later, in a letter to the new secretary of the FMB, she presents reasons missionary salaries should not be cut, then offers for her own annual salary to be reduced to $500. Moon, correspondence to R. J. Willingham, February 28, 1894, in Harper, *Send the Light*, 267.

22. Moon, correspondence to H. A. Tupper, March 13, 1875, in Harper, *Send the Light*, 10–15.

23. Moon, correspondence to H. A. Tupper, October 10, 1878, in Harper, *Send the Light*, 78.

24. See "An Earnest Plea for Helpers" (published in the August 1887 issue of *Foreign Mission Journal*) in *Send the Light*, 215–16, and "From Miss Lottie Moon" (published in the December 1887 issue of *Foreign Mission Journal*) in Harper, *Send the Light*, 222–25.

25. Moon, "An Earnest Plea for Helpers," in Harper, *Send the Light*, 215.

26. Moon, "From Miss Lottie Moon," in Harper, *Send the Light*, 224–25.

27. DMB secretaries who served lengthy and influential tenures during this era include Russell Holman (1845–1851, 1857–1862), Martin Sumner (1862–1875), Isaac T. Tichenor (1882–1899), and B. D. Gray (1903–1928).

28. Barnes, *The Southern Baptist Convention*, 39.

29. *Proceedings of the First Triennial Meeting of the Southern Baptist Convention, Held in Richmond, Virginia, 1846* (Richmond: H. K. Ellyson, 1846), 34–35, accessed October 27, 2024, available at https://sbhla.org/digital-resources/sbc-annuals.

30. *Proceedings of the First Triennial Meeting of the Southern Baptist Convention*, 33–34.

31. Barnes, *The Southern Baptist Convention*, 40–41.

32. *Missionary Journal* I (February 1847): 212, in J. B. Lawrence, *History of the Home Mission Board* (Nashville: Broadman, 1958), 21. The word *Bible* was not capitalized in the original.

33. *Proceedings of the First Triennial Meeting of the Southern Baptist Convention*, 33. Italics added.

34. Lawrence, *History of the Home Mission Board*, 33.

35. Lawrence, *History of the Home Mission Board*, 46–48.
36. William A. Mueller, *A History of Southern Baptist Theological Seminary* (Nashville: Broadman, 1959), 3.
37. A. T. Robertson, "Southern Baptist Ministers of a Hundred Years Ago," *The Seminary Magazine* IV (January 1891): 6–7, in Mueller, *A History of Southern Baptist Theological Seminary*, 4.
38. Mueller, *A History of Southern Baptist Theological Seminary*, 13.
39. Duke McCall, no citation, in Mueller, *A History of Southern Baptist Theological Seminary*, 2.
40. Jeff D. Ray, *B. H. Carroll* (Nashville: Baptist Sunday School Board, 1927), 136–38.
41. Robert A. Baker, *Tell the Generations Following: A History of Southwestern Baptist Theological Seminary, 1908–1983* (Nashville: Broadman, 1983), 120.
42. James T. Spivey Jr., "Benajah Harvey Carroll," *The Legacy of Southwestern: Writings that Shaped a Tradition* (North Richland Hills, TX: Smithfield, 2002), 4.
43. The name was changed to NOBTS in 1946.
44. *Proceedings of the Southern Baptist Convention*, held in Augusta, Georgia, 1845, 15, accessed October 27, 2024, https://sbhla.org/digital-resources/sbc-annuals.
45. The remaining amount of the campus purchase would be paid in annual payments with interest over the next fifteen years.
46. Claude L. Howe Jr., *Seventy-Five Years of Providence and Prayer: An Illustrated History of New Orleans Baptist Theological Seminary* (New Orleans: New Orleans Baptist Theological Seminary, 1993), 18–19.

Chapter 4

1. Bill Sumners, "Swords into Plowshares: Southern Baptists, World War I, and the League of Nations," *Quarterly Review*, April-May-June 1981, 79.
2. Sumners, "Swords into Plowshares," 75–76.
3. Sumners, "Swords into Plowshares," 77.
4. Sumners, "Swords into Plowshares," 79.
5. "Proceedings," *Annual of the Southern Baptist Convention 1917* (Nashville: Marshall & Bruce, 1917), 101, accessed October 28, 2024, http://media2.sbhla.org.s3.amazonaws.com/annuals/SBC_Annual_1917.pdf.
6. H. Leon McBeth, *The Baptist Heritage: Four Centuries of Witness* (Nashville: Broadman, 1987), 618.

7. Robert A. Baker, "The Cooperative Program in Historical Perspective," *Baptist History and Heritage*, July, 1975, 173; Andrew Smith, *Fundamentalism, Fundraising, and the Transformation of the Southern Baptist Convention* (Knoxville, TN: University of Tennessee Press, 2016), 52–53.

8. McBeth, *Baptist Heritage*, 618; and Smith, *Fundamentalism, Fundraising, and the Transformation of the Southern Baptist Convention*, 42–43.

9. L. R. Scarborough, *Marvels of Divine Leadership, or The Story of the Southern Baptist 75 Million Campaign* (Nashville: Sunday School Board, Southern Baptist Convention, 1920), 13.

10. William Leach, *Land of Desire: Merchants, Power, and the Rise of a New American Culture* (New York, NY: Vintage, 1993), 264.

11. Leach, *Land of Desire*, 85, 123, 190, 269–74.

12. Leach, *Land of Desire*, 275.

13. Walter Nathan Johnson, *The Southern Baptist Crisis: A Readjustment for Efficiency* (Thomasville, NC: Presses for Charity & Children, 1914), 7. Pam# 430; SBHLA, Nashville, TN.

14. McBeth, *Baptist Heritage*, 612.

15. *Southern Baptist Handbook, 1921* (Nashville: Sunday School Board, Southern Baptist Convention, 1921), 178–202, accessed October 28, 2024, http://media2.sbhla.org.s3.amazonaws.com/sbc/handbook/SBC_Handbook_1921.pdf; and *Annual of the Southern Baptist Convention 1920*, 2, accessed October 28, 2024, http://media2.sbhla.org.s3.amazonaws.com/annuals/SBC_Annual_1920.pdf.

16. Keith Harper, *The Quality of Mercy: Southern Baptists and Social Christianity, 1890–1920* (Tuscaloosa, AL: University of Alabama Press, 1996), 28; Wayne Flynt, *Alabama Baptists: Southern Baptists in the Heart of Dixie* (Tuscaloosa, AL: University of Alabama Press, 1998), 267; Bill Sumners, *The Social Attitudes of Southern Baptists toward Certain Issues, 1910–1920* (Arlington, TX: University of Texas at Arlington, MA Thesis, 1975), 1–24.

17. George Dallas Faulkner, *The Efficient Country Church* (Louisville, KY: Southern Baptist Theological Seminary, ThD, 1925), 3. MF# 804, SBHLA, Nashville, TN.

18. Fred A. Grissom, "Cooperation through Stewardship," *Baptist History and Heritage*, January 1989, 22.

19. Grissom, "Cooperation through Stewardship," 22, 25; "Report of Committee on Systematic Giving," *Annual of the Southern Baptist Convention 1873*, 21, http://media2.sbhla.org.s3.amazonaws.com/annuals/SBC_Annual_1873.pdf; "Proceedings," *Annual of the Southern Baptist*

Convention 1879, 39–40, http://media2.sbhla.org.s3.amazonaws.com/annuals/SBC_Annual_1879.pdf; "Proceedings," *Annual of the Southern Baptist Convention 1884*, 20, http://media2.sbhla.org.s3.amazonaws.com/annuals/SBC_Annual_1884.pdf; "Proceedings," *Annual of the Southern Baptist Convention 1895*, 18–23, http://media2.sbhla.org.s3.amazonaws.com/annuals/SBC_Annual_1895.pdf; "Proceedings," *Annual of the Southern Baptist Convention 1908*, 26, http://media2.sbhla.org.s3.amazonaws.com/annuals/SBC_Annual_1908.pdf; "Proceedings," *Annual of the Southern Baptist Convention 1913*, 32–37, http://media2.sbhla.org.s3.amazonaws.com/annuals/SBC_Annual_1913.pdf. All accessed October 28, 2024.

20. Alvin Shackelford, "Patterns of Designated Giving in Southern Baptist Life," *Baptist History and Heritage*, January 1986, 35–36.

21. Timothy George, "The Southern Baptist Cooperative Program: Heritage and Challenges," *Baptist History and Heritage*, April 1985, 5–6.

22. McBeth, *Baptist Heritage*, 612, and Karen Bullock, "Southern Baptist Identity: Shaped by Convention Action," *Baptist History and Heritage*, October 1996, 38.

23. *Annual of the Southern Baptist Convention 1913*, 13.

24. George, *The Southern Baptist Cooperative Program*, 6.

25. Bullock, "Southern Baptist Identity," 39–40; Albert McClellan, *Executive Committee of the Southern Baptist Convention, 1917–1984* (Nashville: Broadman, 1985), 43–69.

26. Grissom, "Cooperation through Stewardship," 21; Louise Winningham, "Where Were the Women? Women Played Key Roles in Events Leading up to the Adoption of the Cooperative Program," *Royal Service*, April 1985, 22.

27. Winningham, "Where Were the Women?," 22; Bullock, "Southern Baptist Identity," 37; and Bobby D. Compton, "Cooperation through Missions," *Baptist History and Heritage*, January 1989, 6; Baker, "The Cooperative Program in Historical Perspective," 170.

28. George, *The Southern Baptist Cooperative Program*, 5.

29. "Agencies," *Annual of the Southern Baptist Convention 1849*, 47, accessed October 28, 2024, http://media2.sbhla.org.s3.amazonaws.com/annuals/SBC_Annual_1849.pdf.

30. HMB report, *Annual of the Southern Baptist Convention 1884*, 20, accessed October 28, 2024, http://media2.sbhla.org.s3.amazonaws.com/annuals/SBC_Annual_1884.pdf.

31. B. H. DeMent, Correspondence to I. J. Van Ness, December 4, 1917, Isaac Jacobus Van Ness Papers, SBHLA, Nashville, TN.

32. Compton, "Cooperation through Missions," 6; and James Lee Young, "SBC Cooperative Program Born Out of Adversity," *Baptist and Reflector*, January 23, 1975, 13.
33. McBeth, *Baptist Heritage*, 617.
34. Compton, "Cooperation through Missions," 6.
35. Johnson, *The Southern Baptist Crisis*, 27.
36. James Austin, "Dr. Sullivan, What Are Your Thoughts on the Cooperative Program?," *Baptist Program*, June–July 1992, 11.
37. J. E. Dillard, *Objections to the Cooperative Program Answered* (Nashville: Executive Committee of the Southern Baptist Convention, ca. 1930), 2–3. Pam# 577, SBHLA, Nashville, TN.
38. Faulkner, *The Efficient Country Church*, 1.
39. *Southern Baptist Handbook, 1923*, accessed October 23, 2024, http://media2.sbhla.org.s3.amazonaws.com/sbc/handbook/SBC_Handbook_1923.pdf.
40. *Southern Baptist Handbook, 1923*; McBeth, *Baptist Heritage*, 610; John Lee Eighmy, *Churches in Cultural Captivity: A History of the Social Attitudes of Southern Baptists* (Knoxville, TN: University of Tennessee Press, 1972), 61; Ronald D. Eller, *Miners, Millhands, and Mountaineers: Industrialization of the Appalachian South, 1880–1930* (Knoxville, TN: University of Tennessee Press, 1982), xix, 5, 227; and Wayne Flynt, *Dixie's Forgotten People: The South's Poor Whites*, new ed. (Bloomington, IN: Indiana University Press, 2004), 64–65.
41. *Catalog*, The Southern Baptist Theological Seminary, 1920–1921, 41–42.
42. Grissom, "Cooperation through Stewardship," 26.
43. Selsus E. Tull, Lansing Burrows, M. H. Wolfe, J. T. Henderson, and J. Benjamin Lawrence, *Church Organization and Methods: A Manual for Baptist Churches* (Nashville: Sunday School Board, Southern Baptist Convention, 1917), 3–5.
44. Gaines S. Dobbins, *The Efficient Church: A Study of Polity and Methods in Light of New Testament Principles and Modern Conditions and Needs* (NashvilleN: Sunday School Board, Southern Baptist Convention, 1923), 4.
45. M. Ray McKay, "An Efficient Church in the Modern World," (Louisville, KY: The Southern Baptist Theological Seminary, Th.D, 1928), 158. MF# 4511-198. SBHLA, Nashville, TN.
46. Baker, "The Cooperative Program in Historical Perspective," 172–73.
47. Grissom, "Cooperation through Stewardship," 24.
48. Grissom, "Cooperation through Stewardship," 24.

49. Shackelford, "Patterns of Designated Giving in Southern Baptist Life," 36.

50. Grissom, "Cooperation through Stewardship," 25.

51. E. Y. Mullins, *What the Tithing Movement Means* (Knoxville, TN: Laymen's Movement of the Southern Baptist Convention, ca. 1922), 6. Pam# 6225, SBHLA, Nashville, TN.

52. Melody Maxwell, *The Woman I Am: Southern Baptist Women's Writings, 1906–2006* (Tuscaloosa, AL: University of Alabama Press, 2014), 59, accessed October 28, 2024, https://www.google.com/books/edition/The_Woman_I_Am/lQqUAwAAQBAJ?hl=en&gbpv=1&pg=PR3&printsec=frontcover; and H. Leon McBeth, "The Role of Women in Southern Baptist History," *Baptist History and Heritage*, January 1977, 25.

53. *Southern Baptist Handbook*, 1921, 192.

54. Maxwell, *The Woman I Am*, 4–8.

55. Catherine Allen, *A Century to Celebrate: History of Woman's Missionary Union* (Birmingham, AL: Woman's Missionary Union, 1987), 238–41.

56. Allen, *A Century to Celebrate*, 238–41.

57. Allen, *A Century to Celebrate*, 235–37; Bill Sumners, "Southern Baptists and Women's Right to Vote, 1910–1920," *Baptist History and Heritage*, January 1977, 50.

58. Allen, *A Century to Celebrate*, 235–37; Sumners, "Southern Baptists and Women's Right to Vote, 1910–1920," 50.

59. Maxwell, *The Woman I Am*, 4–5.

60. Allen, *A Century to Celebrate*, 127.

61. Delane Tew, "Baptist Missionary Funding: From Societies to Centralization," *Baptist History and Heritage*, Spring 2006, 58.

62. McBeth, "Role of Women," 19–20; Allen, *A Century to Celebrate*, 126–28.

63. Albert McClellan, "The Leadership Heritage of Southern Baptists," *Baptist History and Heritage*, January 1985, 14; Winningham, "Where Were the Women?," 23.

64. McBeth, "Role of Women," 19–20.

65. Allen, *A Century to Celebrate*, 129.

66. Maxwell, *The Woman I Am*, 15–16.

67. Maxwell, *The Woman I Am*, 15.

Chapter 5

1. Lee Rutland Scarborough, "Article 19 On Co-Operation by L. R. Scarborough," accessed October 29, 2024, http://cdm16969.contentdm.oclc.org/cdm/ref/collection/p16969coll11/id/1133.

2. Lee Rutland Scarborough, "Is Cooperation a New Testament Doctrine by L. R. Scarborough," 4, accessed October 29, 2024, http://cdm16969.contentdm.oclc.org/cdm/ref/collection/p16969coll11/ id/1135.

3. D. Scott Hildreth, *Together on God's Mission: How Southern Baptists Cooperate to Fulfill the Great Commission* (Nashville: B&H Academic, 2018), 20.

4. For more on the inefficiency of the society method of missions funding, see Adam Harwood's chapter 3 in this volume.

5. Glenn Thomas Carson, *Calling Out the Called: The Life and Work of Lee Rutland Scarborough* (Austin: Eakin, 1996), 53.

6. Scott Berg, *Wilson* (New York: G. P. Putnam's Sons, 2013), 444–45, 448.

7. Berg, *Wilson*, 456–57.

8. Berg, *Wilson*, 475–77.

9. Berg, *Wilson*, 481.

10. Calvin Coolidge, *The Autobiography of Calvin Coolidge: Authorized, Expanded, and Annotated Edition*, ed. Amity Schlaes (Wilmington, DE: ISI Books, 2021), 97.

11. For more on how the war affected the missionary spirit of Southern Baptists, see Taffey Hall's chapter 4 in this volume.

12. "Proceedings," *Annual of the Southern Baptist Convention 1919* (Nashville: Marshall & Bruce, 1919), 22, accessed October 29, 2024, http://media2.sbhla.org.s3.amazonaws.com/annuals/SBC_Annual_1919.pdf.

13. "Proceedings," *Annual of the Southern Baptist Convention 1919*, 23.

14. "Proceedings," *Annual of the Southern Baptist Convention 1919*, 32.

15. "Proceedings," *Annual of the Southern Baptist Convention 1919*, 74.

16. Lee Rutland Scarborough, *Marvels of Divine Leadership: Or, the Story of the Southern Baptist 75 Million Campaign* (Nashville: Sunday School Board of the Southern Baptist Convention, 1920), 12.

17. Scarborough, *Marvels of Divine Leadership*, 16.

18. "Foreign Mission Board Report," *Annual of the Southern Baptist Convention 1919*, 198, 201.

19. Lee Rutland Scarborough, *Evangelism, Enlightenment, Enlistment: Millions for the Master* (Nashville: Baptist 75 Million Campaign, 1919), 31.

20. Robert K. Murray, *The Harding Era: Warren G. Harding and His Administration* (Newtown, CT: American Political Biography Press, 1969), 81–82.

21. Murray, *The Harding Era*, 82.

22. F. S. Groner, "The Hour for a Superior Effort," *The Baptist Standard* 37, no. 17 (April 23, 1925), 1.

23. O. E. Bryan, "The Strategy of Simultaneous Action," *Baptist and Reflector*, 91, no. 26 (April 23, 1925), 2.

24. "Proceedings," *Annual of the Southern Baptist Convention 1919*, 82.

25. "Proceedings," *Annual of the Southern Baptist Convention 1919*, 74.

26. Hildreth, *Together on God's Mission*, 17.

27. W. W. Barnes, *The Southern Baptist Convention 1845–1953* (Nashville: Broadman, 1954), 224.

28. Scarborough, *Evangelism, Enlightenment, Enlistment*, 20. "The 75 Million Campaign presents an opportunity for Southern Baptists to show how they can cooperate in a campaign and program which takes in all their combined activities. With charity for all others, malice toward none, we are to throw the full force of our strength into a program somewhat worthy of our great numbers, our commanding influence and the tremendous tasks that confront us."

29. Louis Entzminger, *The J. Frank Norris I Have Known for 34 Years* (Scotts Valley, CA: CreateSpace Independent Publishing, 2015), 287.

30. Entzminger, *The J. Frank Norris I Have Known for 34 Years*, 186–87, 286–87.

31. Scarborough, *Marvels of Divine Leadership*, 93. "Victory Week" marked "Eight Immortal Days" of pledges toward the campaign, from November 30 to December 7, 1919. See also Frank E. Burkhalter, "Seventy-Five Million Campaign," in *Encyclopedia of Southern Baptists*, vol. 2 (Nashville: Broadman, 1958), 1197.

32. Numbers in the center column are taken from the *Annual of the Southern Baptist Convention 1919*, 51. Numbers in the far-right column are taken from the *Annual of the Southern Baptist Convention 1925* (Nashville: Marshall & Bruce, 1925), 23, accessed October 29, 2024, http://media2.sbhla.org.s3.amazonaws.com/annuals/SBC_Annual_1925.pdf.

33. A $27,346 discrepancy in the total of the center column is acknowledged.

34. *Annual of the Southern Baptist Convention 1925*, 22.

35. Numbers in the center column are taken from Burkhalter, "Seventy-Five Million Campaign," 1196. Numbers in the far right column are taken from Annual of the Southern Baptist Convention 1925, 23.

36. A $9.00 discrepancy in the total of the far-right column is acknowledged.

37. Chad Owen Brand and David E. Hankins, *One Sacred Effort: The Cooperative Program of Southern Baptists* (Nashville: B&H Academic, 2005), 95.

38. Andrew Christopher Smith, *Fundamentalism, Fundraising, and the Transformation of the Southern Baptist Convention, 1919–1925* (Knoxville, TN: The University of Tennessee Press, 2016), 103.

39. O. S. Hawkins, *In the Name of God: The Colliding Lives, Legends, and Legacies of J. Frank Norris and George W. Truett* (Nashville: B&H Publishing, 2021), 101.

40. Brand and Hankins, *One Sacred Effort*, 95.

41. "Foreign Mission Board Report," *Annual of the Southern Baptist Convention 1924* (Nashville: Marshall & Bruce, 1924), 165, accessed October 29, 2024, http://media2.sbhla.org.s3.amazonaws.com/annuals/SBC_Annual_1924.pdf. At the instruction of the 1919 convention, in 1924 the board reported outstanding loans to Southwestern Baptist Theological Seminary, New Orleans Baptist Bible Institute, and The Southern Baptist Theological Seminary totaling $257,730.80. By May 1924, the interest on the three school loans rose to approximately $30,000. See 176–77.

42. "Foreign Mission Board Report," *Annual of the Southern Baptist Convention 1924*, 165, 176.

43. "Foreign Mission Board Report," *Annual of the Southern Baptist Convention 1924*, 176.

44. "Foreign Mission Board Report," *Annual of the Southern Baptist Convention 1924*, 165–66, 176.

45. "Foreign Mission Board Report," *Annual of the Southern Baptist Convention 1924*, 165.

46. "Foreign Mission Board Report," *Annual of the Southern Baptist Convention 1924*, 166.

47. "Home Mission Board Report," *Annual of the Southern Baptist Convention 1924*, 318.

48. "Home Mission Board Report," *Annual of the Southern Baptist Convention 1924*, 330.

49. "Home Mission Board Report," "Education Board Report," *Annual of the Southern Baptist Convention 1924*, 370, 445.

50. "Education Board Report," *Annual of the Southern Baptist Convention 1924*, 435.

51. "Education Board Report," *Annual of the Southern Baptist Convention 1924*, 445–46.

52. "Education Board Report," *Annual of the Southern Baptist Convention 1924*, 452–53.

53. "Education Board Report," *Annual of the Southern Baptist Convention 1924*, 454.

54. John Mark Terry and J. D. Payne, *Developing a Strategy for Missions: A Biblical, Historical, and Cultural Introduction* (Grand Rapids: Baker Academic, 2013), 219.
55. Terry and Payne, *Developing a Strategy for Missions*, 221–22.
56. Brand and Hankins, *One Sacred Effort*, 95.
57. H. E. Dana, *Lee Rutland Scarborough: A Live of Service* (Nashville: Broadman, 1942), 98.
58. Scarborough, *Marvels of Divine Leadership*, 151.
59. H. Leon McBeth, *A Sourcebook for Baptist Heritage* (Nashville: Broadman, 1990), 447.
60. "Proceedings," *Annual of the Southern Baptist Convention 1925*, 23–24.
61. "Foreign Mission Board Report," *Annual of the Southern Baptist Convention 1924*, 168. These numbers do not include the board's work in Russia, which had peaked during the years of the campaign to the point of expected successful completion and withdrawal in 1924. See 172.
62. "Foreign Mission Board Report," *Annual of the Southern Baptist Convention 1924*, 168.
63. "Foreign Mission Board Report," *Annual of the Southern Baptist Convention 1924*, 328. Under the subheading "Some Significant Comparisons," the report refers to the numbers in Cuba as the normative "comparison of growth . . . in most of our fields" between 1919–1924.
64. Hildreth, *Together on God's Mission*, 19.
65. Scarborough, *Marvels of Divine Leadership*, 117.
66. McBeth, *A Sourcebook for Baptist Heritage*, 447.
67. Scarborough, *Marvels of Divine Leadership*, 124.
68. Scarborough, *Marvels of Divine Leadership*, 124–25.
69. "Home Mission Board Report," *Annual of the Southern Baptist Convention 1924*, 318.
70. "Home Mission Board Report," *Annual of the Southern Baptist Convention 1924*, 318.
71. "Home Mission Board Report," *Annual of the Southern Baptist Convention 1924*, 328.
72. Scarborough, *Marvels of Divine Leadership*, 64.
73. Scarborough, *Marvels of Divine Leadership*, 63.
74. Scarborough, *Marvels of Divine Leadership*, 243.
75. "Proceedings," *Annual of the Southern Baptist Convention 1925*, 23–24.
76. Terry and Payne, *Developing a Strategy for Missions*, 236.
77. "Proceedings," *Annual of the Southern Baptist Convention 1925*, 24–25.

78. "Home Mission Board Report," *Annual of the Southern Baptist Convention 1924*, 319.
79. "Home Mission Board Report," *Annual of the Southern Baptist Convention 1924*, 330.
80. "Home Mission Board Report," *Annual of the Southern Baptist Convention 1924*, 331.
81. Hildreth, *Together on God's Mission*, 19.
82. Barnes, *The Southern Baptist Convention*, 230.
83. Brand and Hankins, *One Sacred Effort*, 95–97.
84. Dana, *Lee Rutland Scarborough*, 107.
85. Scarborough, *Marvels of Divine Leadership*, 116.
86. "Proceedings," *Annual of the Southern Baptist Convention 1920* (Nashville: Marshall & Bruce, 1920), 49, accessed October 29, 2024, http://media2.sbhla.org.s3.amazonaws.com/annuals/SBC_Annual_1920.pdf.
87. Hildreth, *Together on God's Mission*, 17.

Chapter 6

1. D. Scott Hildreth, *Together on God's Mission: How Southern Baptists Cooperate to Fulfill the Great Commission* (Nashville: B&H Academic, 2018), 17.
2. "Proceedings," *Annual of the Southern Baptist Convention 1925* (Nashville: Marshall & Bruce, 1925), 36, accessed October 29, 2024, http://media2.sbhla.org.s3.amazonaws.com/annuals/SBC_Annual_1925.pdf.
3. "Proceedings," *Annual of the Southern Baptist Convention 1925*, 26.
4. "Proceedings," *Annual of the Southern Baptist Convention 1925*, 28.
5. "Proceedings," *Annual of the Southern Baptist Convention 1939* (Nashville: Executive Committee of the Southern Baptist Convention, 1939), 28–29, accessed October 29, 2024, http://media2.sbhla.org.s3.amazonaws.com/annuals/SBC_Annual_1939.pdf.
6. Austin Crouch, "Cooperative Program," in *Encyclopedia of Southern Baptists*, vol. I (Nashville: Broadman, 1958), 323.
7. Chad Owen Brand and David E. Hankins, *One Sacred Effort: The Cooperative Program of Southern Baptists* (Nashville: B&H Academic, 2005), 97, 187.
8. Hildreth, *Together on God's Mission*, 27.
9. Keith Harper and Amy Whitfield, *SBC FAQs: A Ready Reference* (Nashville: B&H Academic, 2018), 17–18.
10. Robert J. Matz and John M. Yeats, *Better Together: You, Your Church, and the Cooperative Program* (Spring Hill, TN: Rainer, 2019), 48.
11. Matz and Yeats, *Better Together*, 121.

12. Kevin DeYoung and Greg Gilbert, *What Is the Mission of the Church? Making Sense of Social Justice, Shalom, and the Great Commission* (Wheaton, IL: Crossway, 2011), 62.

13. W. W. Barnes, *The Southern Baptist Convention 1845–1953* (Nashville: Broadman, 1954), 231.

14. Hildreth, *Together on God's Mission*, 28.

15. Hildreth, *Together on God's Mission*, 25–26.

16. Brand and Hankins, *One Sacred Effort*, 178.

17. Brand and Hankins, *One Sacred Effort*, 187–88.

18. Matz and Yeats, *Better Together*, 49.

19. DeYoung and Gilbert, *What Is the Mission of the Church?*, 62–63.

20. Brand and Hankins, *One Sacred Effort*, 117.

21. Brand and Hankins, *One Sacred Effort*, 195–96.

22. Harper and Whitfield, *SBC FAQs*, 18.

23. "Proceedings," *Annual of the Southern Baptist Convention 1925*, 36. In their first report, the Future Commission added, as part of its recommendations, "That there be a well co-ordinated [sic] program of teaching stewardship and promoting better financial methods in the churches, especially in assisting the churches to adopt the budget plan."

24. Lee Rutland Scarborough, *Marvels of Divine Leadership: Or, the Story of the Southern Baptist 75 Million Campaign* (Nashville: Sunday School Board of the Southern Baptist Convention, 1920), 241.

Chapter 7

1. Leon McBeth, *The Baptist Heritage: Four Centuries of Baptist Witness* (Nashville: Broadman, 1987), 242.

2. McBeth, *The Baptist Heritage*, 219.

3. McBeth, *The Baptist Heritage*, 366.

4. McBeth, *The Baptist Heritage*, 266.

5. McBeth, *The Baptist Heritage*, 442.

6. "General Information," SBC, accessed October 30, 2024, https://www.sbc.net/about/what-we-do/fast-facts.

7. "Colleges and Universities," SBC, accessed October 30, 2024, https://www.sbc.net/resources/directories/colleges-and-universities.

8. "Colleges and Universities," SBC, https://www.sbc.net/resources/directories/colleges-and-universities.

9. Staff, "Baptist Children's Homes Addressing Family Needs," Baptist Press, May 1, 2016, https://www.baptistpress.com/resource-library/sbc-life-articles/baptist-childrens-homes-addressing-family-needs.

10. "Fast Facts," SBC, accessed October 30, 2024, https://www.sbc.net/about/what-we-do/fast-facts/#SnippetTab.

11. Brian Mastre, "Nebraska Family Looks Back on Barn Moving Event," 6 News WOWT, Omaha, Nebraska, February 20, 2017, https://www.wowt.com/content/news/Family-looks-back-on-barn-moving-event-414295883.html.

Chapter 8

1. Timothy George, *James Petigru Boyce: Selected Writings* (Nashville: Broadman, 1989), 30.

2. The Southern Baptist Theological Seminary, New Orleans Baptist Theological Seminary, and Southwestern Baptist Theological Seminary.

3. All of the seminaries are accredited by regional accreditors. The Association of Theological Schools is the accrediting agency all Southern Baptist seminaries hold in common. More than 270 graduate theological schools are accredited by ATS.

4. L. R. Scarborough, *A Modern School of the Prophet* (Nashville: Broadman Press, 1939), 90.

5. Southern Baptist Convention Press Kit Collection (Southern Baptist Historical Library and Archives Nashville, TN), AR 375, Box 23, Folder 8.

6. "One Faith, One Task, One Sacred Trust: A Covenant between Our Seminaries and Our Churches," New Orleans Baptist Theological Seminary, accessed October 30, 2024, https://catalog.nobts.edu/generalinfo/about/onefaith.

7. "Article I. The Scriptures," *The Baptist Faith and Message 2000*, accessed October 30, 2024, https://bfm.sbc.net/bfm2000.

8. "Proceedings," *Annual of the Southern Baptist Convention 1917* (Nashville: Marshall & Bruce, 1917, 83, accessed October 30, 2024, http://media2.sbhla.org.s3.amazonaws.com/annuals/SBC_Annual_1917.pdf.

9. Chris Chun and John Shouse, *Golden Gate to Gateway: A History* (Nashville: B&H, 2020), 16.

10. Chip Hutcheson, "York Calls Pastoring Buck Run Baptist Church 'a Singular Honor in My Life,'" *Kentucky Today*, January 28, 2024, https://www.kentuckytoday.com/baptist_life/york-calls-pastoring-buck-run-baptist-church-a-singular-honor-of-my-life/article_4cb49763-be3c-11ee-8ef5-c771c66907d0.html.

11. NOBTS Pamphlet, circa 1942. NOBTS Archives.

12. "Seminary Comparative Data," *Book of Reports of the 2023 Southern Baptist Convention*, 134, accessed October 30, 2024, https://www.baptistpress.com/wp-content/uploads/2023/05/2023-Book-of-Reports-Final-Online.pdf.

13. "Annual Data Tables," 2023–2024, Association of Theological Schools, https://www.ats.edu/files/galleries/2023-2024-annual-data-tables.pdf.

14. Each of the seminaries is accredited by a regional accreditor. However, the graduate programs of all six of the SBC seminaries are accredited, along with approximately 270 other theological institutions, by the Association of Theological Schools.

15. "Annual Data Tables for 2022–2023 and 2023–2024," Association of Theological Schools, accessed April 15, 2024, https://www.ats.edu/Annual-Data-Tables.

16. This number does not include all graduates of the institution for NOBTS, SBTS, and SWBTS because their existence predates the 1925 beginning of the Cooperative Program. Golden Gate (now Gateway) was founded in 1944, SEBTS in 1950, and MBTS in 1957. Additionally, this number only represents graduates and not every student who enrolled in the institution.

Chapter 9

1. Barry Hankins, *Jesus and Gin: Evangelicalism, the Roaring Twenties, and Today's Culture Wars* (New York: Palgrave, 2010), 21–40.

2. "Resolution on Lynching and Mob Violence," SBC, May 1, 1936, https://www.sbc.net/resource-library/resolutions/resolution-on-lynching-on-mob-violence.

3. Jesse B. Weatherspoon, "Report of the Social Service Commission," *Annual of the Southern Baptist Convention 1944* (Nashville: Executive Committee of the Southern Baptist Convention, 1944), 129, accessed October 30, 3024, http://media2.sbhla.org.s3.amazonaws.com/annuals/SBC_Annual_1944.pdf.

4. Jerry Sutton, *A Matter of Conviction: A History of Southern Baptist Engagement with the Culture* (Nashville: B&H Publishing Group, 2008),117.

5. Weatherspoon, "Report of the Social Service Commission," 129.

6. Weatherspoon, "Report of the Social Service Commission," 129.

7. Jesse Weatherspoon, "Committee on Race Relations," *Annual of the Southern Baptist Convention 1947* (Nashville: Executive Committee of the Southern Baptist Convention, 1947), 342, accessed October 30, 2024, http://media2.sbhla.org.s3.amazonaws.com/annuals/SBC_Annual_1947.pdf.

8. Alex Ward, *The ERLC and the Cooperative Program: 75 Years of Southern Baptist Advocacy in the Public Square* (Nashville: Leland House Press, 2022), 3.

9. Hugh Brimm, "Report of Social Service Commission," *Annual of the Southern Baptist Convention 1950* (Nashville: Executive Committee of the Southern Baptist Convention, 1950), 378, accessed October 30, 2024, http://media2.sbhla.org.s3.amazonaws.com/annuals/SBC_Annual_1950.pdf.

10. Hugh Brimm, "Report of Social Service Commission," *Annual of the Southern Baptist Convention 1952* (Nashville: Executive Committee of the Southern Baptist Convention, 1952), 408–9, accessed October 30, 2024, http://media2.sbhla.org.s3.amazonaws.com/annuals/SBC_Annual_1952.pdf.

11. A. C. Miller, "Report of the Christian Life Commission," in *Annual of the Southern Baptist Convention 1954* (Nashville: Executive Committee of the Southern Baptist Convention, 1954), 407, accessed October 30, 2024, http://media2.sbhla.org.s3.amazonaws.com/annuals/SBC_Annual_1954.pdf.

12. A. C. Miller, report to SBC Annual Meeting, "Southern Baptist Convention Audio Recordings—1954: Friday Evening—Part 2," Southern Baptist Historical Library and Archive, 7:18, https://sbhla.org/digital-resources/southern-baptist-convention-audio-recordings/sbc-audio-1954.

13. Foy D. Valentine, "Report of the Christian Life Commission," *Annual of the Southern Baptist Convention 1960* (Nashville: Executive Committee of the Southern Baptist Convention, 1960), 273, accessed October 30, 2024, http://media2.sbhla.org.s3.amazonaws.com/annuals/SBC_Annual_1960.pdf.

14. "Recommendation No. 25," *Annual of the Southern Baptist Convention 1961* (Nashville: Executive Committee of the Southern Baptist Convention, 1961), 60, accessed October 30, 2024, http://media2.sbhla.org.s3.amazonaws.com/annuals/SBC_Annual_1961.pdf.

15. Sutton, *A Matter of Conviction*, 168.

16. Dwayne Hastings, "Foy Valentine, Dead at 82, Led SBC Moral Concerns Arm 27 Years," Baptist Press, January 9, 2006, https://www.baptistpress.com/resource-library/news/foy-valentine-dead-at-82-led-sbc-moral-concerns-arm-27-years.

17. Foy D. Valentine, "Report of the Christian Life Commission," *Annual of the Southern Baptist Convention 1964* (Nashville: Executive Committee of the Southern Baptist Convention, 1964), 228–29, accessed October 30, 2024, http://media2.sbhla.org.s3.amazonaws.com/annuals/SBC_Annual_1964.pdf.

18. Tim Fields, "Call Still Rings Clearly for Christian Life Leader," Baptist Press, February 24, 1982, http://media.sbhla.org.s3.amazonaws.com/5413,24-Feb-1982.pdf.

19. Sutton, *Matter of Conviction*, 279.

20. Hastings, "Foy Valentine," *Baptist Press*.

21. Sutton, *A Matter of Conviction*, 274–75.

22. Sutton, *A Matter of Conviction*, 280.

23. Jerry Sutton, *The Baptist Reformation* (Nashville: B&H Publishers, 2000), 316–17.

24. Implementation Task Force, "Transition Plan for Covenant for a New Century," *Baptist Press*, August 1, 1997, https://www.baptistpress.com/resource-library/sbc-life-articles/transition-plan-for-covenant-for-a-new-century-2.

25. Manhattan Declaration, November 20, 2009, https://www.manhattandeclaration.org.

26. *Russell D. Moore: Inauguration Address*, 2013, https://www.youtube.com/watch?v=hrVfcbRNpwo.

27. "Organization Manual—SBC.Net," accessed December 12, 2023, https://www.sbc.net/about/what-we-do/legal-documentation/organization-manual.

28. "Here We Stand: An Evangelical Declaration on Marriage," ERLC, accessed December 12, 2023, https://erlc.com/resource-library/statements/here-we-stand-an-evangelical-declaration-on-marriage.

29. "The Importance of Bylaws," ERLC, accessed December 26, 2023, https://erlc.com/wp-content/uploads/2022/10/ERL2066_PastorAppreciateMonthPDF2_FINAL_10142s-Digital.pdf.

30. "Nashville Statement," CBMW, accessed December 13, 2023, https://cbmw.org/nashville-statement.

31. "Racial Justice and the Uneasy Conscience of American Christianity," Russell Moore, April 10, 2018, https://www.russellmoore.com/2018/04/10/king-and-kingdom-racial-justice-and-the-uneasy-conscience-of-american-christianity.

32. "Artificial Intelligence: An Evangelical Statement of Principles," ERLC, accessed December 13, 2023, https://erlc.com/resource-library/statements/artificial-intelligence-an-evangelical-statement-of-principles.

33. "Abuse of Faith," *Houston Chronicle*, accessed October 30, 2024, https://www.houstonchronicle.com/news/investigations/abuse-of-faith.

34. "On Transgender Identity," SBC.Net, accessed December 13, 2023, https://www.sbc.net/resource-library/resolutions/on-transgender-identity.

Chapter 10

1. Lyle Daly, "The Largest Companies by Market Cap in 2023," *The Motley Fool*, January 2, 2024, https://www.fool.com/research/largest-companies-by-market-cap/#:~:text=of%20January%202024.-,Key%20findings,and%20Amazon%20(%241.57%20trillion).

2. Chris McCoy, "The City that Sam Built," *Memphis Magazine*, October 17, 2022, https://memphismagazine.com/travel/the-city-that-sam-built.

3. "Who We Are," North American Mission Board, accessed January 5, 2024, https://www.anniearmstrong.com/resource/north-american-mission-board-who-we-are.

4. Leisa Hammett-Goad, *A History of Home Missions* (Atlanta: Home Mission Board, 1993), 1.

5. Hammett-Goad, *A History of Home Missions*, 2.

6. Eddy Oliver, *A Heritage of Caring People* (Atlanta: Home Mission Board, 1994), 2–3.

7. Hammett-Goad, *A History of Home Missions*, 2, 4.

8. Rosalie H. Hunt, *The Story of WMU* (Birmingham, AL: Woman's Missionary Union, 2006), 28, 35.

9. Hammett-Goad, *A History of Home Missions*, 11.

10. Oliver, *A Heritage of Caring People*, 13.

11. Oliver, *A Heritage of Caring People*, 13.

12. Hammett-Goad, *A History of Home Missions*, 16.

13. Hammett-Goad, *A History of Home Missions*, 16, 19.

14. Oliver, *A Heritage of Caring People*, 16–17.

15. Oliver, *A Heritage of Caring People*, 17.

16. Oliver, *A Heritage of Caring People*, 18.

17. Hammett-Goad, *A History of Home Missions*, 21.

18. Hammett-Goad, *A History of Home Missions*, 25.

19. Implementation Task Force, "Transition Plan for Covenant for a New Century," *Baptist Press*, August 1, 1996, https://www.baptistpress.com/resource-library/sbc-life-articles/transition-plan-for-covenant-for-a-new-century.

20. Staff, "SBC Wrapup: Messengers Pass GCR Report, Elect New President in First Runoff since '82," Baptist Press, June 17, 2010, https://www.baptistpress.com/resource-library/news/sbc-wrapup-messengers-pass-gcr-report-elect-new-president-in-1st-runoff-since-82.

Chapter 11

1. "175 Years," International Mission Board, accessed November 1, 2024, https://www.imb.org/175.
2. "175 Years—1840s," International Mission Board, accessed November 1, 2024, https://www.imb.org/175/decades/1840s.
3. "175 Years—1860s," International Mission Board, accessed November 1, 2024, https://www.imb.org/175/decades/1860s.
4. "175 Years—1870s," International Mission Board, accessed November 1, 2024, https://www.imb.org/175/decades/1870s.
5. "175 Years—1880s," International Mission Board, accessed November 1, 2024, https://www.imb.org/175/decades/1880s.
6. "175 Years—1910s," International Mission Board, accessed November 1, 2024, https://www.imb.org/175/decades/1910s.
7. "175 Years—1920s," International Mission Board, accessed November 1, 2024, https://www.imb.org/175/decades/1920s.
8. "Proceedings," *Annual of the Southern Baptist Convention 1925* (Nashville: Marshall and Bruce, 1925), 34, accessed November 1, 2024, http://media2.sbhla.org.s3.amazonaws.com/annuals/SBC_Annual_1925.pdf.
9. "175 Years—1930s," International Mission Board, accessed November 1, 2024, https://www.imb.org/175/decades/1930s.
10. "175 Years—Missionary Profiles: Orvil Reid," International Mission Board, accessed November 1, 2024, https://www.imb.org/175/missionary-profiles/orvil-reid.
11. "175 Years—1940s," International Mission Board, accessed November 1, 2024, https://www.imb.org/175/decades/1940s.
12. "175 Years—1950s," International Mission Board, accessed November 1, 2024, https://www.imb.org/175/decades/1950s.
13. "175 Years—1940s," International Mission Board, accessed November 1, 2024, https://www.imb.org/175/decades/1940s.
14. "175 Years—1960s," International Mission Board, accessed November 1, 2024, https://www.imb.org/175/decades/1960s.
15. "175 Years—Missionary Profiles: Mary Sue Thompson," International Mission Board, accessed November 1, 2024, https://www.imb.org/175/missionary-profiles/mary-sue-thompson.
16. "175 Years—1970s," International Mission Board, accessed November 1, 2024, https://www.imb.org/175/decades/1970s.
17. "175 Years—Missionary Profiles: George Braswell," International Mission Board, accessed November 1, 2024, https://www.imb.org/175/missionary-profiles/george-braswell.

18. "175 Years—1980s," International Mission Board, accessed November 1, 2024, https://www.imb.org/175/decades/1980s.

19. "175 Years—Missionary Profiles: Yvette Aarons," International Mission Board, accessed November 1, 2024, https://www.imb.org/175/missionary-profiles/yvette-aarons.

20. "175 Years—1990s," International Mission Board, accessed November 1, 2024, https://www.imb.org/175/decades/1990s.

21. "People Groups," International Mission Board, accessed November 1, 2024, https://peoplegroups.org.

22. "175 Years—Missionary Profiles: George and Veda Rae Lozuk," International Mission Board, accessed November 1, 2024, https://www.imb.org/175/missionary-profiles/george-and-veda-rae-lozuk.

23. "People Groups," International Mission Board.

24. "175 Years—2000s," International Mission Board, accessed November 1, 2024, https://www.imb.org/175/decades/2000s.

25. "175 Years—Missionary Profiles: Martha Myers," International Mission Board, accessed November 1, 2024, https://www.imb.org/175/missionary-profiles/martha-myers.

26. "175 Years—2010s," International Mission Board, accessed November 1, 2024, https://www.imb.org/175/decades/2010s.

27. "175 Years—Missionary Profiles: Brennan and Veronica Masterson*," International Mission Board, accessed November 1, 2024, https://www.imb.org/175/missionary-profiles/brennan-and-veronica-masterson.

28. https://www.baptistpress.com/resource-library/news/imb-leaders-announce-plan-to-balance-budget/

29. Stella McMillian, "Southern Baptists Explore East Asia Virtually," International Mission Board, April 7, 2021, https://www.imb.org/2021/04/07/southern-baptists-explore-east-asia-virtually. Tessa Sanchez, "Easter Video from Missionary Leads to Long-term Discipleship of Teenager," International Mission Board, April 6, 2023, https://www.imb.org/2023/04/06/easter-video-from-missionary-leads-to-long-term-discipleship-of-teenager. Jennifer Waldrep, "Missionary Family Spreads Hope," International Mission Board, March 30, 2020, https://www.imb.org/2020/03/30/missionary-family-spreads-hope.

30. "Markers: The Cooperative Program," Kentucky Historical Society, accessed November 1, 2024, https://history.ky.gov/markers/the-cooperative-program.

31. Paul Chitwood, "First-Person: Partnership Requires Perseverance," *Baptist Press*, May 1, 2023, https://www.baptistpress.com/resource-library/news/first-person-partnership-requires-perseverance.

Chapter 12

1. This definition, it is worth noting, does not depend on any formal connection with the convention itself: entities defined largely by the service they provide and the support they receive from Southern Baptist churches would include not only the twelve entities related to the Southern Baptist Convention but also the various state conventions, the various local associations, the entities related to those state conventions and local associations, a whole host of networks, alliances, and institutions which exist in the broader penumbra of all things Southern Baptist.

2. Bebbington's Quadrilateral works well as a definition here: evangelical churches are biblicist, crucicentric, conversionist, activist churches. David Bebbington, *Evangelicalism in Modern Britain: A History from the 1730s to the 1980s* (London: Routledge, 1988).

3. Aaron M. Renn, *Life in the Negative World: Confronting Challenges in an Anti-Christian Culture* (Grand Rapids: Zondervan), 2024.

4. Ligonier Ministries and Lifeway Research, "The State of Theology," accessed November 1, 2024, https://thestateoftheology.com.

5. Preamble, *The Baptist Faith and Message 2000*, 21, accessed November 1, 2024, https://bfm.sbc.net/wp-content/uploads/2024/08/BFM2000.pdf.

6. "NC Pastor's Motion for 'Fellowship Meal Sunday' to Receive Consideration," N. C. Baptists, June 24, 2021, https://ncbaptist.org/article/nc-pastors-motion-for-fellowship-meal-sunday-to-receive-consideration.

Chapter 13

1. "Gen Z: The Culture, Beliefs and Motivations Shaping the Next Generation," Barna Group, January 23, 2018, https://barna.gloo.us/reports/gen-z.

2. Abraham Kuyper, "Inaugural Address at the Free University: The Summa of Kuyper's Thought," in *Abraham Kuyper: A Centennial Reader*, ed. James D. Bratt (Grand Rapids, MI: Eerdmans, 1998), 488.

3. John M. Perkins, "The Christian and Biblical Justice," in *Transforming Our World: A Call to Action*, ed. James Montgomery Boice (Portland, OR: Multnomah, 1988), 112.

4. Barna Group, "The Trust Factor," Barna Access, September 18, 2023, https://barna.gloo.us/reports/trust-factor.

5. Barna Group, "Making Space from Generation to Generation," Barna Access, November 27, 2023, https://barna.gloo.us/briefing/making-space-generations.

6. John Stott and Christopher J. H. Wright, *Christian Mission in the Modern World*, 3rd ed. (Downers Grove, IL: IVP, 2015), 30.

7. Carl F. H. Henry, *Aspects of Christian Social Ethics* (Grand Rapids, MI: Eerdmans, 1964), 100.

8. Barna Group, "Making Space from Generation to Generation."

Chapter 14

1. "Historical Population Change Data (1910–2020)," United States Census Bureau, April 26, 2021, https://www.census.gov/data/tables/time-series/dec/popchange-data-text.html.

2. "U.S. Population Projected to Begin Declining in Second Half of Century," United States Census Bureau, November 9, 2023, https://www.census.gov/newsroom/press-releases/2023/population-projections.html.

3. William H. Frey, "Census Day Is Here. How Is Our Nation Changing?," May 31, 2020, https://www.brookings.edu/articles/the-2020-census-is-here-what-will-it-tell-us.

4. Leon E. Truesdell, U.S. Department of Commerce, *Fifteenth Census of the United States: 1930 Population Volume 2* (Washington: United States Government Printing Office, 1931), 25.

5. C. L. Kincannon, U.S. Department of Commerce, "Characteristics of Population, Chapter C General Social and Economic Characteristics Part 1, United States Summary," *1980 Census of Population*, vol. 1 (Washington: U.S. Government Printing Office, 1981), 11–13.

6. "Table 4: Hispanic or Latino Origin by Race: 2010 and 2020," U.S. Census Bureau, accessed December 30, 2023, https://www2.census.gov/programs-surveys/decennial/2020/data/redistricting-supplementary-tables/redistricting-supplementary-table-04.pdf.

7. "U.S. Population Projected to Begin Declining in Second Half of Century," United States Census Bureau, November 9, 2023, https://www.census.gov/newsroom/press-releases/2023/population-projections.html.

8. Todd M. Johnson and Gina A. Zurlo, eds., World Christian Database, accessed January 2023, www.worldchristiandatabase.org, "Status of Global Christianity, 2023, in the Context of 1900–2050," https://www.gordonconwell.edu/wp-content/uploads/sites/13/2023/01/Status-of-Global-Christianity-2023.pdf.

9. "The Future of World Religions: Population Growth Projections 2010–2050," Pew Research Center, April 2, 2015, https://www.pewresearch.org/religion/2015/04/02/religious-projections-2010-2050.

10. J. Clifford Tharp Jr., *Standing out of Sight: A History of Denominational Statistics in the Southern Baptist Convention 1882–2009* (Bloomington, IN: CrossBooks, A Division of LifeWay, 2010), 124–26.

11. Hight C. Moore and Joseph Henry Burnett, eds., *Annual of the Southern Baptist Convention 1925* (Nashville: Marshall & Bruce Co., 1925), 86, http://media2.sbhla.org.s3.amazonaws.com/annuals/SBC_Annual_1925.pdf.

12. Tharp, *Standing out of Sight*, 124–25.

13. Landry Homes, *It's Worth It: Uncovering How One Week Can Transform Your Church* (Nashville: LifeWay Christian Resources 2018), 39–41, 51.

14. Tharp, *Standing out of Sight*, 124–26.

15. Tharp, *Standing out of Sight*, 128.

16. Scott McConnell, "5 Wrong Ways to Think about Church Growth," Lifeway Research, May 25, 2023, https://research.lifeway.com/2023/05/25/5-wrong-ways-to-think-about-church-growth.

17. Tharp, *Standing Out of Sight*, 125–28.

18. Aaron Earls, "Southern Baptists Decline in Membership, Grow in Attendance, Baptisms," May 9, 2023, https://lifeway.com/2023/05/09/southern-baptists-decline-in-membership-grow-in-attendance-baptisms.

19. Charles Willis, "Southern Baptist Church Membership Hits Record, Approaches 16 Million," April 16, 2001, https://www.baptistpress.com/resource-library/news/southern-baptist-church-membership-hits-record-approaches-16-million. BP Staff, "Southern Baptists Grow in Number of Churches, Plant 588 New Congregations amid COVID-19 Pandemic," May 20, 2021, https://www.baptistpress.com/resource-library/news/southern-baptists-grow-in-number-of-churches-plant-588-new-congregations-amidst-covid-19-pandemic.

20. "SBC Congregations by Racial and Ethnic Groups: Congregations 2000–2020," Ethnic Research Network, accessed December 30, 2023, https://baptistresearch.com.

21. "SBC Congregations by Racial and Ethnic Groups: Congregations 2000–2020," Ethnic Research Network, accessed December 30, 2023, https://baptistresearch.com.

22. John L. Yeats, *Annual of the Southern Baptist Convention 2021* (Nashville: Executive Committee of the Southern Baptist Convention, 2021), 171.

23. Analysis by Lifeway Research for this publication.

24. Scott Barkley, "SBC Diversity Has Entered a New Age, Newly Compiled Data Shows," February 17, 2022, https://www.baptistpress.com/resource-library/news/sbc-diversity-has-entered-a-new-age-newly-compiled-data-show.

25. Todd M. Johnson and Gina A. Zurlo, eds., World Christian Database, "Status of Global Christianity, 2023, in the Context of 1900–2050."

26. Todd M. Johnson and Gina A. Zurlo, eds., World Christian Database, "Status of Global Christianity, 2023, in the Context of 1900–2050."

27. Todd M. Johnson and Gina A. Zurlo, eds., World Christian Database, accessed October 2016, www.worldchristiandatabase.org, Infographic, "500 Years of Protestantism 1517–2017," https://www.gordon conwell.edu/wp-content/uploads/sites/13/2019/04/136e0d3b6-d706-4bcf-a892-87a608c59104-18.pdf.

28. Todd M. Johnson and Gina A. Zurlo, eds., World Christian Database, accessed April 2018, www.worldchristiandatabase.org, Infographic "Global Christianity: A Look at the Status of Christianity in 2018," https://www.gordonconwell.edu/wp-content/uploads/sites/13/2019/04/GlobalChristianityinfographic.pdfPg1_.pdf.

29. "How Many Languages Are There in the World?," Ethnologue, accessed December 30, 2023, https://www.ethnologue.com/insights/how-many-languages.

30. "2023 Global Scripture Access," Wycliffe Global Alliance, September 1, 2023, https://www.wycliffe.net/resources/statistics.

31. Todd M. Johnson and Gina A. Zurlo, eds., World Christian Database, "Status of Global Christianity, 2023, in the Context of 1900–2050."

32. East-West Intern, "The History of Unreached People Groups," accessed December 30, 2023, https://blog.eastwest.org/the-history-of-unreached-people-groups.

33. Orville Boyd Jenkins, "What Is a People Group?," International Mission Board, accessed December 30, 2023, https://www.peoplegroups.org/understand/313.aspx.

34. "What Is a People Group?," Joshua Project, accessed December 30, 2023, https://joshuaproject.net/resources/articles/what_is_a_people_group.

35. "Global Status of Evangelical Christianity: GSEC Overview," International Mission Board, Global Research, October 2023.

36. "Global Impact Guide 2023: Impacting Lostness Together," International Mission Board, June 2023, 6, 32, https://www.imb.org/wp-content/uploads/2023/06/IMB_GIG-2023-Eng_FINAL_spreads.pdf.

37. "Global Dashboard," Joshua Project, accessed January 2, 2024, https://Joshuaproject.net/peoplegroups/dashboard.

38. Todd M. Johnson and Gina A. Zurlo, eds., World Christian Database, accessed January 2023, www.worldchristiandatabase.org, "Status of Global Christianity, 2023, in the Context of 1900–2050," https://swww.gordonconwell.edu/wp-content/uploads/sites/13/2023/01/Status-of-Global-Christianity-2023.pdf.

39. "World Watch Research: WWL 2023 Country Scores and Ranks," Open Doors International/World Watch Research, January 2023, 3–4, https://opendoorsanalytical.org/wp-content/uploads/2023/01/WWL-2023-Country-scores-and-ranks.pdf.

40. "World Watch List 2023: The Persecution of Christians Globally," Open Doors, 2023, https://www.opendoors.org/en-US/theadvocacyreport.

41. Stephen C. Neill, *A History of Christian Missions*, rev. ed. (London: Penguin, 1990), 421.

42. Jason Mandryk, "A Clarion Call to Missions from a Century Ago," Operation World, December 1, 2023, https://operationworld.org/2023/12/01/a-clarion-call-to-missions-from-a-century-ago.

43. John P. Jones, *The Missionary Challenge* (New York: Fleming H. Revell, 1910), 251.

Chapter 15

1. Chad Owen Brand and David Hankins, *One Sacred Effort: The Cooperative Program of Southern Baptists* (Nashville: Broadman and Holman Academic, 2006).

2. Mark Twain, quoted in Sanjiv Chipra and Gina Vilds, *The Two Most Important Days* (New York: Thomas Dunne Books, 2017), introduction.

3. "Proceedings," *Annual of the Southern Baptist Convention 1845* (Richmond: H. K. Ellyson, 1845), 13, accessed November 1, 2024, http://media2.sbhla.org.s3.amazonaws.com/annuals/SBC_Annual_1845.pdf.

4. George Mueller, "How I Ascertain the Will of God," George Mueller, May 9, 2016, https://www.georgemuller.org/devotional/how-i-ascertain-the-will-of-god.

5. Charles S. Kelley Jr., *How Did They Do It?: The Story of Southern Baptist Evangelism* (Chicago: Insight Press, 1993), 4–53.

6. Steve W. Lemke, "Education," Article XII in *The Baptist Faith and Message 2000: Critical Issue's in America's Largest Protestant Denomination*, ed. Douglas K. Blount and Joseph D. Wooddell (Maryland: Rowman and Littlefield Publishing Group, 2007), 123.

7. D. Martyn Lloyd Jones, *Studies in the Sermon on the Mount* (Grand Rapids: Eerdmans, 1971).

8. Charles Spurgeon, "The Conditions of Power in Prayer," preached March 23, 1873, found in *Charles H. Spurgeon's Sermons, Vol. 19*, accessed November 2, 2024, https://www.spurgeon.org/resource-library/sermons/the-conditions-of-power-in-prayer/#flipbook.

9. For a definition on the clear teachings of Scripture, see Steven B. Cowan and Terry L. Wilder, *In Defense of the Bible: A Comprehensive Apologetic for the Authority of Scripture* (Nashville: B&H Publishing Group, 2013), 119–463.

10. Graeme Goldsworthy, "What Is the Bible," in *Preaching the Whole Bible as Christian Scripture* (Grand Rapids: Eerdmans, 2000), 11–21.

11. See James C. Hefley, *The Truth in Crisis: The Controversy in the Southern Baptist Convention*, 4 vols. (Hannibal, MO: Hannibal Books, 1986).

12. V. Raymond Edman, *They Found the Secret: 20 Transformed Lives that Reveal a Touch of Eternity* (Grand Rapids: Zondervan, 1984).

13. See Darrell W. Robinson, "The Priority of Personal Evangelism," in *Evangelism in a Changing World, Essays in Honor of Roy Fish,* ed. Timothy Beougher and Alvin Reid (Eugene, OR: Wipf and Stock Publishers, 1995), 11–126.

14. "David Livingstone: Missionary-Explorer of Africa," *Christianity Today,* accessed November 2, 2024, https://www.christianitytoday.com/history/people/missionaries/david-livingstone.html.

15. "SBC Annuals," Southern Baptist Historical Library and Archives, https://news.lifeway.com/2024/05/07/southern-baptist-membership-decline-slows-baptisms-and-attendance-grow/.

16. See John Mark Terry, "The Great Commission and International Missions," in *The Challenge of the Great Commission: Essays on God's Mandate for the Local Church,* ed. Chuck Lawless and Thom S. Rainer (Bemidji, MN: Pinnacle Publishers, 2005), 65–78.

17. This quote is often attributed to David Livingstone.

18. Jim Elliot, quoted in Elisabeth Elliot, *Through Gates of Splendor* (Carol Stream, IL: Tyndale, 1981), 20.

Afterword

1. "Proceedings," *Annual of the Southern Baptist Convention 1924* (Nashville: Marshall & Bruce, 1924), 69, accessed November 2, 2024, http://media2.sbhla.org.s3.amazonaws.com/annuals/SBC_Annual_1924.pdf.